Arms Control and
European Security

Joseph I. Coffey

Published for the International
Institute for Strategic Studies

The Praeger Special Studies program—utilizing
the most modern and efficient book production
techniques and a selective worldwide distribution
network—makes available to the academic, government, and business communities significant,
timely research in U.S. and international economic,
social, and political development.

Arms Control and European Security

A Guide to East–West Negotiations

PRAEGER SPECIAL STUDIES IN INTERNATIONAL POLITICS AND GOVERNMENT

Praeger Publishers New York London

Library of Congress Cataloging in Publication
Data

Coffey, Joseph I.
    Arms control and European security.

    (Praeger special studies in international
politics and government)
    Includes index.
    1. Atomic weapons and disarmament.
    2. Disarmament.   3. Security, International.
    4. Europe—Defenses.
I. Title.
JX1974.7.C53   327'.174   76–29615
ISBN 0–275–24340–0

PRAEGER PUBLISHERS
200 Park Avenue, New York, N.Y. 10017, U.S.A.

Published in the United States of America in 1977
by Praeger Publishers

© 1977 by the International Institute for
Strategic Studies

Printed in the United Kingdom

CONTENTS

PREFACE

This book was begun during the year I spent as a Research Associate at the International Institute for Strategic Studies. I therefore owe a large debt of gratitude to the directorial staff of the Institute (at that time François Duchêne, Kenneth Hunt, Christoph Bertram and Ian Smart) who, collectively and individually, encouraged me in my efforts, increased my understanding and constructively criticized my successive drafts. I owe an equal debt, if of a different nature, to the administrative staff: most notably to Meryl Eady, who helped locate and acquire essential material; to Vera Sands, who transformed my recorded speech into intelligible English; to Patricia Evans, who arranged for the retyping, reproduction and distribution of my initial draft; and to John Wheelwright, who edited it. And to my fellow Research Associates, notably Robert Kleiman and Hannes Adomeit, I owe thanks for both their professional and their personal contributions, as I also do to Christopher D. Carr, who assisted with research; without them, my year in England would have been duller, my work harder.

That year was made possible by a sabbatical leave from the Graduate School of Public and International Affairs of the University of Pittsburgh, and my research was aided by a grant from the University Center for International Studies. My continuing work on the book was also aided by my long-suffering students, a number of whom spent a term assessing the problems of arms control and security in Europe (and my draft manuscript on the subject) and three of whom (Artis Francis Allen, Richard Asplund and Richard Herrmann) sought out the information needed to keep that manuscript more or less up to date. In that task they were abetted by Mary Ellen Bayuk, who incorporated into the several versions the numerous changes necessitated by a changing world.

Finally, I should like to thank all those—Russian as well as American and Canadian, East European as well as West European—who answered my questions, set forth their own views and challenged mine; if I do not list them all by name it is only because their number is too great. Although I cannot claim that I have reflected their (sometimes divergent) opinions on European security and ways in which arms control could affect it, I can truly say that my book is the better for their contributions. If, after all this, the product has shortcomings, I have no one to blame but myself!

Pittsburgh, Pennsylvania
October 1976

J. I. Coffey

GLOSSARY

ABM	anti-ballistic missile(s)
ALCM	air-launched cruise missile(s)
AWACS	airborne warning and control system(s)
ASROC	anti-submarine rocket(s)
ASM	air-to-surface missile(s)
ASW	anti-submarine warfare
CEP	circular error probable
CES	Committee on European Security
CSCE	Conference on Security and Co-operation in Europe
DRG	Democratic Republic of Germany
EDIP	European Defense Improvement Program
ENF	European Nuclear Force
FBS	forward-based system(s)
FRG	Federal Republic of Germany
ICBM	intercontinental ballistic missile(s)
MARV	manoeuvrable re-entry vehicle(s)
MFR	Mutual Force Reductions
MIRV	multiple independently targetable re-entry vehicle(s)
MRBM	medium-range ballistic missile(s)
MRCA	multi-role combat aircraft
MR/IRBM	medium-range/intermediate-range ballistic missile(s)
NATO	North Atlantic Treaty Organization
NGA	NATO Guidelines Area
R & D	research and development
RV	re-entry vehicle(s)
SACEUR	Supreme Allied Commander Europe
SACLANT	Supreme Allied Commander Atlantic
SALT	Strategic Arms Limitation Talks
SAM	surface-to-air missile(s)
SLBM	submarine-launched ballistic missile(s)
SLCM	sea-launched cruise missile(s)
SNDV	strategic nuclear delivery vehicle(s)
SRAM	short-range attack missile(s)
SRBM	short-range ballistic missile(s)
SSM	surface-to-surface missile(s)
TNDV	tactical nuclear delivery vehicle(s)
TNF	tactical nuclear forces
TNW	tactical nuclear weapons
VRBM	variable-range ballistic missile(s)
VSRM	very short range missile(s)
WTO	Warsaw Treaty Organization

Chapter 1

THE SEARCH FOR SECURITY
IN EUROPE

For almost thirty years the United States and her North Atlantic Treaty Organization (NATO) allies have confronted the Soviet Union and her fellow-members of the Warsaw Treaty Organization (Warsaw Pact) in the centre of Europe. Over this period both sides have expended vast sums on the development of new weapons and the maintenance of large forces in an effort to ensure their security. In the process they have once again turned Europe[1] into an armed camp: a million NATO soldiers, sailors and airmen in West Germany and the Low Countries confront a million Warsaw Pact troops in East Germany, Poland and Czechoslovakia, while hundreds of thousands more armed men are ranged against each other in southern and in northern Europe.

Those endorsing this build-up of military power insist that it is essential. They argue that the presence of armed men along the line of confrontation discourages encroachments and so stabilizes the political situation. They maintain that the availability of back-up forces inhibits attempts to exploit weak spots, and that the deployment of nuclear-armed units inhibits larger-scale military operations as well. They also point out that the existence of cohesive alliances serves to avoid misunderstandings about the consequences of employing force, thereby helping to preserve peace in Europe.

These are weighty arguments and must be given due consideration; however, not even those who advance them would list military power as the sole factor contributing to peace. Moreover, whatever the

[1] Technically, Europe extends from the Urals to the mid-Atlantic (taking in the Azores in the south and Iceland in the north) and from the North Cape to the Bosphorus. However, since Turkey spans the Bosphorus, her territory in Asia is included in this book under both the geographic and the political definitions of Europe. Conversely, the Union of Soviet Socialist Republics is not considered here as politically part of Europe but as a separate entity. Thus, the phrase 'European security' refers to the interests and the problems of the thirty-one states west of the Soviet border, six of which are allied with the Soviet Union, thirteen of which are members of NATO, and twelve of which do not formally belong to either grouping.

contribution of military power, it has not achieved the larger goal of ruling out threats to the territorial integrity, economic viability and political freedom of choice of the countries of Europe–that is to say, it has not sufficed to ensure European security.

THE SOURCES OF INSECURITY

The sense of insecurity derives in part from the mere presence of armed forces in large numbers, which heightens awareness of particular military threats (such as a Soviet amphibious landing on the north coast of Norway or a NATO nuclear strike against targets in Poland) and increases concern about the intentions of those who have deployed these forces. It also derives from the fact that much of Europe is divided into two blocs with opposing ideologies, differing socio-economic systems and conflicting interests. The feelings of insecurity created by this division are intensified by the fact that the leaders of these two blocs, the United States and the Soviet Union, see Europe not only as a prize of great value but as an arena within which to compete for power, influence and prestige. Finally, these feelings are enhanced because the United States and the Soviet Union have not hesitated to use their overwhelming power to achieve political gains or avoid political losses–even to the extent of using force or the threat of force.

Perhaps the most significant contribution to the sense of insecurity is the awareness that if either of the super-powers chose to unleash its full might, no country in Europe could stand against it. For one thing, only the most advanced states possess the technical knowledge required to develop modern weapons and the industrial base needed to build them. For another, few such states can afford to produce in quantity the range of equipment used by armed forces today; even countries like France and Britain must concentrate on a few types of weapons, while Italy–which spends less on defence research in a year than the United States spends in a week–is literally priced out of the market. Furthermore, not even West Germany, the most populous country in Europe, could match the numbers of troops available to the super-powers (which have three or four times as many men to draw on), so that–even if they wanted to–the individual nations of Europe could not create armed forces comparable with those that could be brought against them.

The two super-powers muster not only powerful conventional forces but even more powerful nuclear ones as well, with delivery vehicles numbering in the thousands. If even a few of these weapons were ever employed they could devastate any country on the face of the globe.[2]

[2] By way of illustration, 200 1-megaton (MT) warheads delivered on the United States could kill 80 million Americans; a similar number dropped

Even the lesser nuclear powers are at a disadvantage compared with the United States and the Soviet Union, since they can hope to deter only gross and direct threats (such as that of a disarming strike or an all-out assault by conventional troops), and then only by threatening actions which could result in their own annihilation. Those countries relying solely on conventionally armed units are at even more of a disadvantage, since such units are so vulnerable to nuclear weapons and so incapable of coping with their means of delivery that in the event of all-out war they can, in the words of General André Beaufre, 'only disperse, dig in, and take part as best they can in . . . rescue operations'.[3] Most of the nations of Europe are therefore exposed to threats which they themselves have no means of deterring or countering.

This disparity in military strength is of added concern because each of the super-powers has established a more-or-less permanent presence on the continent of Europe, a presence which others perceive as threatening. Thus many in Western Europe (and some in the non-aligned countries) see the Soviet presence in Eastern Europe as inimical to their security, since the large numbers of troops deployed there, their closeness to important Western positions, and their ability to utilize the terrain, the economies and the armed forces of their East European allies enable the Russians to mount operations which would be difficult to resist.[4] Moreover, many Europeans are conscious of the Soviet Union's continuing attempts to extend her influence over those countries not within her zone of control, attempts which have in the past been marked by threats to utilize power if necessary.

These concerns have persisted despite the recent improvement in relations between East and West. One reason is fear lest the Soviet Union revert to her previous policies. Another is doubt as to whether the more democratic societies and more responsive governments in Western Europe will sustain the policies and programmes required to ensure national security and uphold national interests. Still another is awareness that, even if their own publics were prepared to support larger and better-equipped defence forces, West European countries could not hope to match the capabilities of the Warsaw Pact without assistance and support from the United States, whose steadfastness many question.

This questioning of American purpose and reliability arises from a

[3] André Beaufre, *Deterrence and Strategy*, translated by Major-General R. H. Barry (London: Faber, 1965; New York: Praeger, 1966), p. 123.
[4] See Chapter 2, pp. 36-9 below.

on the Soviet Union could kill 50 million Russians. In each case, 200 MT equivalents represents about 5 per cent of the amount available.

number of circumstances. One of them is the advent of strategic parity between the United States and the Soviet Union, which has exacerbated long-held doubts about the former's willingness to respond to Soviet aggression by initiating a retaliatory strike on the Soviet Union, hence further diluting belief in the effectiveness of the American deterrent. A second is the apparent importance which the United States Government attaches to the maintenance of good relations with the Soviet Union—which has led many to question whether *détente* might not be pursued at the expense of cohesion within the Atlantic alliance, if not at the cost of sacrificing West European interests. A third is the increasing opposition among the American people (and in the United States Congress) to the role of the United States as leader of the free world, and the growing unwillingness to commit American resources—much less American forces—to the defence of others. A fourth is the preoccupation of successive administrations with other areas, such as South-East Asia or the Middle East, or with other problems, such as balance of payments deficits or inflation. Taken together, these have aroused fears that the United States may be less ready to make sacrifices and to run risks for the defence of Western Europe.[5]

If the European members of NATO are worried about the loss of cohesion in that alliance, the members of the Warsaw Pact are concerned about its continuation and improvement. They see NATO, through ideologically tinted glasses, as militaristic, imperialistic, and as planning aggressive war. More significantly, they see NATO as committed to the support of West Germany, a country viewed, at least until recently, as a revisionist power seeking to obtain a position of strength from which to dictate changes in the boundaries and institutions resulting from World War II. Moreover, they view NATO as a prime source of pressure for changes in their systems, changes which could undermine political stability in Eastern Europe, encourage the development of alternatives to the present economic and social structures, and lead to the erosion of Communist power. As one writer put it, '*Détente* and co-operation do indeed reduce the possibility of a

---

[5] In some sense these fears may reflect a misunderstanding of American opinion, since polls showed that 48–56 per cent of the people interviewed felt that the United States should come to the defence of her European allies if any of these were attacked—with the percentage so believing increasing in 1976. William Watts and Lloyd A. Free, 'Nationalism, Not Isolationism', *Foreign Policy*, No. 24 (Fall 1976), p. 17. Moreover, support by leadership groups was put as high as 77 per cent—and, as was noted by the author, it is elite support that counts. Charles R. Foster, 'American Elite and Mass Attitudes Towards Europe', *NATO Review*, Vol. 23, No. 3 (June 1975), p. 14.

military conflict, but they increase the possibilities of ideological "infection" '.[6]

Under these circumstances, the Soviet presence in Eastern Europe is seen as having two major benefits: protecting the area from hostile military action and precluding political moves aimed at altering the *status quo*. It is also seen as ensuring political stability, in that the Soviet Army is a guarantor against upheavals, whether indigenous in origin or 'imported' from the West. Against this must be set the fact that the Soviet Union has in the past employed force against its associates in Eastern Europe when the ruling group in a country was unable or unwilling to adhere to the Soxiet version of Marxism–Leninism, and still preserves the option of employing it again. Moreover, the massive weight and pervasive scope of the Soviet presence inhibits the governments of the region from exercising freedom of choice, thereby restricting their political independence and, some would say, undermining their economic viability. Thus the Soviet presence in Eastern Europe is viewed ambivalently when it comes to ensuring the security of the countries of that area.

So too is the American presence. On the one hand, this is recognized as a restraining influence on West European behaviour and as a damper on developments which would adversely affect East European security, as could the creation of a [West] European Nuclear Force (ENF). On the other hand, it is this presence (and all that it implies) which makes NATO a formidable military machine, which lends weight to pressures for change in Eastern Europe, and which otherwise might have been settled on terms favourable to the East.

As for the non-aligned countries, these are primarily worried lest they be dragged into a new war in Europe, as so many were dragged into World War II. Many of them see the maintenance of powerful military forces by NATO and the Warsaw Pact as indicators that such a war is conceivable, and hence tend to regard such forces as undesirable *per se*. Some see them as posing specific threats to their security: either directly, by making possible armed intervention, or indirectly, by lending weight to threats and pressures. Understandably, these

[6] Peter Bender, *East Europe in Search of Security*, translated from the German by S. Z. Young (London: Chatto and Windus for IISS, 1972), p. 7. Evidence that the leaders of the area share this view is provided by Erich Honneker's comment that the security of East Germany comes ahead of freer travel between East and West, and that implementation of the agreements on humanitarian co-operation reached at the Conference on Security and Co-operation in Europe depended on 'the extent to which *détente* proceeds and the principles of Helsinki [barring interference in internal affairs] are implemented' (The *New York Times*, 9 August 1975, p. 4).

concerns are more marked on the part of those directly exposed to assault by a powerful neighbour, as is Finland, or caught between the two blocs, as are Austria and Yugoslavia, but they are not uncommon throughout much of Europe.

Obviously, not all threats to the security of the countries of Europe derive from the confrontation between East and West or from the presence on the continent of the two super-powers. Broadly speaking, however, it is the division of Europe into opposing armed camps that constitutes the greatest threat to the greatest number of countries, and it is the imbalances between the capabilities of the two super-powers and those of the states of Europe which makes it so difficult for the latter to assure security and to protect their national interests. The fundamental question for these countries is, therefore, how to change the present situation to one in which the threats posed by the super-powers and their respective alliances would be reduced in magnitude, in likelihood, or both.

THE SEARCH FOR SECURITY

One way of doing this would be to change the international system so that greater and more certain constraints could be imposed upon the exercise of force by one state against another. In the long run, security must rest upon the perfection of controls over the exercise of power, since untrammelled competition can lead only to destruction on a scale unimagined even by Genghis Khan. In the short run, however, a host of obstacles stand in the way. For one thing, political as well as ideological differences preclude early agreement on a code of behaviour, with the Communists insisting that fraternal aid to national-revolutionary movements should not be ruled out, and others calling for controls which would do just that. For another, it is easier to agree on principles than on their application in particular instances–as evidenced by the continuing dispute over the implementation of Security Council Resolution 242, which ended the Six Day War between Israel and the Arab States. And if, by some miracle, agreement should be reached on institutions and procedures for adjudicating disputes, there is still the problem of enforcement, which would require the establishment of a world government–or at least of a world police force–with all that this could imply in terms of shared powers and changed attitudes.

Even lesser efforts have foundered on the same obstacles. Thus the post-war attempt to create world-wide collective security arrangements under the United Nations came to nought, largely because of differences among the great powers who were to be the guarantors of peace. Nor have the prescriptions in the Charter of the United Nations against the use of force other than for defence against aggression been binding, partly because it is so hard to determine who is the aggressor (or at least the *provocateur*) and partly because the members of the Security Council have tended to divide on issues brought before it. Although it may be useful in settling disputes which might lead to war, discouraging military operations and mobilizing opinion against those who launch them, the United Nations cannot be counted upon to preclude armed conflict between states, much less to bar other and more subtle uses of force; indeed, in most East–West crises and confrontations the UN has played only a minor role.

If, then, the world cannot readily be transformed, can those Europeans dissatisfied with the present state of affairs create a power base which would ensure their security, even against a super-power? The answer to this, for any given country, is probably 'No'.

To begin with, an independent power-base presupposes a national nuclear deterrent, and these are not easy to create. Most European countries which 'go nuclear' will still find themselves at a disadvantage compared with the super-powers, in that their economic and financial resources may not support the development and procurement of strategic weapons-systems on anything like a similar scale. They may also suffer other disadvantages, in that their small size and dense population make them particularly vulnerable to a nuclear strike, erode the credibility of their deterrent posture and weaken their bargaining power in a crisis or confrontation. Moreover, they may find it difficult to produce the panoply of conventional equipment which both extends the capabilities of the super-powers and enables them to choose options other than the employment of nuclear weapons.

One way of overcoming the economic difficulties mentioned earlier, and of providing both the space and the resources needed to create a powerful deterrent, would be to combine into regional groupings–a suggestion often made with respect to the countries of Western Europe. Unfortunately for those promoting this, the creation of a new political entity is a slow and painful task. It has taken the European Economic Community some fifteen years to reach its present stage of development and will probably take it another ten years to achieve even limited political cohesion.[7] While charismatic leadership, an appealing issue or an enlarged threat may speed up this process, it is doubtful whether Western Europe will in the foreseeable future

---

[7] The schedule laid out by the leaders of the nine EEC member states calls for the creation by 1980 of additional common institutions and arrangements, including a Political Consultative Committee. Whether this schedule will be met is perhaps doubtful, even though the French government–until recently a strong opponent of moves towards political unity–has now pronounced in their favour (The *New York Times*, 30 May 1975, p. 3).

achieve the degree of political and economic integration deemed necessary for the development of a strategic nuclear force, or, if it does, for its control.

Even should a more unified Western Europe come into existence, it would not necessarily attempt to create an independent power-base. Unless the situation in Europe changes drastically, there would be strong opposition to any significant military build-up, and particularly to the creation of a sizeable European Nuclear Force. This might well raise all kinds of difficult issues, such as the role West Germany should play and the degree of control she should have over nuclear weapons and means of delivering them.[8] It could arouse old fears in Eastern Europe, generate new difficulties with the Soviet Union, and lead to a worsening of relations with the members of the Warsaw Pact. It could also induce the United States to dissociate itself from the consequences of unco-ordinated employment of the ENF, and possibly to disavow any responsibility for the defence of Western Europe. Hence, the countries of Western Europe may be neither willing nor able to replace the American nuclear guarantee with an indigenous one—much less to create a military posture which would ensure their security against all possible threats.

This suggests that both the countries of Western Europe and those elsewhere on the Continent will have to look to other ways of maintaining their security and their freedom of political action.

One way of doing this would be to preserve a careful neutrality, relying on non-involvement in the 'cold war' and passivity in inter-state relations to reduce the risk of war, and on support from other powers, singly or in concert, should it actually break out. To countries like Ireland or Switzerland this is attractive and feasible, since they are not directly threatened by either neighbours or outsiders and have no ambition whose realization requires them to play the game of international politics. Others, like Hungary, may be forced to play whether or not they wish, or, like West Germany, may find it necessary to enter the game in order to achieve their national objectives. Thus not all countries can—or wish to—avoid involvement in the struggle between East and West.

Those countries which are involved, either from choice or of neces-

[8] In this connection, see the comment in the *Frankfurter Rundschau*, 4 October 1973, on the proposals of the Group of Nine for a European Nuclear Force based on the British and French potential (reprinted in the *German Tribune*, No. 601, 18 October 1973, p. 29), and the specific disclaimer by Defence Minister Georg Leber of West German support for an ENF, pending the creation of a politically united Europe (*Financial Times*, 8 October 1973, reprinted in *The Bulletin of the German Press and Information Service*, Vol. 21, No. 36, 16 October 1973, p. 276).

sity, face the problem of ensuring their security (and obtaining support for actions designed to advance their interests) in other ways. One way is for a country to balance between one super-power and the other, seeking to maintain a position in both camps which will ensure that its interests are taken into account and that it will not be left unsupported should a regional conflict develop. This, however, presupposes that the country in question is not tied politically, economically or ideologically to one of the super-powers, which is true of relatively few European states. It also assumes that both super-powers deem it in their interest to maintain the country's political independence, territorial integrity and economic viability, an assumption which may be hard to validate. Moreover, the balancing country can never be sure that either super-power will be willing to go to war in its defence, or even to run risks on its behalf. Those states which feel threatened may therefore prefer to form an alliance with one of the two super-powers, even though this restricts their freedom of action.

In today's world, however, such an alliance is necessarily unequal, in that the lesser power can contribute only marginally (if at all) to the security of the greater, while the greater suffers because of the guarantees the weaker ally may demand and the requirements for help it may generate. The larger the difference in capabilities, the less a small state can contribute to an alliance and the less its ability to influence the policy of that alliance. Even in an integrated alliance like NATO it may be difficult for the lesser members to depend fully on their super-power ally, especially if it is their interests that are threatened and not the super-power's.

All this suggests that East–West security cannot be achieved by any single policy but must be sought in a variety of ways, some of which are available to all countries, some of which are open only to a few. In the past, most members of NATO and the Warsaw Pact, and some non-aligned countries, have relied heavily upon military strength to ensure security. But the very process of arming arouses fears and heightens perceptions of threat, in that weapons and forces which seem reassuring to one state may seem threatening to another.[9] There have been changes in these perceptions in the course of time, but a general feeling of insecurity seems to have persisted. Were this not so, there would be less concern about military imbalances between East and West and less effort devoted to redressing them.

[9] J. I. Coffey and Jerome H. Laulicht, *The Implications for Arms Control of Perceptions of Strategic Weapons Systems*, a study Prepared for the United States Arms Control and Disarmament Agency, by the Graduate School of Public and International Affairs and the Research Office of Sociology, University of Pittsburgh (Pittsburgh, Pennsylvania: November 1971), ACDA E-163, Vol. I: *Summary*, p. 2.

In all likelihood this concern will persist, since the fears and suspicions which give rise to it will not soon pass away. And, failing other
alternatives, the members of both alliances may continue in efforts
to counter adversary capabilities which seem potentially dangerous.
The question, then, is whether one can devise and implement policies
which could ameliorate concerns and reduce threats, thereby enhancing security in ways different from those followed in the past.

One way of doing this would be energetically and meaningfully to
pursue the search for accommodation between East and West, with a
view to resolving differences which could lead to a clash of arms,
creating vested interests in the maintenance of good relations, and
changing perceptions of the adversary's behaviour. To some extent
this process has been going on since the early 1970s. The Government
of West Germany has removed a major thorn in the side of the countries of Eastern Europe by its *Ostpolitik* and its treaties with Poland,
the Soviet Union and East Germany. Additionally, West Germany,
France and other powers have sought to increase East–West trade, to
encourage the freer flow of people and information between East and
West, to improve co-operation in science and technology, and in these
and other ways to normalize relations. Perhaps most significantly, the
United States, the mainstay of the Western Alliance, has not only
joined in these kinds of measures but has also sought to reach an
understanding with the Soviet Union on the ways in which force
should be used and the purposes for which it should be employed.[10]

For their part, the Soviet Union and the countries of Eastern
Europe have, with varying degrees of enthusiasm, moved to improve
relations with the West, sought to open up new channels of communication and means of exchange, and by and large pursued a policy
of *détente*. This policy has been marked by some degree of Soviet co-
operation in damping down potentially explosive conflicts in other
areas, such as the fourth Arab–Israeli War. And it has been evidenced
by a Soviet willingness to forswear the use of force against the United
States, its allies, or any other country 'in circumstances which may
endanger international peace and security'.[11]

While these agreements between the two super-powers are impor-

[10] See the First, Second and Third articles of the 'Basic Principles of
Relations between the United States of America and the Union of Soviet
Socialist Republics', 29 May 1972, in *Weekly Compilation of Presidential
Documents*, Vol. 8, No. 23, (5 June 1972), pp. 943–4 (Washington: Office
of the Federal Register, National Archives and Records Service, 1972),
reprinted in *Survival*, July/August 1972, pp. 191–2.

[11] 'Nixon–Brezhnev Agreement on the Prevention of Nuclear War'
The Times (London), 23 June 1973, p. 4, reprinted in *Survival*, September/
October 1973, pp. 245–6.

tant, their effect on perceptions of threat depends more on their observance than on their adoption. Moreover, even if they are honoured, they do not cover all conceivable threats to the various countries of Europe, some of whom have noted that the Nixon–Brezhnev agreement does not preclude threats of force, pressure backed by force, or military actions which would *not* endanger international peace and security, actions such as Soviet intervention in Eastern Europe. For these reasons, and on the sound principle that a web of agreements is harder to break than a single (or even double) strand, many European nations sought, in the Conference on Security and Co-operation in Europe (CSCE), to obtain new promises that the participants would refrain from the threat or the use of force, acknowledge the inviolability of frontiers and the territorial integrity of European states, and eschew intervention in the internal affairs of their neighbours.

These measures are symptomatic of a wider range, embracing legal prescriptions, institutional constraints, political liabilities and perhaps economic sanctions, which can inhibit the use of force, and in this way contribute to East–West security. However, while these certainly increase the cost of taking military action, they do not necessarily preclude it. Some regimes may be comparatively insensitive to such inhibitions; others may be so convinced of the importance of the interests at stake as to be willing to pay the price attaching to the use of force, as was the Soviet Union when she sent troops into Czechoslovakia in 1968, and the United States when she landed Marines in the Dominican Republic in 1965. Thus it is understandable that some Europeans should seek not only to strengthen inhibitions on the use of force but also to reduce the ability of others to employ force, should they choose to do so: in short, to limit and control armaments.

THE APPROACH

The first step in this process will be to look at the military balance between East and West (i.e. between the Warsaw Pact and NATO) with particular reference to those elements of the armed forces of the two alliances which are deployed in, or available for operations in, the European theatre. This step is essential both because one cannot assess the implications of arms-control measures without a knowledge of the military situation, and because this same situation (or, rather, perceptions of the military balance and of what it allegedly reveals concerning the intentions of one's adversary) affects interest in, and the acceptibility of, measures for the limitation of armaments.

The second step will be an examination of the ways in which arms control can affect capabilities for military operations and perceptions of threat, and of the probable limits to arms control, which derive in part from the interests and concerns mentioned above, and in part from the very nature of modern armed forces. This will be followed in turn by a more detailed assessment of strategic arms limitations, of constraints on tactical nuclear forces, of mutual force reductions in Europe and of overall restrictions on armaments. The final step (and final chapter) will consist of a summary of what has been said previously about arms control, and of an assessment of the applicability of the measures proposed to a changing–and uncertain–future.

Before we climb these steps, however, a number of cautions are in order. Security is not the only objective of states, nor arms control their only instrument of policy – which suggests that we look at the interests and the policies of the various states. But here, three problems arise. The first is that even governments find it difficult to determine in advance how they will respond to a range of arms-control proposals, each of which will have a different effect on their military capabilities, political relations and economic balance-sheets; for an analyst to attempt this for twenty or thirty countries is palpably absurd. The second is that national policies–if not national interests–adjust to changes in the international environment, so that one would have to look not only at the present but also at the future, indeed at many possible futures, some of which would involve new weaponry and new institutional arrangements as well as different political trends. The third is that the process of negotiation involves multiple interactions within any government, with other elements of the body politic, with allies and with adversaries. Since the outcomes of these interactions are influenced by personal predilections, political rivalries, bureaucratic infighting and a host of other factors, they are extremely hard to determine. This suggests an approach which assesses subjective as well as objective components of East–West security, but which stops well short of attempting to evaluate all national concerns, interests and probable positions.

The second caution is that security :

1. is never absolute; we cannot hope for a world (or even for a Europe) where peace is guaranteed, and no one need fear threats of force;
2. applies to the countries of Eastern Europe as well as those of Western Europe, to the non-aligned states as well as those allied or associated with one of the super-powers;
3. is not an end in itself but a means to an end, which in the short run may be increasing accommodation and promoting East–West[12]

---

[12] 'Eastern Europe' and 'Western Europe' are political rather than geographical expressions, referring in the first instance to the six countries which are associated with the Soviet Union in the Warsaw Pact (Bul-

détente, in the longer run ensuring that both domestic and international changes take place peacefully and in accordance with the will of the peoples concerned.

A third caution is that the focus of this study is both wider than and narrower than that of European security. It is wider in that it must necessarily take into account the global interests and the far-flung presence of the United States and of the Soviet Union; the East–West confrontation is by no means limited to Europe. It is narrower in that it will consider primarily the views about arms control of the members of the two alliances, rather than those of all the thirty-five states of Europe. This does not mean that the neutral and non-aligned states are uninterested in arms control (or in security); only that they are not now involved in the negotiations on arms limitations[13] and are unlikely to become involved in the near future.

The approach I have outlined has certain advantages and certain disadvantages. The advantages are that the problem will be examined from a single perspective, that of what arms control can and cannot do to enhance security, and on the basis of a single judgment: that of the author. The disadvantages are, first of all, that perspectives will obviously colour judgment; for instance, if one looks at European political and military integration in terms of its implications for arms control one may arrive at a conclusion different from that reached by those who are looking solely at the security of Western Europe or at the desirability of European integration. Another disadvantage is that my judgment will certainly differ from that of others—as far as East–West security is concerned, we are all blind men examining an elephant. This disadvantage I hope to offset by reporting the views of other examiners, that is, by marshalling arguments for and against issues before indicating my own views on the subject. Finally, and perhaps most importantly, my judgment may be faulty; I lay no claim to omniscience. I can only hope to provide enough information to enable the reader to make his own judgments about the utility and the acceptability of measures for the control of armaments.

---

[13] They were, of course, participants in the Conference on Security and Co-operation in Europe (CSCE), which did consider—and may again consider—confidence-building measures.

---

garia, Czechoslovakia, East Germany, Hungary, Poland and Rumania) and in the second case to members of NATO other than the United States and Canada.

Chapter 2

THE MILITARY BALANCE

As the first step on this 'journey of a thousand miles', I will describe briefly the forces at the disposal of NATO and the Warsaw Pact and assess their capabilities for various types of military operations. Unfortunately this description and evaluation cannot be limited to those forces deployed within the geographical area we call Europe. For one thing, both the super-powers maintain strategic nuclear forces which, though not directly involved in the confrontation in Europe, significantly—and perhaps decisively—affect European security. For another, both the Soviet Union and the United States deploy substantial elements of their armed forces outside the boundaries of Europe, as, to a lesser extent, do others among the Western allies. I shall, therefore, discuss the military balance in Europe under three headings:

1. *Strategic nuclear forces*, i.e. those capable of striking with nuclear weapons at military targets, governmental centres, industrial facilities and populated areas in an adversary's homeland, or those deployed to defend against such strikes. For convenience, these will be further subdivided into global (intercontinental) strategic forces and regional strategic forces, i.e. those of shorter range or more limited deployment.
2. *Tactical nuclear forces*, i.e. those nuclear-armed elements of armies, navies and air forces which are primarily designed and intended for employment against military targets in a theatre of operations, such as Central Europe.
3. *Conventional forces*, i.e. those elements whose mission is similar, but which do not employ nuclear weapons.

In the second and third categories I will distinguish between those forces based in Europe and those outside it (including by definition those east of the Soviet frontier), which will be considered under the heading of reinforcement capabilities.

STRATEGIC NUCLEAR FORCES

Global forces

For almost thirty years the United States has been building nuclear warheads and the means of delivering them over intercontinental distances—a path subsequently followed by the Soviet Union. In the process, these two powers have developed a range of atomic and thermonuclear weapons and a variety of launch vehicles, including bombers, intercontinental ballistic missiles (ICBM) and submarines carrying both ballistic and cruise missiles. (In this connection, see Table 1. Strategic Nuclear Forces, mid-1976.) Moreover, they have so multiplied the number of these delivery vehicles that each country is capable of devastating the other, regardless of its attempts to defend itself.[1] Furthermore, each has the technical skills, industrial base and economic resources to maintain this capability, despite anything the other can do. Although either can disturb the strategic balance, neither can upset it if the other takes prudent counter-measures in the form of either weapons programmes or measures for the limitation of armaments.[2] Although their inability to 'win' a strategic nuclear war means that the employment of global forces *en masse* would be self-defeating, it does not necessarily rule out their use on other missions. They could, for example, be employed to launch limited strikes against an adversary's weapons systems, against other military targets or against civilian facilities and installations; in fact, their enormous potential means that such missions could be undertaken without diminishing retaliatory capabilities. They could also be used to supplement theatre nuclear forces, should war ever rise to such a pitch that their controlled employment would be necessary and feasible. They could be employed against concentrations of naval forces, directed against single targets in third countries (such as air or submarine bases), and in these and other ways used to cope with lesser threats. Thus, the possession of global strategic forces enables the two super-powers to dominate lower-level conflicts and to deter a wide spectrum of threats to their security—albeit with some risk of escalation into nuclear war.

Regional forces

The situation of Britain and France is very different. For one thing, their strategic nuclear forces are not large, amounting at most to 5 per cent of those of the United States or the Soviet Union (see Table 1). For another, the size and the characteristics of these forces rule out any counter-force strikes, save as a symbolic gesture; in fact, some of the two countries' launch vehicles are vulnerable to a disarming strike

[1] See note 2, Chapter 1.
[2] For a fuller discussion of the capabilities of Soviet and American strategic nuclear forces, and of the difficulties which both countries face in attempting to secure meaningful strategic advantages, see J. I. Coffey, *Strategic Power and National Security* (Pittsburgh: University of Pittsburgh Press, 1971), esp. pp. 21–45.

by one of the super-powers. Furthermore, the relatively small economic bases of the two European states and their lag in weapons technology (in part a function of available resources) mean that neither can hope to match the super-powers in the foreseeable future.

This does not mean that their strategic nuclear forces are unimportant, either as military instruments or as political ones. Even small forces could inflict levels of damage on a non-nuclear power which could be decisive; should France ever again have cause to fear invasion by her neighbour to the east, the *force de frappe* should serve to reassure her. And while these might be relatively less effective against one of the super-powers, calculations have shown that even the British or French submarine-launched ballistic missile (SLBM) force could inflict some millions of fatalities on the Soviet Union (or, conceivably, upon the United States).[3]

In addition, these lesser powers could signal their determination to resist aggression by a controlled launch against high-value targets, such as the Soviet nuclear-production facilities at Alma Ata. They could escalate any conflict which did arise by using strategic (as well as tactical) nuclear forces against advancing troops or, as a last resort, by launching their bombers and missiles against the homeland of a nuclear-armed adversary. Moreover, possession of these forces enables Britain and France to create uncertainties in the mind of a potential adversary about their responses to aggression and, conceivably, to trigger off a super-power nuclear exchange.

In sum, the nuclear forces of Britain and France are more useful for deterring wars than for fighting them, and of greater symbolic than actual importance. They cannot, however, be ignored by potential adversaries, nuclear or non-nuclear. And they may help enhance the security of these two countries by enabling their leaders to resist political pressures and to influence the course of events in time of crisis.

The role of Soviet regional nuclear forces is very different. Although they can contribute to deterrence by holding Europe hostage for American behaviour, and although they could inflict significant damage should deterrence fail, these are not their primary missions. One primary mission is to disrupt governmental and military control systems and to destroy industrial and logistic facilities which directly support the war effort—in effect carrying out what one analyst has

[3] Geoffrey Kemp and Ian Smart, 'SALT and European Nuclear Forces', in William R. Kintner and Robert L. Pfaltzgraff, Jr. (Eds.), *SALT: Implications for Arms Control in the 1970s* (Pittsburgh: University of Pittsburgh Press, 1973), pp. 217–18, 225–6.

called 'counter-center' operations.[4] Another is to strike at an enemy's nuclear delivery vehicles, major troop concentrations and other military targets in rear areas, with the aim of clearing the way for operations by mobile units, especially tank and airborne forces. In this sense, they extend and complement the 'tactical' and 'operational–tactical' weapons of the Army and the Tactical Air Force, which will strike at similar targets of lesser importance, closer to the front line, or of a more fleeting nature.[5] Thus the Soviet Union's regional strategic nuclear forces are given a major responsibility for ensuring the success of any campaign in Europe–which may explain why they total over a thousand launch vehicles, compared to approximately two hundred for their British and French counterparts (see Table 1, p. 247).[6]

TACTICAL NUCLEAR FORCES

In addition to regional delivery vehicles, which have effective ranges of 2,000–3,000 miles, each alliance also musters artillery, rockets, short-range ballistic missiles (SRBM), cruise missiles and strike aircraft with ranges varying from ten miles to over 1,000 miles.[7] Within Europe proper, there are thousands of nuclear-capable aircraft, each side deploying hundreds in Central Europe alone (see Table 2, p. 248, Nuclear-Capable Tactical Delivery Vehicles in Europe, Mid-1976). Moreover, each side has scores of SRBM, such as the NATO *Pershing* and the Warsaw Pact *Scaleboard*. In addition, each has hundreds of free rockets, very short range missiles (VSRM) and artillery pieces which are capable of delivering low-yield nuclear warheads at relatively short ranges against troop concentrations, artillery positions and other battlefield targets. The warheads required for these weapons, for surface-to-air missiles and for other uses amounted in 1976 to

[4] Leon Goure, Foy D. Kohler and Mose L. Harvey, *The Role of Nuclear Forces in Current Soviet Strategy* (Coral Gables, Florida: Center for Advanced International Studies, University of Miami, 1974), p. 17.

[5] For a more detailed discussion of the role of Soviet theatre nuclear forces see John Erickson, *Soviet Military Power* (London: Royal United Services Institute for Defence Studies, 1971), pp. 69–70.

[6] In addition, the United States has allocated at least five missile submarines to NATO. These submarines would presumably be employed in theatre operations in Europe. Since these are technically part of the American strategic forces, however, they are not counted here. Neither, for the same reason, are the 100 variable-range ballistic missiles (VRBM) deployed in the western part of the Soviet Union.

[7] For technical characteristics of these tactical nuclear delivery vehicles, see *The Military Balance 1976–1977* (London: IISS, 1976), pp. 73–4, 76–7.

about 7,000 for NATO and perhaps 3,500 for the Warsaw Pact (some, if not all, of the latter stored inside Soviet territory).[8]

The warheads and delivery vehicles in Europe are, of course, only a small part of the total. The United States Air Force, Navy and Marine Corps would be able to muster between them well in excess of 1,000 nuclear-capable aircraft, some of which could be redeployed to Europe within days, if not hours. Moreover, the United States Army has additional surface-to-surface missiles and nuclear-capable artillery battalions which, in time, could also be redeployed to Europe. Even if one allows for the fact that some of these aircraft are on carriers in the Pacific, and that not all would necessarily be sent to Europe, the United States could quickly double the number of strike aircraft available for employment in Europe and could, given time, add significantly to the number of shorter-range delivery vehicles deployed in the theatre.

Similarly, in any campaign in Europe the Soviet Union could employ as many as 1,000 light bombers and nuclear-capable ground-attack planes now USSR-based, even after allowing for possible requirements in other theatres. For operations against ships and coastal targets, she could augment these with nuclear-armed SLCM (submarine-launched cruise missiles) and again with elements of the medium bombers assigned to the Naval Air Force. For employment on the battlefield, she could bring in the *FROG* rockets organic to her divisions, the nuclear-capable artillery and very short-range missiles normally attached to a Soviet Tank or Combined Arms Army, and the *Scud* and *Scaleboard* SRBM assigned to a 'Front' or Army Group. Thus the Soviet Union also could double the nuclear-capable aircraft available for operations in Europe and could add significantly to the numbers of other types of tactical nuclear-delivery vehicles (TNDV).

As with regional nuclear forces, the tactical nuclear forces of both sides have different missions. It might almost be said that the primary mission of NATO forces is deterrence, by holding out the prospect of escalating a conventional conflict (with unpredictable consequences). This mission would be carried out by limited and selective attacks upon military targets at varying distances from the battle area. A second mission is that of inflicting heavy damage on Pact units

---

[8] *Report of the United States Delegation to the Fourteenth Meeting of Members of Parliaments from the North Atlantic Assembly Countries held in Brussels, 11 November through 15 November 1968*, 28 March 1969, p. 29, quoted in Trevor Cliffe, *Military Technology and the European Balance*. Adelphi Paper No. 89 (London: IISS, 1972), p. 4. See also *The Military Balance 1976–1977, op. cit.* above, hereafter cited as *The Military Balance 1976–7*, appendix 'Theatre Balance between NATO and the Warsaw Pact', p. 103.

should these employ nuclear weapons or should an advance by the Pact threaten major NATO forces or areas important to NATO. This second mission would be fulfilled by suppressive strikes against airfields and missile sites in Eastern Europe (and conceivably in the western regions of the Soviet Union), by interdictory attacks on bridges, marshalling yards and other key points in the network of communications running through Eastern Europe, and by launches against stockpiles of supplies and concentrations of troops, both on and off the battlefield. In short, the war-fighting role of NATO tactical nuclear forces would be to knock out Warsaw Pact air and missile systems and to preclude the Soviet Union and its allies from bringing to bear the full weight of their conventional forces.

Soviet writers do not assign to their tactical nuclear forces either a deterrent or an escalatory role; instead they assume either that NATO will employ nuclear weapons at the outset of hostilities or that any conventional conflict will almost inevitably escalate, and become a large-scale nuclear war. Under these circumstances, Soviet tactical nuclear forces would have two missions: decimating the adversary's nuclear strike forces, and blasting a way for mobile ground and airborne units which would exploit the results achieved by these shattering blows.[9] Thus, Soviet tactical nuclear forces are designed to support offensive operations, rather than, as in NATO, to bolster defensive ones.

Although it is not possible to assess precisely the capabilities of the two sides, it is possible to draw inferences from this crude portrayal of tactical nuclear capabilities in Europe. The first is that, given the number of delivery vehicles, the variety of types, their wide dispersal, and the measures taken to protect them (such as placing quick-reaction aircraft in concrete igloos or revetments) it is virtually impossible for either side successfully to deliver a tactical nuclear disarming strike. A second is that the delivery vehicles remaining after such an attempt should be sufficient to blunt any advance, with artillery and rockets delivering nuclear warheads on assault forces, their supporting artillery and local supply-points, while short-range missiles and aircraft struck at airfields, staging areas, depots and vulnerable points on lines of communication, like the bridges across the Rhine and the Oder. If this were not enough, nuclear-capable aircraft from the United States or the Soviet Union could be used for interdiction strikes and attacks against large concentrations of enemy forces, or even to lay down a barrage which could create lethal radioactive zones. A third inference

[9] Erickson (*op. cit.* in note 5), pp. 67–73. For further details see A. A. Sidorenko, *The Offensive: A Soviet View*, translated and published under the auspices of the United States Air Force (Washington, DC: USGPO, 1970), pp. 40–4 and 111–18.

is that, even if every effort were made to minimize damage to civilian targets, millions of people in both Eastern and Western Europe would suffer; one exercise which simulated the use of tactical nuclear weapons in a limited area containing no large towns caused the 'deaths' of more than $1\frac{1}{2}$ million German citizens.[10] Less restraint in their employment, extensive interdiction or the use of area weapons like medium-range ballistic missiles could lead to the deaths of 100 million East and West Europeans–which is why most are so anxious to avoid a tactical nuclear war in Europe. Finally, the use of nuclear weapons on any scale would tend to change the nature of a conflict and to heighten the danger of all-out nuclear war, which makes them indeed a double-edged sword.

CONVENTIONAL THEATRE FORCES

The risks and dangers inherent in any use of tactical nuclear weapons, however limited, have inclined many in the West to view these as a last resort and to call for a balance between NATO and Warsaw Pact conventional forces, which could deter or check aggression by other conventional forces. Unfortunately, such a balance is not only more difficult to maintain but also more difficult to ascertain. Conventional capabilities are usually expressed in terms of the number of ground-combat units (infantry, armoured and airborne divisions, artillery brigades, armoured reconnaissance regiments, etc.), squadrons of aircraft (interceptors, fighter-bombers and reconnaissance) and numbers of major warships. These are, for a number of reasons, less meaningful indicators of capability than numbers of strategic nuclear-delivery vehicles, or even tactical nuclear weapons systems. Variables in armament, equipment, organization and less tangible areas mean that there will be important differences in the combat capabilities of troops from different countries, under varying circumstances.

Ground forces

Ignoring these qualitative factors for the moment, if one looks only at formations in place, it is obvious that the Warsaw Pact has significant advantages. Table 3, NATO and Warsaw Pact Ground and Air Forces Immediately Available for Operations in Europe, Mid-1976, p. 250, shows its preponderance in tanks, which reflects not only its emphasis on armoured formations but also the larger number of divisions at its disposal–all of them fully equipped, even though some are at cadre strength. It also shows the Warsaw Pact's relative advantage in tactical aircraft, even after those NATO squadrons deployed in Western Europe are weighed in the balance.

[10] Sir Solly Zuckerman, 'Judgement and Control in Modern Warfare', *Foreign Affairs*, Vol. 40 No. 2 (January 1962), p. 201.

The table indicates why many in NATO are concerned over the possibility of a surprise attack which could exploit those advantages, and perhaps shatter Western defences, but it does not show local groupings of forces which could affect significantly the success of such an operation. One such is in the north of Norway, where a single Norwegian brigade faces markedly superior Soviet forces. Another is in North Germany, where the strategy of forward defence stretches troops so thin that one West German division may have to defend a front fifty miles long. A third is in Southern Europe, where geography renders *hors de combat* the quarter-million-man Italian Army, thereby eliminating NATO's seeming advantage in that region.

On the other hand, NATO tanks are generally more modern than those of the Warsaw Pact: while the new T-72 tank just being introduced may equal the *Chieftain* and *Leopard* tanks of Britain and West Germany, the latter outclass the T-62s now in the hands of Pact armoured units. Moreover, NATO's relative weakness in tanks is to some extent offset by its superiority in ground anti-tank weapons and by more effective airborne anti-tank weapons, such as the missiles carried by fighter aircraft and helicopters. Although the Warsaw Pact musters larger numbers of artillery pieces, those of NATO tend to be of larger calibre, and their ammunition is more lethal, and NATO's greater logistic capability enables them to sustain higher rates of fire. Transport lift (which enhances logistic capacity and staying power) is about half as high again in NATO as in Warsaw Pact divisions. Thus NATO has both advantages and disadvantages in ready forces compared to the Warsaw Pact.

The same is true of reinforcement capabilities. As mentioned previously, many of the Warsaw Pact divisions are manned at levels well below their combat strength, some at cadre level, i.e. less than one-third. The mobilization of reservists would enable the East Europeans to fill out their fifty-odd divisions to full strength; selected elements of these could probably be ready for action in 7–10 days, but the bulk would not be available until later. It would also enable the Soviet Union to bring up to strength the sixty-odd divisions in the western military districts of the USSR, only about one-third of which are combat-ready. (Of the remainder, some would require only limited augmentation, while the others would need more substantial inputs of –presumably less well-trained–personnel and, possibly, additional equipment.) Although the actual allocation of these particular divisions cannot be determined, it is reasonable to assume that within 30 days after mobilization the Soviet Union and its allies could at least double the forces available for operations against NATO.[11]

[11] No two authorities agree on either the states of readiness of Soviet divisions inside the USSR nor on the time required to redeploy these

Similarly, most NATO allies plan only to flesh out existing units. In Northern Europe, however, Denmark and Norway would mobilize additional infantry brigades, plus home guards, as, on the central front, would Belgium, Holland and West Germany. While Britain could provide modest reinforcements, and France more significant ones, the bulk of the requirements must come from North America. The United States has earmarked for Europe several divisions, whose equipment is stored in West Germany. In addition, five other Army divisions and at least one Marine Division could be made available, once shipping could be assembled for the transport of their heavy equipment. In time the United States could also make available most of the units of the Reserve and National Guard, which are at varying levels of equipment, training and readiness; however, in the short run only some eight division-equivalents of the reserve combatants would be ready for combat.[12]

The question, however, is not only the number of reserve divisions and their readiness, but their proximity to a possible confrontation between NATO and the Warsaw Pact. Broadly speaking, most of the divisions in eastern Europe and the western Soviet Union are relatively close to potential battlefields and have the advantage of land lines of communication, enabling them to move more rapidly. On the other hand, although NATO can mobilize Belgian, Dutch, Danish and Norwegian reserve brigades and the fillers for the units of other

---

to the battle areas in Europe. *The Military Balance 1976–1977*, p. 100, suggests that the 27 Soviet divisions in the countries of the Northern tier (Poland, East Germany and Czechoslovakia) 'could be increased to over 80 in a few weeks. . . .' an augmentation of 53. Jeffrey Record, *Sizing up the Soviet Army* (Washington, DC: The Brookings Institution, 1975), pp. 22–23, projects increases in that area by M+30 of only 28–32 divisions, including four redeployed from Hungary, and introduces 53 additional divisions only by M+60. An official American estimate is that by M+60 the Soviet Army could mobilize and deploy a total of 113 divisions; however, some 60 of these are in the Far East or in Central Asia. (*Report of Secretary of Defense James R. Schlesinger to the Congress on the FY 1976 and Transition Budgets, FY 1977 Authorization Request and FY 1976–1980 Defense Programs*, 5 February 1975, mimeograph, p. III-14. Hereafter, this document will be cited as *Schlesinger Report, 1975*.) My own opinion is that by M+30, the Soviet Union and its allies could add 2 divisions on the Northern flank, about 20–22 in the Central Region and perhaps 6 in South-Eastern Europe, for a maximum of 30. By M+60 another 30 divisions could conceivably be introduced into combat, including 16 from the East European members of the Warsaw Pact; only after M+120, when Soviet Category III (cadre) divisions complete their mobilization could this figure be increased significantly.

[12] For details, see *The Military Balance 1975–76*, pp. 99–100.

countries reasonably quickly (within one to two weeks), it has more of a problem with other potential reinforcements. The US divisions whose equipment is stored in West Germany can be rapidly transported by air, as can, with greater difficulty, the American 82nd Airborne Division and 101st Air Assault Division (bringing their equipment with them) and the United Kingdom Mobile Force, which is air-transportable. Other units, whether redeployed from the United States or from Italy, need time to assemble, move to ports, load men and equipment, sail to disembarkation points, disembark, collect equipment and move to their area of responsibility. This means that, if mobilization precedes conflict, or is uninterrupted, the Warsaw Pact could probably enhance its current advantages in northern and central Europe during the first 30 days, even though not all divisions from the western Soviet Union could—or probably would—be moved forward by that time.[13] Within 90 days the balance might begin to shift in favour of the West, with the arrival of transports from the United States but, nonetheless, many units could not be redeployed to Europe until at least six months after the order for mobilization.[14]

Air Forces

Because of their mobility and the speed with which reinforcing squadrons can be deployed to prepared airfields, aircraft in place in Europe are perhaps less important than divisions or their weapons. The number of aircraft on station does, however, indicate something about initial capabilities for attack and defence. Moreover, these numbers are useful in looking at the possible effects of arms-control measures in Europe. For these reasons, approximate totals for combat aircraft by region are given in Table 3 (p. oo), and further details in Chapter 6.

[13] Richard D. Lawrence and Jeffrey Record, *US Force Posture in NATO: An Alternative* (Washington: The Brookings Institution, 1974), pp. 46, 104 and 112, come up with ratios somewhat more favourable to NATO:

	Ratio M-Day (with France)	Ratio M + 30 (with France)
Total military manpower	1.1:1	1:1
Ground combat troops	0.9:1	0.7:1
Divisions	0.5:1	0.4:1
Tanks	0.6:1	0.4:1
Tactical aircraft	0.5:1	0.6:1

[14] Apparently the United States is counting on 23 days of warning time prior to conflict and on a war which will last 30–180 days thereafter. (The *New York Times*, 24 September 1976, p. A7.)

As in the case of ground troops, numbers are not the only factor which must be noted with respect to air power: the types of aircraft, their capabilities, the quality of their pilots, and so on, will affect significantly the ability of air forces to operate against one another and against targets on the ground or at sea. In general, NATO has a higher proportion of multi-purpose aircraft which can operate flexibly in various missions and are superior to most Warsaw Pact planes in range, payload and armament. This gives it a long-range deep-strike capability which the Warsaw Pact cannot match. Moreover, NATO is probably also superior in the sophistication of its equipment and the training of its air crews. On the other hand, the Warsaw Pact has in recent years introduced new types of aircraft, such as the MiG-23, which are possibly superior to their NATO counterparts. Moreover, most Pact aircraft, being designed to operate from dispersed natural airfields serviced by mobile systems, can be more widely and speedily deployed; they also have the great advantage of standard ground-support equipment, which enables any airfield to service any plane.

Unfortunately, all these different factors are not measurable in precise terms. Differences in numbers of aircraft are, and here the Warsaw Pact has a local advantage and NATO a global one. The Warsaw Pact could quickly augment the number of aircraft on the central and southern fronts, thereby increasing its marginal peacetime advantages over the short run.[15] However, as American planes began to arrive, which they could in a matter of days, the balance would begin to tip the other way. Some years ago the then US Secretary of Defense, Robert S. McNamara, estimated that 'NATO tactical air-

---

[15] *The Military Balance 1976–77*, p. 102, gives the overall totals as follows:

Tactical aircraft in operational service	Northern and Central Europe			Southern Europe		
	NATO	Warsaw Pact	(of which USSR)	NATO	Warsaw Pact	(of which USSR)
Light bombers	185	225	200	–	50	50
Fighter/ground attack	1,250	1,375	950	450	250	100
Interceptors	375	2,050	950	275	700	200
Reconnaissance	275	550	400	150	100	50
TOTAL	2,085	4,200	2,500	875	1,100	400

These totals include Soviet aircraft redeployed from the western military districts of the Soviet Union, and NATO aircraft currently based in Britain and in Spain (where the United States has several wings of fighter-bombers), but not reinforcements from the United States nor French aircraft numbering about 500.

craft reinforcements would about equal the Pact's in the early stages of mobilization, after which we could add considerably more aircraft than the Pact',[16] and the situation has not changed markedly since then.

Whether either side will in fact have numerical superiority at any given time will depend in part on the willingness of the United States and the Soviet Union to redeploy forces from other areas, such as the Far East. It will depend also on their ability to do this quickly, which is a function of the range of the aircraft, the number of airfields which they can use *en route* and on arrival, their degree of operational readiness, and whether fuel, ammunition and other supplies are prestocked or must be transported along with the aircraft. It will also depend significantly on whether this redeployment is uninterrupted or impeded; if local airfields are bombed, oil-storage tanks destroyed, depots attacked and so on, then the numbers of aircraft in the Moscow Military District or in the American Mid-west may be relatively unimportant. But at least they are there–and must be reckoned with.

Naval Forces

As shown in Table 4, Naval Forces Available for Operations in Europe, Mid-1976, p. 251, there are almost as many asymmetries in the naval forces of NATO and the Warsaw Pact as there are in their ground and air forces. Thus NATO has more attack carriers and major combat surface ships (as well as more specialized anti-submarine warfare (ASW) vessels and minesweepers), whereas the Soviet Union and her allies have more attack submarines (and patrol craft). The Soviet Black Sea Fleet and Baltic Fleet operate in restricted waters, whose exits are controlled by NATO, and only the Northern Fleet, based on the Kola Peninsula, has relatively free access to the Atlantic Ocean. Conversely, the Western allies have many more bases and much greater freedom of transit, but could find it difficult to operate in the Baltic and the Eastern Mediterranean, and possibly in the Norwegian Sea. Whereas the Soviet Union would find it almost impossible, once hostilities had begun, to redeploy elements of its Far Eastern fleet, the

---

[16] Although Mr McNamara gave no basis for his judgment, he apparently assumed that the Soviet Union would deploy to Central Europe only part of her 4,500-plane Tactical Air Force and little or none of her Air Defence Force. If sizeable elements of the latter, which, as of 1976 numbered about 2,600 aircraft, were redeployed, the Pact could probably maintain its numerical advantage–at the risk of leaving the Soviet Union more vulnerable to bombing attacks, should the war escalate. See *Statement by Secretary of Defense Robert S. McNamara before the Senate Armed Services Committee on the FY 1969–73 Defense Program and 1969 Defense Budget*, mimeograph, p. 81.

United States could bring in additional ships from its Pacific Fleet and others from its sizeable reserve.

These asymmetries in part reflect historical accidents, but they also reflect the differences in the missions of the navies of the two alliances. That of the Warsaw Pact (which is to say basically that of the Soviet Union) is first and foremost to shield the USSR from attacks by missile submarines based in the Mediterranean and the North Atlantic. Its second major mission is that of coastal defence, which accounts for the large numbers of patrol craft and torpedo boats in the navies of the Warsaw Pact countries. A third mission is anti-shipping, employing primarily attack submarines with torpedoes and cruise missiles, and a fourth is ship-to-shore bombardment, using the same submarines but with nuclear-armed missiles. The Warsaw Pact also has a very limited amphibious capability, concentrated mostly in the Baltic, where Poland and East Germany maintain some four amphibious brigades and the Soviet Union two. The NATO naval forces exist primarily to control the seas, a mission which includes not only the destruction of Soviet surface warships but also the neutralization of Soviet submarines and the secure passage of convoys, should any conflict last long. A second mission, particularly important in the Mediterranean and in the north-east Atlantic, is that of providing air support, conducting offshore bombardments and landing amphibious forces to reinforce threatened points or attack key positions in enemy-held coastal areas. A third mission is the attrition of Soviet missile submarines, but this is minor compared to the other two (even for American forces, which devote considerable resources to the task).

THE NON-ALIGNED COUNTRIES

So far we have spoken only of the military forces of the NATO and Warsaw Pact countries, but there are other forces in Europe. The eight largest non-aligned nations[17] have a total population of 90 million, almost equal to that of France and Italy combined, and not far short of that of the six countries of Eastern Europe. As of 1976, their armed forces number almost 800,000, and include about 55 division-equivalents, over 1,500 combat aircraft, and some 500 warships.[18] Thus, taken together, they possess considerable military power.

The rub is, of course, that they cannot be taken together, including, as they do, nations with divergent political philosophies and different interests. Moreover, they are scattered across Europe from the North Cape to the Iberian Peninsula, and are in many instances separated

[17] Albania, Austria, Eire, Finland, Spain, Sweden, Switzerland, and Yugoslavia.
[18] See *The Military Balance 1976–77*, pp. 27–30.

from one another by political as well as geographical distances. Nevertheless, some of them have important influences on the military balance in Europe.

In some instances, this is because of their location. Finland–and, even more, Sweden–shield most of Norway from attack from the east, Austria protects the southern flank of NATO forces in the Federal Republic of Germany, and, together with Yugoslavia, separates Italy from the Soviet forces in South-Eastern Europe. Spain occupies an important position at the exit from the Mediterranean into the Atlantic, and Albania a scarcely less important one where the Adriatic Sea joins the main body of the Mediterranean. Their neutrality, therefore, could be a positive advantage, to one side or the other, while their adherence to one of the alliances could give it access to key geographic positions from which to further extend its air and naval operations.

Furthermore, some of these countries (like Spain, Sweden, Switzerland, and Yugoslavia) possess sizeable and comparatively well-equipped forces which could tip the scales one way or another in regional military operations. For instance, Admiral Horacio Rivero, USN, former Commander-in-Chief Allied Forces Southern Europe, estimated that the Warsaw Pact forces available for an attack on Northern Italy would outnumber the defenders by two to one on the ground and two-and-a-half to one in the air.[19] However, if Yugoslavia resisted any efforts by Warsaw Pact units to advance through her territory (which offers the quickest and least defensible route into Italy), her forces would almost redress the balance on the ground and would materially alter the imbalance in numbers of tactical aircraft.

In isolated operations, the capabilities of the individual countries are perhaps less significant, partly because overwhelming power could be brought to bear against any one of them and partly because it might not have access to the supplies and equipment it would need for sustained conventional operations. Even so, Sweden or Yugoslavia could offer strong resistance to external attacks, as, of course, could Switzerland. Even Finland or Albania, with much smaller forces, could put up stubborn resistance over difficult terrain for at least short periods of time.

Conversely, these countries have comparatively limited capabilities for offensive operations. This in part reflects the level of equipment, the state of organization and the training of their armed services, but it also reflects the fact that they would immediately come up against one or other of the alliances, with potentially dire consequences.

[19] 'The Defence of NATO's Southern Flank', *Royal United Services Institute Journal* (June 1972), p. 4.

Moreover, none of these countries has any unsatisfied territorial ambitions which would cause it to take such action, nor such ideological differences with a neighbour as to make conflict seem probable; even Albania and Yugoslavia have settled down to 'hostile co-existence'.

MILITARY CAPABILITIES

Obviously, any estimate of the capabilities of the forces of the two alliances is highly dependent on scenarios, warning time, the duration of the war, whether or not it stays conventional and a host of other variables. To examine all possible scenarios is obviously impossible, as it is to estimate precisely the outcomes of any conflicts, a task which is beyond the ability of the most experienced planner supported by the most extensive analyses. It is, however, feasible–if risky–to select for examination some rather obvious military options and to make some very crude comparisons of capabilities.

1. The Warsaw Pact is capable of launching local operations against limited objectives with little or no warning, examples being the airfields and ports in Northern Norway, the Danish island of Bornholm, and conceivably Hamburg or Kiel in West Germany, all of which are close to Warsaw Pact troop concentrations and bases. It could also–albeit with greater difficulty–land small forces on the northern coast of Turkey or smash through Grecian Thrace to the Aegean Sea. NATO has relatively fewer potential targets available to it, and is handicapped in attempting similar operations by its inferiority in ground forces, and by its inability to penetrate the Baltic or the Black Seas in strength.

2. The Warsaw Pact could also launch sizeable air strikes (and/or ship-to-shore missile strikes) at isolated targets, such as Tromsö in Norway or Samsun in Turkey. NATO, in part because of the longer ranges of its land-based aircraft, and in part because of its carrier-borne units, is even better able to carry out this type of attack, for instance on Murmansk and the associated military facilities on the Kola Peninsula.

3. The Warsaw Pact could conduct limited naval operations in the Black, Baltic and Norwegian Seas, designed to destroy or drive off NATO ships; however, it would itself be vulnerable to similar operations in the Mediterranean and, in the longer run, in the Norwegian Sea.

4. Each alliance could conduct anti-shipping campaigns, with the Warsaw Pact probably able to interrupt the flow of commodities to countries of Western Europe (at the cost of losing its own shipping at sea), at least until NATO ASW forces were augmented, convoys were organized and the slow process of protection and

attrition took effect. It is conceivable that such a campaign could be isolated as part of a crisis or confrontation in Europe, but, given the stakes and the risks of any such enterprise, it is more likely to be part of a broader conflict.

5. The Warsaw Pact could launch a sizeable surprise attack with conventional forces, taking advantage of the fact that not all NATO units are deployed in blocking positions; that even where they are, the defending troops are thinly spread (especially on the Central Front); that the Warsaw Pact is superior in mobile elements; and that the ability to choose the time and place of such an attack would give it further advantages. By such an attack it might hope to disrupt NATO defences, perhaps to shatter the opposing forces, and possibly to overrun considerable territory, including most of Germany east of the Rhine. How successful the attack might be would depend on the degree of surprise, on how far the Warsaw Pact was willing to extend the theatre of operations (a broad attack would risk escalation and a narrow one would leave untouched the tactical air squadrons in Spain, France and England) and on the nature of the NATO response. If the response remained conventional, the Warsaw Pact might, according to some Western estimates, have a good chance of making sizeable gains. But if NATO reacted by using tactical nuclear weapons, as prescribed by its present doctrine, all bets would be off. Conversely, NATO lacks the ability to launch a surprise attack under normal circumstances. Only if both the Warsaw Pact units immediately available, such as the East German and Czechoslovak divisions and the Soviet troops in those countries, were caught up in an internal upheaval, could NATO hope to succeed in limited conventional operations. Only when instabilities in Eastern Europe led to uprisings, therefore, would Western intervention be practicable.[20]

6. Instead of attacking with the forces in place, the members of the Warsaw Pact could first undertake partial or total mobilization, which would enable them to increase their advantages in divisions, tanks and aircraft and provide the transport units and other logistic support elements needed for extended conflict. As before, they might hope to penetrate Western defences, to turn these by a flank move (for example, through Austria against Southern Germany) or by amphibious landings to take in the rear the Turkish forces in Thrace. Here again, the likelihood of success, based on the balance of forces and the terrain, is greatest in West

[20] Theoretically, similar upheavals in Western Europe could also help the Soviet Union, but such upheavals are both less likely and less essential to the success of conventional operations.

Germany and in Denmark. However, to all the other uncertainties—about the degree of success in conventional operations, whether or not NATO would employ nuclear weapons, and so on—they would have to add uncertainties about allied behaviour during the mobilization period, since interdictory attacks at this time could have a shattering effect, particularly if made with nuclear weapons. For its part, NATO would have great difficulty in carrying out such an attack, which could at best achieve minor and local gains.

7. The Warsaw Pact is also capable of launching a combined nuclear–conventional attack, either with or without significant warning; indeed, this kind of operation is consistent with the doctrine, training and, to some extent, equipment of Warsaw Pact forces. NATO, of course, is also capable of launching such an attack, and its numerical and qualitative superiority in nuclear-capable aircraft might give it a meaningful advantage. A problem for both sides is that, as indicated earlier, neither can count on knocking out all the tactical delivery vehicles of the other, and that each side has weapons outside the theatre which could if necessary be used: the MR/IRBM in the Soviet Union and the missile submarines and carrier aircraft in the Mediterranean, to give just two illustrations. Furthermore, the number of weapons available is such that any ground advance could literally be pulverized; it is only restraint on their employment that enables conventional (or mixed) operations to proceed in anything resembling an organized fashion.[21] Finally, whatever the likelihood that other levels and forms of attack might escalate, this type would be almost certain to do so, since the adversary would be shocked into taking action, deprived of the normal means of response, and, in the case of the Soviet Union, confronted with independent nuclear powers whose interests and preconceptions might lead them to take actions which their super-power ally would prefer not to see carried out.

8. It is even more clear that a strategic strike would be likely to lead to a nuclear exchange between the United States and the Soviet

[21] For the view that God is on the side of the heavier battalions, even in tactical nuclear war, see Wolfgang Heisenberg, *The Alliance and Europe, Part I: Crisis Stability in Europe and Theatre Nuclear Weapons*, Adelphi Paper No. 96 (London: IISS, Summer 1973), pp. 8–13. However, most of the studies which led to this (not uncommon) opinion were carried out in an era of nuclear scarcity, which no longer exists. Moreover, some at least of these studies were essentially self-serving, in that they were designed to 'prove' that land armies had significant roles, even in nuclear war.

Union. As indicated previously, neither country can disarm the other, and each can inflict tremendous damage in retaliatory strikes. If, under these circumstances, it makes little sense to risk such a response, it makes no sense at all to take action which could provoke it—as the leaders of the two super-powers have agreed.[22]

9. Obviously, either NATO or the Warsaw Pact would be better able to bring overpowering military force to bear against one of the non-aligned countries than against the other alliance. Its actual ability to do so would depend on the geographic position of the country, with Finland, for example, exposed to Soviet invasion and Spain secure against that particular threat. It would also depend on whether the military operation was an isolated one, in which case one could expect constraints on the scale and scope of any attack, or whether it was part of a larger conflict, in which case these constraints might not apply. In general, the non-aligned countries would be helpless against a nuclear strike, vulnerable to the exercise of air and naval power, and open, in varying degrees, to attacks by ground forces. More importantly, some of them would be susceptible to limited operations aimed at sapping their strength or their will to resist pressures: operations such as the interception of shipping, the sinking of naval vessels, the shooting down of civil or military aircraft, and so on.

10. To sum up, NATO and the Warsaw Pact are more or less evenly matched in their capabilities for waging nuclear war, strategic or tactical. The Warsaw Pact has some advantages in conventional capabilities, arising out of geography, the readiness for combat of its forces and the structure of that organization and its member nations (which allows them to decide on military operations without public debate and to carry them through with little or no warning). However, these advantages hold largely at the higher levels of conventional conflict, where the risks of escalation are the greatest and the potential consequences of operations are least predictable. Both sides are well able to launch selective air strikes, but NATO has a significant advantage in its ability to conduct major naval operations and to land amphibious forces. However, asymmetries in terrain, troop deployments, and so on, mean that neither capabilities nor advantages can be exploited fully; thus it may be relatively easy for the Soviet Union to land small forces in northern Norway, but difficult to maintain them there in the face of allied counter-actions, and virtually impossible for these forces to press southwards.

[22] See Chapter 1, note 11.

PERCEPTIONS OF SECURITY

The view from NATO

Security in Europe cannot be considered solely in terms of what each side can do, but of what the leaders and peoples of the other side (and of the non-aligned nations) are concerned that it may do. In this and subsequent sections, I will try to aggregate their varying perceptions, as revealed in published works, the press, speeches and interviews, in order to obtain an intelligible, and I hope accurate, assessment of concerns about security.

As suggested in Chapter 1,[23] most of those speaking for and about NATO tend to see the balance of capabilities in Europe as tilting in favour of the Warsaw Pact. They point to the achievement by the Soviet Union of rough strategic parity with the United States, and to her continuing possession of powerful theatre nuclear forces. They refer to the steady improvement of her conventional capabilities, and especially to the imbalance between Warsaw Pact and NATO forces on the central front and, in a more limited context, in the far north. They seem to be particularly concerned about the deployment of Soviet naval forces to new areas of the world, and about the build-up of the Soviet flotilla in the Mediterranean and of the Northern Fleet, which the former British Secretary of State for Defence, Lord Carrington, described as 'a powerful threat against the northern flank of Europe . . . a powerful threat in the Atlantic, and . . . as powerful a threat to the land-mass of Europe itself as the land forces under the Warsaw Pact'.[24] Thus, even though NATO has undoubted naval superiority, as well as more men under arms and more combat aircraft, current trends are seen as favouring the Warsaw Pact.

Somewhat surprisingly, this assessment of Soviet/Warsaw Pact military capabilities has not resulted in perceptions of direct threats to the security of Western Europe. There seems to be no fear that the Soviet Union will employ its overwhelming nuclear power to initiate nuclear war—in fact this possibility is almost never mentioned. Even the specific threats posed by the Soviet MR/IRBM are seldom discussed—and then only in the context of a counter to NATO tactical nuclear delivery vehicles, rather than as the instrument for a Soviet onslaught against NATO Europe. As for Warsaw Pact tactical nuclear

[23] See pp. 11–2.

[24] *Hansard*, 23 February 1973, p. 1314. For a Norwegian view of the threat, see Jann T. Lund, 'North Sea Defense and National Security', *Aftenposten*, 27 January 1975, p. 4, translated in Foreign Broadcast Information Service (FBIS), Western Europe (Norway), 7 February 1975, pp. 41–3.

forces, these may figure in military plans, but they do not seem to be salient in perceptions of threat.

Moreover, while both national and NATO officials tend to place great stress on imbalances in conventional forces which could enable the Soviet Union to launch a successful attack, little fear of such an attack is actually apparent. Thus, French President Valéry Giscard d'Estaing asserted that 'the Soviet Union's leaders have no aggressive military programmes or intentions against West Europe'.[25] In 1974 the British Secretary of State for Foreign Affairs, James Callaghan (now Prime Minister), reminded his NATO colleagues that 'none of us believes that the present Soviet leaders have any desire or intention to engage in acts of military aggression against the West'.[26] The German White Paper of 1970 admitted that 'a major aggression aimed at the annihilation or annexation of the Federal Republic and our neighbours is not beyond the military capabilities of the Warsaw Pact. It would, however, touch off the process of deliberate escalation on the part of NATO and, if the aggressor continued his operations, it could easily develop into a general nuclear war ... Therefore, a major aggression against Western Europe is at present not very likely.'[27] And not only Dr Joseph Luns, the Secretary-General of NATO, but other high officials also have indicated that they consider such an attack unlikely.[28]

As for limited attacks or attempted *coups de main*, these are also viewed as unlikely, largely because of the dubious gains and potential costs of such undertakings. Even though some elements in particular countries seem to be concerned about local attacks, such as an amphibious invasion of northern Norway, it is hard to determine whether they see these as independent operations serving military ends, or as threats which could be used to back up political pressures.

The main concern seems to be not direct and deliberate assaults, whether massive or small-scale, but the initiation of actions which could eventually lead to larger conflicts. The one most frequently mentioned is Soviet intervention in the event of a new upheaval in Eastern Europe (and specifically in the German Democratic Republic)

[25] *Le Monde*, 28 May 1975, pp. 2–3, translated and reprinted in FBIS, Western Europe (France), 29 May 1975, p. K12.

[26] The Rt. Hon. James Callaghan, MP, 'Britain and NATO', *NATO Review*, Vol. 22, No. 4 (August 1974), p. 14.

[27] *White Paper 1970 on the Security of the Federal Republic of Germany and on the State of the German Federal Armed Forces* (Bonn: Press and Information Office of the German Federal Government, 20 May 1970), hereafter cited as *German White Paper, 1970*, para. 26, p. 20.

[28] Joseph Luns, 'The Present State of East–West Relations', *NATO Review*, Vol. 24, No. 2, April 1976, pp. 3–7.

–an action which could trigger off a Western counter-intervention, or could involve units attempting to put down the upheaval in combat with Western troops deployed along the borders. A second possibility which causes concern is that of a Soviet/Warsaw Pact operation against a non-NATO country which threatened the security of NATO members–a concern which was so strong after the Soviet intervention in Czechoslovakia in 1968 that the NATO Council of Ministers issued an explicit warning against such operations.[29] A third is that the Soviet Union (or the United States) might take action outside Europe which could lead to a conflict in Europe–this being one reason for opposition to any extension of the war in Vietnam.

The major cause of this concern is the development by the Soviet Union of 'globally mobile forces', notably an ocean-going surface fleet and a small but élite naval infantry. Some worry lest these be used to interdict the sea lines of communication which are vital to the countries of Western Europe; others fear that they might enable the Soviet Union to intervene in unstable areas where small forces could secure a rich prize–such as Bahrein, Kuwait and other oil-producing areas in the Persian Gulf. Still others are afraid that the Soviet Navy might attempt to preclude intervention by NATO members to alleviate threats to their security from third parties,[30] in the process starting a conflict which could have incalculable–but presumably dire–consequences.

There is even greater concern about Warsaw Pact or Soviet political actions involving threats of force or indirect uses of force than there is about the employment of military power. In this sense, threats to cut sea lines of communication or to disrupt the flow of oil from the Middle East to Europe could be reminders of Soviet presence and power, aimed at inducing a change in policy or affecting bargaining and decision-making in times of crisis.[31] So too could be the dispatch of Soviet submarines into Norwegian fjords, the shadowing of Norwegian merchant-vessels by Soviet warships, and the conduct of amphibious manoeuvres off the north coast of Norway, all of which could reinforce demands for bases in northern Norway or pressures for

[29] Final Communiqué of the Ministerial Meeting of the North Atlantic Council, 14–16 November 1968, para. 6. Reprinted in *NATO Facts and Figures* (Brussels: NATO Information Service, 1970), p. 338.

[30] Sir Bernard Burrows and Christopher Irwin, *The Security of Western Europe* (London: Charles Knight, 1972), p. 82.

[31] Johan Jorgen Holst, 'The Soviet Build-up in the North-East Atlantic', *NATO Review* (October 1971), reprinted in *Survival* (January/February 1972), p. 27. See also *The Future of the Netherlands Defence Effort*, Report to the Government of the Netherlands by the Commission of Civilian and Military Experts, March 1972, English Version, mimeograph, p. 14.

the ousting of NATO personnel from Norway. As the West German Government put it, 'The narrowing, through pressure or threats, of their freedom of political decision is the real danger which the Federal Republic and her allies might have to face.'[32]

The most widespread concern, however, is a more general one: that the continued growth of Soviet power in relation to that of the Western allies may enable the Soviet Union to over-awe the Europeans. By discreet warnings of what 'overwhelming power can accomplish if more palatable methods do not work', the Soviet Union may be able to bring about changes in behaviour.[33] More importantly, she may be able to promote a feeling that accommodation is the only possible policy. While this is deemed unlikely at the present, there is a feeling that if NATO were further weakened and/or the American presence were significantly scaled down, the sheer disparity of military strength would leave Western Europe with no convincing strategy and no confidence in its ability to sustain a confrontation if one occurred. Under these circumstances, to quote Edward Heath, 'a process of disintegration could begin which would lead to the ultimate prize, an extension of the Soviet sphere of influence gradually into countries at present members of the Alliance and, if possible, to the Atlantic'.[34] And this process could lead to what is sometimes termed 'Finlandization', that is to a Europe whose member states, while preserving their autonomy, would of necessity avoid anti-Soviet policies and would be responsive to the wishes of the Soviet Union.

Under these circumstances, it is understandable that the European members of NATO should value above all else the American commitment to the defence of Europe, which alone can redress imbalances in power and safeguard the West Europeans against Soviet threats, real or fancied. It is also understandable that they should seek to ensure the validity of that commitment (and the viability of NATO defences) by keeping strong American forces in Western Europe, and that they should attempt to overcome the crisis of confidence arising from the Soviet development of counter-deterrent forces by attempting to link conventional operations with strategic nuclear ones, through the medium of tactical nuclear forces. Finally, it is understandable that some among them, concerned both about that linkage and about the firmness of the American commitment, should wish to strengthen indigenous nuclear capabilities, either through closer Anglo–French co-operation or through joint action by a larger number of states.

[32] *German White Paper, 1970*, para. 29, p. 21.
[33] Nils Ørvik, 'Scandinavian Security in Transition: The Two-Dimensional Threat', *Orbis*, Volume XVI, No. 3 (Fall 1972), p. 23.
[34] *Hansard*, 2 March 1971, p. 1418.

Thus the West Europeans have assets they would wish to keep throughout negotiations on arms control, as well as liabilities of which they would like to dispose.

The outlook from the Warsaw Pact

The Warsaw Pact assessment of military capabilities is understandably different from that of NATO. Soviet and East European writers have referred continually to the overall superiority of NATO in manpower, ships and aircraft; have admitted that the West is at least equal in terms of strategic nuclear capabilities; and may feel that it is ahead in advanced military technology. Perhaps more importantly, NATO is seen as having a particular and immediate advantage in tactical nuclear delivery vehicles, which are, moreover, more versatile, more capable and more mobile than their Soviet counterparts. Thus it is no wonder that the Soviet Union has striven to achieve reductions in American strike aircraft in Europe (the so-called Forward Based Systems),[35] which also seem particularly threatening to its associates in the Warsaw Pact.

Within this context, the Warsaw Pact has placed major reliance on Soviet strategic nuclear forces to preclude an attack against members of the Socialist Commonwealth. Other elements of the armed forces are seen less as contributing to deterrence than as a means of defence and an instrument for the exploitation of Soviet counter-blows. Thus Soviet naval deployments, which many in the West view as threatening, may well be intended to keep at a distance Western missile-submarines and aircraft-carriers, and the mobile armoured and motorized units in Central Europe may be seen as ancillary to a nuclear exchange, and not as designed for independent conventional operations.

Nevertheless, when one puts on Warsaw Pact glasses, one sees some similarities in perceptions of threat, as well as some significant differences. The most marked similarity is that neither the Soviet Union nor the countries of Eastern Europe seem to fear a strategic nuclear attack: first, because there is no reason for this to be directed against Eastern Europe, and second, because it is deterred by Soviet nuclear power. Thus while an American strategic strike is still, in official military doctrine, both the threat which must be countered and the probable *casus belli*, apparently it carries even less weight among political leaders than does the threat of an all-out Soviet conventional assault among their Western counterparts.

One major difference is that there is considerable concern in the Soviet Union—and even more in Eastern Europe—about the possibilities of tactical nuclear war. This could occur as a result of the

---

[35] See Chapter 4, p. 82.

all-out nuclear–conventional assault by NATO, an *idée fixe* in Warsaw Pact military thinking, or as a result of the NATO doctrine of flexible response. It could arise out of political instability in Eastern Europe, leading to Western intervention or to armed clashes between the peoples of East and West (again, East Germany seems to be the most feared cause of such instability, and the most likely country from which a conflict could spill over into the West). A tactical nuclear war could also result from attempts by a revanchist West Germany armed with nuclear weapons to recoup the losses of World War II–although this threat seems diminished recently, due as much to political changes in the West German leadership as to FRG ratification of the Nuclear Non-Proliferation Treaty. Finally, a tactical nuclear war could come about as a result of a conflict elsewhere spreading to Europe. In any case, limited war is seen as impossible and nuclear devastation as a likely consequence of any war between East and West. In the words of one Polish writer, 'Even the kind of "Brest-to-Brest" engagement contemplated by some American strategists–a theatre, in other words, running from the River Bug to the Atlantic–would amount to an all-out war with the most appalling consequences.'[36]

Although there are apparently discussions in military circles of other threats, such as strikes by American carrier-borne aircraft against Murmansk, it seems that these are visualized as general war operations and not as limited and localized attacks. Moreover, concerns about such threats do not seem to be serious outside the Soviet Union–nor even very great within it. While there are frequent references to Western aggression and intervention in the Third World, there is little or no discussion of attacks on the Mediterranean Squadron, threats to Soviet shipping, or the esoteric scenarios involving crisis behaviour and bargaining which are so common in the West. Thus the Soviet Union and its allies do not seem greatly worried about direct military operations by Western air and naval forces, even though their superiority is generally acknowledged.

As is true in NATO, the members of the Warsaw Pact seem much more concerned with political threats than with military ones, and with indirect threats rather than direct ones. Some of these concerns are passive, as is the one that a strong Western Europe might act to curb Soviet influence and to restrict the ability of the Soviet Union to use her political, economic and military power. Other, and more active, concerns are that West Germany may seek some form of association with East Germany, some adjustment in the present situation.

[36] Ryszard Frelek, 'Some Remarks on European Security and Co-operation' *Sprawy Miedzynarodowe*, Special [English Language] Edition, 1970, p. 7.

There is also the fear that close association with the West may undermine political stability in Eastern Europe, encourage the development of alternatives to the present economic and social structures, and lead to the erosion of Communist power. Thus, *détente* may lessen the fear of war, but it does not necessarily enhance the sense of security among the members of the socialist camp.[37]

Here it is necessary to make two important distinctions between the perceptions of threat in Eastern Europe and those in the West. The first is that we are talking about various forms of political association, rather than about the actual or threatened use of force—and hence are in some sense discussing issues outside the scope of our definition of security. The second is that this fear of political moves affects differently various elements in the Soviet Union and Eastern Europe. It is safe to say that all the regimes are concerned lest this association create developments which threaten their political power—or at least force the pace of change and alter its direction. The Soviet Union is particularly concerned lest it undermine bloc solidarity (which is not all that the Soviet leaders would desire), increase their problems in dealing with their associates and perhaps require tighter and costlier controls over the other members of the Warsaw Pact. As for the countries of Eastern Europe, they are concerned in varying degrees lest associations with the West introduce changes which would prompt action by the Soviet Union, either in the form of armed intervention such as took place against Hungary and Czechoslovakia, or in the form of a threat to resort to armed intervention—a threat which is even more meaningful after the 1968 operations against Czechoslovakia. Thus they would like at least to shape the Soviet presence and to restrict Soviet military actions in ways which, while not depriving them of support, would give them a greater freedom of choice as to when to call for that support, and would increase their ability to prescribe the form that it should take.

---

[37] Adam B. Ulam, 'The Destiny of Eastern Europe', *Problems of Communism*, Vol. 23, No. 1 (January/February 1974), especially pp. 7 and 12. *See also* Robert Hirg and Robert Dean (eds.), *East European Perspectives on European Security and Co-operation* (New York: Praeger, 1974).

Chapter 3

THE SCOPE OF ARMS CONTROL[1]

Many of the perceptions of threat listed previously are based on assessments of what a potential opponent is capable of doing, not on estimates of what he will necessarily do: i.e., they reflect capabilities rather than intentions. However, even those who deem it unlikely that particular threats will be implemented, or who argue that the development of military capabilities implies nothing about their potential uses, must consider the fallibility of human judgments and the uncertainties associated with political prognoses. Accordingly, most prudent leaders will seek to offset potential threats to national security, either by building forces which can deter or counter these threats or by adopting arms-control measures which can ameliorate them, or by doing both. In this chapter we will look at what arms control can offer that 'prudent leader' who chooses arms control as one of his instruments of policy.

ARMS CONTROL AND MILITARY CAPABILITIES

In this context, arms-control measures may afford benefits far exceeding potential costs or contingent liabilities. If a country is concerned about the possibility that another state may launch limited conventional operations against vulnerable points to achieve political gains, there are a number of ways dealing with such a threat. One would be to develop nuclear-capable forces and a doctrine for their employment which would virtually ensure their being used in the event of such operations; however, such a policy implies both willingness and ability to produce atomic weapons and also enough confidence in their deterrent effect to adopt a policy which, should it fail, would almost inevitably precipitate a nuclear war. An alternative would be to build up local defences; however, no country can be strong everywhere, and an aggressor can choose both the place and the time of an attack. A third option would be to develop mobile tactical forces, which could block or seal off penetrations. This, however, can be costly and may be ineffective, particularly if the opponent

[1] As used here, 'arms control' includes any measure limiting or reducing forces, regulating armaments or restricting the deployment of troops and/or weapons which is intended to induce responsive behaviour, or which is taken pursuant to an understanding with another state or states.

possesses greater resources or is able to deploy his forces in positions from which surprise attacks can be launched.

A different way of coping with limited conventional attacks would be to press for arms-control measures which would both reduce the ability to initiate such attacks and preclude their being launched with little or no warning. To this end, one could aim at restricting the deployment of forces in particular areas, either by establishing de-militarized zones, by reaching agreement on troop ceilings, or by prohibiting the stationing of units particularly suited for offensive operations, such as amphibious brigades. Alternatively, one could reduce the percentage of offensive forces, replacing them with less mobile and less powerful units, or cut down on those weapons most useful in an offensive, such as tanks, armoured personnel-carriers and self-propelled guns. In either case, one could set up joint observation posts which would give evidence of gross violations and warning of steps taken preparatory to an attack, could introduce third-party missions into the zone of control, and so on. While nobody might be willing, at this stage of affairs, to rely completely on such measures, it is obvious that they could both complement preparations for defence and eliminate the necessity for more expensive and more provocative steps, such as building up one's own military establishment.

Similarly, arms control can be used to avoid or to limit clashes between forces confronting one another, a possibility of continuing concern to many planners. Thus, the establishment of demilitarized zones would preclude troops (although not necessarily police or civilians) from firing on one another, and restrictions on the introduc-tion into such zones of additional forces or particular types of weapons would militate against intensification of any conflict. Separating nuclear warheads from conventional ones and keeping the former well back from any zone of confrontation would inhibit escalation of any clash by depriving local commanders of the possibility of using nuclear weapons and by avoiding the prospect of their being overrun and seized, which might induce a political decision to fire them before capture. The exchange of liaison missions and the establishment of 'hot lines' between the military headquarters of the two sides could also help, by enabling rapid communication with trusted subordinates 'on the spot'. (Admittedly, all these measures look to settle clashes rather than to exploit them, and thus may run counter to the interests of some countries or the fears of others; however, the point is that they do offer alternatives to the more typical kinds of military response which might otherwise be adopted.)

In the same way, large-scale surprise attacks can be deterred or countered by some combination of military and arms-control measures. Militarily, strong screening forces along frontiers, the fortification and garrisoning of key points, preplanned demolitions, and the creation of larger and more mobile field forces can all deter surprise attacks or enable one to cope with them. So, alternatively, could restrictions on the size and location of manoeuvres, which would make it more difficult for troops to preposition themselves for an attack under the guise of engaging in routine training exercises. Restrictions on the number of men in active service would also have the same effect, since these would reduce the number of units available for a surprise attack, possibly necessitate partial mobilization of reserves (thereby decreasing the likelihood of achieving surprise) and probably affect the capability of troops for offensive operations more markedly than their ability to engage in defensive fighting. Surprise attacks could be further inhibited by agreement not to interfere with national means of surveillance, such as flights along national borders by aircraft equipped with side-looking radar, or to authorize limited and selective aerial reconnaissance over the territory of another state, on either a national or a multinational basis. If one wished to go still further, the deployment of neutral troops in key areas or the creation of joint patrols from the armies of the opposing powers could afford further guarantees against surprise attack. Moreover, such measures would be cheaper and less provocative than improvements in defensive forces and would perhaps achieve more.

Carried a step further, such measures could also reduce the possibility of a deliberate attack succeeding, thereby further inhibiting such an attack. Reserve forces, which are usually less well trained and frequently less well equipped than those on active duty, are correspondingly likely to be less effective in an attack; hence, cuts in active forces could tip the scale in favour of the defender. So, in a different way, could eliminating or drastically reducing reserve units, which might be needed to achieve the degree of superiority essential to a successful attack. Budgetary restrictions could affect not only the size and state of readiness of armed forces but also their equipment, and particularly the production of highly mobile, long-range—and generally very expensive—offensive weapons. Alternatively, selective constraints could be imposed on offensive weapons such as tanks and fighter-bombers, leaving unrestricted the production and deployment of anti-tank guns, surface-to-air missiles and possibly interceptor aircraft. In these and other ways the ability of an attacker to exploit any military successes could be reduced without putting the defender at a corresponding disadvantage.

So far we have been talking largely about the implications of arms control for land warfare, but this is not the only milieu in which constraints on forces may be desirable. For many countries, even in Europe, naval power poses particular threats: intervention in a crisis, quick assaults to seize territory, interdiction of sea lines of communication, and sea and air attacks on lucrative targets. Given the mobility of warships (which, even in fleet formation, can steam 500 miles in 24 hours) and the presence of powerful flotillas in most of the major seas, it is hard to envisage measures which would effectively preclude these threats, much less be acceptable to the countries capable of carrying them out. Despite this, there are some possibilities worth considering.

One would be an agreement limiting the size of amphibious forces, afloat or ashore, in a given region. Although there are certainly cases where a battalion could achieve results, there are many more where only a brigade or a division could hope to intervene successfully or to seize and hold territory; demobilizing or redeploying larger-sized units would thus increase the security of small powers – albeit at the expense of larger ones. A complementary measure would be to put ceilings on the number and types of ships permitted in crucial areas such as the Barents Sea, the Baltic Sea and the Mediterranean, ceilings which could be exceeded only after due notice and for limited periods of time. A third would be to accept restrictions on movement of naval vessels into the territorial waters of countries undergoing potential crises or internal convulsions, thereby inhibiting armed intervention (if not the kind of silent pressure exerted by warships deployed farther offshore).

While one could conceivably place limits on attack submarines (in which the Soviet Union leads) and on attack carriers (of which the United States has a monopoly), it is doubtful that any conceivable ceilings would eliminate the ability of either country to disrupt sea traffic, should it choose to do so. More promising would be arrangements to curb the number of hunter-killer submarines and patrol aircraft, and to prescribe the areas in which these could operate, thereby giving additional safeguards to ballistic-missile submarines. Although these are almost invulnerable to present anti-submarine warfare forces, and are likely to become more so as their propulsion systems are made quieter and the ranges of their missiles increase, 'sanctuaries' could protect them against unforeseen technological innovations and could help to ensure the survival of retaliatory forces. Moreover, if these 'sanctuaries' were located away from the coasts of other countries they would give these countries longer warning of attack and hamper depressed-trajectory launches against vulnerable weapons sites.[2]

---

[2] Normally missiles (including SLBM) are fired on minimum-entry trajectories, which carry them far above the atmosphere, thereby increasing both range and the time within which they can be detected. 'Depres-

If one is interested in preserving retaliatory forces, then other arms-control measures could also contribute to this end. Restrictions could be placed on multiple independently targetable re-entry vehicles (MIRV) and limitations imposed on the size and/or weight of delivery vehicles, thereby reducing the number of targets which could be attacked and the yield of the warhead(s) employed. Even more important might be constraints on accuracy, since halving the CEP[3] of a warhead has the same net effect on the probability of destroying a point target as a tenfold increase in yield. And perhaps most important might be freedom to shift from one type of delivery vehicle to another, a measure which can substitute for (or complement) the super-hardening of missile silos, the development of mobile ICBM and the deployment of ballistic missile defences—all of which are expensive and some of which might stimulate offsetting measures by an adversary concerned to maintain his own strategic deterrent.

Since such measures usually take the form of increasing the number of weapon sites and multiplying the number of targets against which each weapon can retaliate, they tend to increase the damage from a nuclear exchange. Reconciling the objective of preserving the deterrent with that of reducing damage should deterrence fail is extremely difficult—not least because the level of damage which will deter aggression is both imprecise and variable.[4] To some extent this can be achieved by restricting the number of warheads carried by a plane or a missile and the yield of those warheads, which goes up rapidly with weight; however, only very drastic—and very unlikely—reductions in Soviet (or American) delivery vehicles would achieve any significant drop in damage. Thus, arms-control measures can more readily preserve weapons than people, especially if they also curb strategic defensive systems such as ABM.

The same is true at a tactical level, with the difference that there is less to be gained by striking at civilian installations and the number of military targets to be attacked is correspondingly greater, including not only air bases and missile sites but artillery positions, troop concentrations, stockpiles of equipment, key bridges and other logistic and communications facilities. Reductions in the number of available

---

[3] Circular Error Probable: the radius from the centre of a target of a circle within which half the warheads aimed at that point can, on the average, be expected to fall.

[4] J. I. Coffey, *op. cit.* in Chapter 2, note 2, esp. pp. 49–51.

---

sed-trajectory' missiles, as the name suggests, are fired at lower altitudes (and hence necessarily at shorter ranges), thus reducing the time-to-target and the amount of warning received.

warheads or tactical nuclear-delivery vehicles, or both, may thus lessen the ability to wage tactical nuclear war. The effects would, of course, vary with the nature of the cuts. 'Across the board' cuts might alter the intensity of such a war but not its nature. Disproportionate cuts in fighter-bombers and short-range missiles would make it more difficult for an attacker to launch disarming strikes or blast a path for advancing forces and for a defender to interdict such an advance – at least until one or both re-introduced nuclear-capable aircraft or employed strategic nuclear weapons. Conversely, cuts in dual-capable artillery, free rockets and other battlefield weapons would diminish the danger of inadvertent escalation without necessarily affecting the form or extent of a deliberate nuclear *riposte*. Which option, if any, reduces the danger of war depends largely on one's concept of deterrence, one's perceptions of the 'enemy' and what weapons one possesses; it was more than coincidental that French strategic concepts changed after France developed tactical atomic weapons and at least one vehicle which could deliver them.

ARMS CONTROL AND PEACEFUL INTENTIONS

As indicated previously, national security depends not only on net military capabilities but also on perceptions of threat. Arms control, therefore, must affect subjective as well as objective factors if it is to enhance national security; that is, it must influence estimates of the intensions of an adversary as well as assessments of his capabilities.

In assessing the contributions which arms control can make to reducing fears, diminishing tensions, and otherwise affecting perceptions of security, we must start with the fact that while a nation may have many reasons for building up its armed forces (bureaucratic pressures, domestic interests, inertia), its opponents tend to see these forces as directed largely at themselves. Conversely – and happily for our concern about the ways in which arms control can influence perceptions of threat – reductions in armaments tend to be viewed as expressing a desire for peace and indicating no intention of applying power in the conduct of political relations. Obviously, unilateral reductions in armaments, without a corresponding phase-down by others, would be even more impressive than arms-control measures; probably no single Soviet move would so disarm NATO (literally, by inciting pressures for arms reductions, as well as psychologically) as the withdrawal of Soviet divisions from East Germany. However, it is perhaps too much to expect adversaries who are still competing, and who may view security as a zero-sum game (in which increases in the power position of one nation adversely affect that of another), to practise unilateral disarmament. The question then is how one state can use lesser measures, including both agreements on the limitation of armaments and actions designed to induce responses by another country, to change the impressions of that country's leaders concerning its intentions.

It is obvious from the previous section that the best way to change perceptions of intent is to eliminate or reduce forces and weapons which pose particular threats, which is why I singled out unilateral reductions in the powerful and mobile Soviet divisions in East Germany. Putting this principle into practice, an agreement on mutual force reductions which provided for asymmetrical decreases in Soviet combat formations (and especially armoured units) would give assurance of peaceful intent to the Western allies, just as disproportionate cuts in Western fighter-bombers and other dual-capable tactical nuclear delivery vehicles would give increased assurance to the countries of Eastern Europe that the West was not preparing for war.

It does not follow that arms-control measures designed to be reassuring need always take the form of cuts. To give one illustration, redeployment to the Eastern Baltic of existing Polish and East German amphibious forces, or provisions for continuous surveillance of those units, would ease Danish fears of a surprise attack and hence reassure the Danes about the peaceful intentions of their neighbours. Similarly, ceilings on strategic nuclear weapons might obviate fears that an adversary is aiming for a first-strike counter-force capability. In more general terms, agreements which preclude the attainment of 'superiority' or prevent the development of gross imbalances in military capabilities would ease fears and ameliorate concerns. Thus, many who feel that the continuing modernization and improvement of Soviet forces will eventually give the Soviet Union a position of strength from which to exert pressures for political accommodations would be reassured by ceilings on defence expenditures or freezes on levels of weapons which would preclude this.

Entirely apart from their direct effects on the perceptions of an adversary, arms-control measures can have other favourable results. They can demonstrate the ability of the political leadership to overcome the 'forces for war' among bureaucratic and business élites—a point of some importance to those sharing the Soviet view of Western political–economic structures. They can create a vested interest in maintaining good relations, since otherwise one of the participants may invoke the escape clauses implicit in any agreement and explicit in most. (It is hard, for example, to imagine the SALT agreements surviving, say, Soviet intervention in Yugoslavia or Western support for that hypothetical East German uprising mentioned earlier.) And they can contribute to the betterment of relations among states, which is why so many people in Eastern Europe are interested in 'military détente', i.e. limitations on armaments.

THE LIMITS TO ARMS CONTROL

All this suggests that arms-control measures can affect perceptions of security both directly and indirectly. There are, however, basic limits to what arms control can accomplish in offsetting imbalances between states and curtailing the military advantages possessed by some of them; not even total disarmament could erase the knowledge of weapons technology from the minds of Soviet or American nationals, nor preclude the two super-powers from re-establishing their military pre-eminence, should they choose to do so.[5] There are almost equally severe limits to what it can accomplish in Europe in today's context.

One such limit derives from the sheer complexity of the problem. As indicated earlier, the forces which could influence the outcome of any conflict in Europe include strategic elements as well as tactical ones, nuclear-armed units as well as those equipped with conventional weapons, and troops deployed off the Continent as well as those stationed in Europe. Moreover, the troops in Europe come from the armies, navies and air forces of many different countries and are accordingly organized, equipped and trained differently. (This applies particularly in the West.) Some are deployed on their home territories while others are stationed on foreign soil; some are combat ready, while others require the infusion of reservists or the call-up of transport, signal and supply elements before they can fight at full capacity. This means that any decisions on arms control, which necessarily will have to take account of these factors, will be slow in coming and narrow in scope.

Another limit to arms control derives from the fact that almost any measure adopted will affect differently the military capabilities of the two alliances—and we do not know how to assess accurately these effects. Even units of the same type and size (such as tank battalions) may differ in the number of men in the battalion, their state of training, the technical characteristics of their tanks, etc., and hence their effectiveness in combat will differ also. When it comes to evaluating the relative contributions of a tank battalion and a fighter-bomber squadron, the problem is even more difficult, since each performs different (though partially overlapping) missions. Moreover, technological innovations such as laser-guided anti-tank rockets, 'smart' bombs and heat-seeking, shoulder-fired surface-to-air missiles, will affect the performance of each in ways which cannot fully be foreseen. All this means that evaluations of the overall capabilities of a given force posture (and of measures affecting that posture) are

[5] Thomas C. Schelling, 'The Role of Deterrence in Total Disarmament', *Foreign Affairs*, Vol. 40, No. 3 (April 1962), pp. 392–406.

essentially judgments—and reasonable men may come to quite different judgments.

This is particularly true in the case of Europe, where the members of the two alliances have very different perceptions of the military balance and of the resultant threats to their security.

As far as NATO is concerned the major military threat is that arising out of imbalances in ground and tactical air capabilities, notably on the Central Front. These imbalances are seen as facilitating both local operations designed to seize important objectives and larger-scale ones intended to pierce Western defences and eventually roll up and destroy the defending armies; in fact, this particular threat is the one against which NATO has been preparing since its inception. NATO tactical nuclear forces are seen as partially offsetting Warsaw Pact conventional superiority, as a deterrent to the exercise of that superiority, and as a link with strategic nuclear forces which can enhance the credibility of the strategic deterrent. Thus, NATO would logically be, and is, largely interested in arms-control measures which would disproportionately reduce Warsaw Pact—and especially Soviet—divisions and air squadrons in Eastern Europe.

Conversely, the Warsaw Pact apparently regards these NATO nuclear forces as a primary threat and their early employment as inevitable, if not deliberate. Its own tactical (and regional) nuclear forces are intended to retaliate to a NATO nuclear strike and to pave the way for operations by Pact tank, mechanized and airborne divisions giving the *coup de grâce* to a devastated Europe. Thus, the Warsaw Pact could be expected to seek cuts in Western strike aircraft, SRBM and other nuclear launch vehicles, as well as in the warheads which they can deliver, while opposing marked cuts in their own conventional troops, which the military planners may deem barely capable of conducting a theatre campaign and the political leaders may consider barely sufficient to ensure political stability.

The same dichotomy of interests also holds with respect to Warsaw Pact (and especially Soviet) naval and amphibious forces, which some members of NATO see as able to cut sea lines of communication, seize isolated ports and airfields (for advanced bases in time of war or for bargaining purposes in time of peace) and to intervene in distant areas. While the Russians may admit to some of these capabilities, and while they acknowledge the importance of naval forces in 're-buffing imperialism' throughout the world, their major deployments are apparently aimed at coping with American missile submarines on station in the Mediterranean and the North Atlantic. Moreover, those forces deployed outside the Black and Baltic Seas are markedly inferior to those possessed by NATO, and extremely vulnerable to

Western counter-action.[6] Hence, while NATO and the Warsaw Pact may both be interested in measures to curtail the modernization of naval forces or restrict their deployments, the specific proposals of the two alliances may be diametrically opposed.

The same is likely to be true in other areas. For example, both the United States and the Soviet Union may be interested in curbing strategic nuclear forces, but in different ways.[7] Moreover, the Russians and the East Europeans would undoubtedly like to preclude or to hamper the development of a European nuclear force, particularly one in which West Germany would play a significant role, while most West Europeans would like to keep open the possibility of strengthening and possibly combining British and French regional nuclear forces. Finally, the East Europeans may be desirous of loosening bloc ties, both because this reduces the danger that any confrontation between super-powers will lead to war in Europe and because it may give them greater freedom of action vis-à-vis the Soviet Union, whereas many in Western Europe would see a further decline of cohesion within NATO as weakening their security.

Moreover, arms-control measures may achieve a measure of effectiveness in enhancing security against one threat at the price of decreasing the ability to cope with another. For example, while the SALT agreements further reduced the likelihood that the Soviet Union could muster the forces required for a first-strike counter-force attack against the United States, by constraining ballistic-missile defences, they also made it harder for the United States to do anything to reduce the damage to its cities from a nuclear exchange. Furthermore —and paradoxically—measures to reduce armaments may arouse fears rather than assuage them, in that many people tend to view their own weapons as enhancing security. Hence, even if one is more amenable to change and more optimistic about its consequences than are many officials, it is possible to judge that arms-control measures can diminish national security.

Even where particular measures enhance rather than diminish perceptions of security, their acceptability may depend on their side-effects. Measures which require the abandonment of cherished objectives, such as the establishment of a European Defence Community, may be rejected for that reason alone. So may measures which would require changes in national policies; thus denuclearized zones may be ruled out because they could require greater NATO reliance on conventional forces, any build-up of which would cause political and

---

[6] Michael MccGwire, Kenneth Booth and John McDonnell (eds.), *Soviet Naval Policy: Objectives and Constraints* (New York: Praeger, 1975).

[7] See Chapter 4, pp. 79–83.

economic strains, and a change to a strategic doctrine which emphasized defence rather than deterrence.

The acceptability of arms-control measures may also depend on perceptions of the adversary; for example, those Americans who fear that a shift in the strategic balance would prompt more aggressive Soviet behaviour, leading to local wars and super-power confrontations,[8] are unlikely to be proponents of SALT. And it may also be affected by the structure of government (which determines whether those leaders can direct or sway public policy); by the power and influence of various élites and interest-groups, such as the armed forces; by the philosophies or ideologies espoused by political parties; and by the practical consideration of whether support of a given measure will strengthen one leader's position *vis-à-vis* other leaders, interest-groups, and factions. Thus, even where basic doctrine favours arms control, as it does in the Soviet Union, powerful elements within the Party leadership, the bureaucracy and the 'econocrats' in charge of heavy industry may oppose cuts in forces or reductions in expenditures which could adversely affect their influence and prestige.

There are also differences with respect to the implications of the arms-control process. As suggested earlier, some in Eastern Europe see this process as easing the confrontation in Europe, providing additional assurances against the use of force and improving relations among the nations of Europe; if this process also results in a loosening of bloc ties, so much the better. On the contrary, some in Western Europe fear arms-control negotiations as serving to divide the allies, by playing upon the fear of some and the eagerness of others for *détente* and disarmament. They also see these negotiations as a temptation for the United States to reduce her forces in Europe and to do so through bilateral agreements with the Soviet Union, even though these might be disturbing to its allies. Above all, they worry lest successful negotiations could institutionalize controls over the armaments and armed forces of some of the allies, as could happen if mutual force reductions were restricted to a relatively limited area in Europe. Thus the fact of negotiations, as well as the subject-matter, tends to be perceived as inimical to West European security.

This does not mean that there are no possibilities of agreement between East and West; were that so, I should scarcely have troubled to write this book. Asymmetries in military postures, differences in perceptions of threat and variations in concern over alliance solidarity may militate against rapid agreement on far-reaching changes but

---

[8] See, for example, the testimony in US Congress, Joint Committee on Atomic Energy, Subcommittee on Military Applications, *Hearings* [on the] *Scope, Magnitude, and Implications of the United States Antiballistic Missile Program*, 90th Congress, 2nd Session, 1969, esp. pp. 55, 58–61, 72–3.

they do not rule out the lesser alternatives in which forces and weapons which seem 'threatening' to one side could be traded against those which seem threatening to the other. Moreover, we have not taken into account the economic advantages of curbing defence expenditures and public pressures to do so, pressures which may induce cuts in force levels if not changes in their composition. Nor have the various countries proceeded far with their negotiations (save for those on the limitation of strategic armaments), and these negotiations will require both compromises among divergent positions and political decisions which might not otherwise be made. Finally, we have not looked in any detail at arms-control measures which could alleviate perceived threats. These tasks we will now undertake, beginning with an examination of measures for the limitation of strategic armaments.

Chapter 4

STRATEGIC ARMS LIMITATIONS

Relatively few people in Europe, East or West, seem fearful that either of the super-powers will deliberately initiate strategic nuclear war. East Europeans apparently see the Soviet strategic nuclear forces as assurance that such a war will not start, while West Europeans view American forces (and, to a lesser extent, British and French ones) as providing a similar guarantee. This does not, however, mean that the Europeans have no interest in limitations on strategic armaments, which could head off shifts in the strategic balance that might be disturbing, lessen either quantitative or qualitative competition in armaments, and in these and other ways reduce tension between East and West.

The Europeans recognize, however, that strategic arms limitations are primarily matters for decision by the two super-powers. In this chapter, therefore, we will consider first of all the effects of the SALT I and Vladivostok agreements on the forces and programmes of the United States and the Soviet Union. We will then look at those areas which were not affected by the agreements and therefore may be the subject of negotiations in current or future meetings, with particular reference to the technical feasibility of additional controls and the military implications of establishing them—or not establishing them. We will next study the interests of the United States and the Soviet Union in particular measures, in order to get some feeling for the kinds of things that may emerge from these negotiations. Lastly we will examine the interests and concerns of the Europeans, and discuss the extent to which various likely outcomes may affect these, with particular reference to their interest in maintaining a military balance between East and West and their concerns about security.

THE PRESENT SITUATION

In 1972, after almost two years of negotiations, the Soviet Union and the United States signed agreements designed to limit their strategic forces.[1] The Treaty on the Limitation of Anti-Ballistic Missile

[1] For details see the Treaty between the United States of America and the Union of Soviet Socialist Republics on the Limitation of Anti-Ballistic Missile Systems, 26 May 1972 (hereafter cited as Treaty on the Limitation of Anti-Ballistic Missile Systems) and the Interim Agreement between

Systems precludes each party from deploying such systems or their components except for one network of no more than 100 launchers and interceptor missiles around each party's national capital and one other network of similar size elsewhere in the country, with the proviso that this second network does not overlap and reinforce the first one.[2] Moreover, the Treaty so restricts the number and deployment of radars as to make difficult any significant strengthening or extension of these systems, rules out both multiple launchers and automatic launchers for interceptor missiles, and prohibits the development, testing or deployment of sea-based, air-based, space-based or mobile land-based ABM. In short, the Treaty bars measures which could enable either side to protect its industry and population against nuclear attack by the other, or which could arouse concern that it was attempting to develop a capacity to do this.

The Interim Agreement with Respect to the Limitation of Strategic Offensive Arms, its protocol and the associated understandings issued by the two parties halt the construction of additional fixed land-based ICBM as of 1 July, 1972, preclude conversion of land-based launchers for light ICBM (or for older ICBM deployed before 1964) into launchers for heavy ICBM of types deployed after that time, and set limits to the number of submarines which each party may possess.[3] And although both sides have the right to scrap older types of ICBM or missile submarines and to replace them with more modern submarine-launched missiles, extreme shifts are barred by the overall limitations of 950 ballistic missile launchers on submarines and 62 modern submarines for the Soviet Union and 44 modern submarines with 710 SLBM for the United States.[4]

[2] Article III, Treaty on the Limitation of Anti-Ballistic Missile Systems; Agreed Interpretations (with Respect to the) ABM Treaty, the *New York Times*, 14 June 1972, p. 18, reprinted in *Survival*, July/August 1972, pp. 196–7. (By subsequent agreement, the United States relinquished the right to deploy ABM around her capital, and the Soviet Union gave up her second network, leaving only the system around Moscow.)

[3] Articles I, II, III, Interim Agreement with Respect to the Limitation of Strategic Offensive Arms.

[4] Protocol to the Interim Agreement with Respect to the Limitation of Strategic Offensive Arms. For a more detailed discussion of both the

the Union of Soviet Socialist Republics and the United States of America on Certain Measures with Respect to the Limitation of Strategic Offensive Arms (hereafter cited as Interim Agreement with Respect to the Limitation of Strategic Offensive Arms) in *Weekly Compilation of Presidential Documents*, Vol. 3, (Monday, 5 June 1972), pp. 926–8 (Washington: Office of the Federal Register, National Archives and Records Service, 1972), reprinted in *Survival*, July/August, 1972, pp. 192–6.

The programmes on which the two countries embarked in the after-math of this agreement gave the Soviet Union a marked advantage in numbers of ICBM (many of which are larger than their American counterparts and carry heavier payloads) and a slight edge in SLBM; however, they left the United States with a three-to-one superiority in intercontinental strategic bombers, and an even greater superiority in the payloads these bombers can carry and the number of warheads they can deliver (see Table 5, Strategic Nuclear Forces, 1976–1980, p. 252). The United States is numerically superior in MIRV-equipped launch vehicles –and hence in the number of warheads she can direct against different targets. This capability tends to offset the Soviet advantage in throw-weight; in fact, if one looks at the 'megaton equivalents' (MTE) of the weapons possessed by the two super-powers, they are approximately equal.

This picture could change over the coming years. Even though the Vladivostok Accord (which is scheduled to supersede the Interim Agreement in October 1977) places a ceiling of 2,400 on strategic launch vehicles and a sub-ceiling on ICBM silos (as did the Interim Agreement), the overall ceiling is so high that the Soviet Union could keep all of her modern ICBM, even while adding further to her fleet of missile-submarines. More importantly, the 15 per cent increase in the diameter of missile silos allowed by the Interim Agreement is enough, especially when coupled with 'cold launch' techniques,[5] to enable the Russians to build considerably larger missiles, with greater throw-weight.[6] And the limit of 1,320 placed on MIRV-equipped launchers would not preclude the Soviet Union from installing multiple warheads on most of her ICBM–as she is apparently in the process of doing.[7]

---

[5] These use compressed gases to eject the launch vehicle from the silo prior to firing, rather than igniting it in the silo.

[6] Similarly, a new, cold-launched *Minuteman* could have three times the throw-weight of the current models, and one using a larger silo a still higher ratio. For example, the SS-17, one of the two potential follow-ons to the SS-11 ICBM, carries four times the payload of its predecessor. Michael Nacht, 'The Vladivostok Accord and American Technological Options', *Survival*, May/June 1975, p. 107.

[7] All four new Soviet missiles tested in 1974–5 carry MIRV 'buses', and three of the four have been tested with MIRV (*ibid.*). For further details see the *Report of Secretary of Defense Donald H. Rumsfeld to the Congress on the*

Treaty and the Interim Agreement see the Stockholm International Peace Research Institute, *Strategic Arms Limitation, Part I: The First Agreements*, SIPRI Research Report No. 5, September 1972 (Stockholm: Almqvist & Wiksell; New York: Humanities Press; London: Elek, 1972).

Equally, however, the Vladivostok Accord does not preclude the United States from further augmenting her SLBM force (as she currently plans to do), from increasing the throw-weight and payload of her ICBM to levels comparable to those of the new Soviet missiles, or from installing additional re-entry vehicles in her 1,320 MIRV-equipped launchers—as she will with *Trident II*.[8] Thus, during the period covered by the Vladivostok Accord, the United States should maintain her lead in deliverable warheads and could strike an approximate balance in deliverable megatonage and in MTE[9] (see Table 5, p. 252).

These projections suggest that the Moscow Agreement and the Vladivostok Accord have either registered or permitted asymmetries between the United States and the Soviet Union which largely offset each other, at least as far as the ability to inflict damage on the other party is concerned. In addition, the treaty and the subsequent agreement so constrict ballistic missile defence as to ensure that these will be minimal rather than meaningful, thereby ratifying the fact that both countries are open to destruction from a strategic nuclear exchange.

Were this all, we could cease to worry about either future weapons developments or further limitations on armaments; but unfortunately it is not. For one thing, the mere fact that asymmetries exist has generated worries lest they should affect perceptions of the strategic balance (whether by adversaries or on the part of allies) thereby diminishing the credibility of the American deterrent, and has given rise to calls for 'essential equivalence' in 'the design of new offensive and defensive systems, in such areas as accuracy and reliability and, if

[8] For a discussion of these and other options open to the United States see the Background Briefing by Dr Henry A. Kissinger, US Secretary of State, 3 December 1974, reprinted in *Survival*, July/August 1975, esp. p. 196.

[9] Dr Kissinger (*ibid.*) indicated that the United States would have 'somewhat above 10,000' warheads in 1985, and the Soviet Union would have fewer; however, General George S. Brown, USAF, Chairman of the Joint Chiefs of Staff, stated that if the Soviet Union continues her current rapid effort at modernization she could overtake the United States by mid-1979 and 'dominate this measure of the balance' (*US Military Posture for FY 1976*, Senate Armed Services Committee, Washington, D.C., pp. 36–7). It seems clear that Dr Kissinger was counting all re-entry vehicles whereas it may be that General Brown was counting only ICBM—in which case he is correct.

FY 1978 Authorization Request and the FY 1977–1981 Defense Program, 27 January 1976, offset, p. 52 (hereafter cited as the *Rumsfeld Report, 1976*).

necessary, in throw-weight and its management'.[10] Furthermore, the prospect that, as the numbers of re-entry vehicles grow and their accuracies increase, both American and Soviet ICBM may become vulnerable to a disarming strike has aroused concern among American officials that the ability to conduct limited and selective first strikes may be diminished, and with it the ability to deter similar operations by the Soviet Union. Finally, the deployment in quantity of weapons not covered by existing agreements (such as cruise missiles) could conceivably alter the strategic balance—or at least perceptions of it—this time to the detriment of the Soviet Union. Thus, much remains to be done.

What will be done in SALT II, and subsequently, depends in large measure on the interests and the objectives of the super-powers. If they are seeking to economize, they may try not only to bring under control those weapons not now covered but also to head off new weapons programmes and to reduce existing forces. If they are concerned about strategic stability, they may be more selective in the programmes they attempt to control and more cautious about constraining technical developments or innovations in weaponry which they regard as important to the maintenance of that balance. If they are interested in maintaining options other than assured retaliation, they may be even more reluctant to choke off certain possibilities, such as increases in missile accuracy. If they are looking to limit damage, or to reverse the situation under which each side remains vulnerable to the other, they may wish to remove the constraints on defences and to impose additional ones on offensive systems. Without prejudging decisions by the United States or the Soviet Union, it may be worth examining those areas over which controls could be imposed and the potential consequences of imposing them.

POTENTIAL STRATEGIC ARMS LIMITATIONS

Bringing other weapons systems under control

One of the most obvious and most important measures would be that of bringing under control weapons which are not now covered, such as medium bombers,[11] strike aircraft and cruise missiles. All these can be

[10] *Report of Secretary of Defense James R. Schlesinger to the Congress on the FY 1976 and Transition Budgets, FY 1977 Authorization Request and FY 1976–1980 Defense Programs*, 5 February 1975, mimeograph, pp. II-18 (hereafter cited as the *Schlesinger Report, 1975*).

[11] The Vladivostok Accord counted heavy (intercontinental) bombers in the 2,400 delivery vehicles authorized for each side, thereby bringing

used by at least one of the super-powers to strike at the other's homeland, all are therefore at least potential candidates for control – and all
present problems to anyone seeking to improve controls.

One argument for attempting to limit numbers of medium bombers
is that these may be virtually indistinguishable militarily from their
heavier brethren; for example, the American FB-111A, which is
classified as a medium-range bomber, has almost two-thirds of the
operational reach and twice the payload of the long-range Soviet
Mya-4 *Bison*. Another is that even medium-range bombers can strike
at intercontinental targets if refuelled by tanker aircraft or if
launched from advanced bases. A third is that they can carry weapons
which extend their reach and expand their capabilities to attack
strategic targets: weapons such as the short-range attack missile
(SRAM) and the air-launched cruise missile (ALCM), of which more
later.

Against this is the fact that the asymmetries in numbers mean that
the Soviet Union would either have to cut her overall forces drastically, or else be permitted higher ceilings – thereby violating the principle of 'equality' to which both sides agreed in the Vladivostok
Accord.[12] Another factor is that the Soviet medium bombers, unlike

[12] Under the terms of the Interim Agreement with Respect to the
Limitation of Strategic Offensive Arms, the forces of the two sides were
fixed as follows:

	US	USSR
ICBM	1,054/1,000	1,618/1,408
SLBM	656/710	740/950
	1,710	2,358
Add: Heavy bombers currently in operation, mid-1976	397[a]	135
	2,107	2,493
Medium bombers currently available mid-1976	66	480[b]
Total	2,142	2,973

[a] Excluding 153 B-52 in active storage, but including 71 used in training
squadrons.
[b] Excluding some 30 *Backfire* and 280 *Badger* in the Naval Air Force,
configured for attacks on shipping. These could, in theory, deliver nuclear
weapons.
SOURCE: *The Military Balance 1976–7*, pp. 8–9.

these, as well as SLBM and ICBM, under control. It also covers air-to-surface
ballistic missiles of more than 600 km (340 miles) range, which will be
counted against the total launch vehicles allowed to each side (Background Briefing by Dr Kissinger, *op. cit.* in note 8, p. 191).

their American counterparts, are directed primarily at military targets on the Eurasian mainland. Furthermore, efforts to limit all the aircraft capable of delivering nuclear weapons on the United States or the Soviet Union would immediately open up all kinds of other issues, including that of whether and how to count the bombers in the hands of France and Britain.

Thus the simplest, and perhaps the best, solution would be to leave medium bombers uncontrolled–unless a partial inclusion (as of American FB-111A and certain versions of the new Soviet *Backfire*) are needed to reconcile differences between the super-powers over what should or should not be counted under the Vladivostok Accord.[13]

Unfortunately, as the Soviet Union has pointed out, bombers are not the only planes capable of delivering nuclear weapons. If one looks at the aircraft-carrier as a weapons system, the thirteen attack carriers which the United States currently operates and the two ASW carriers which the Soviet Union has operational or under construction are theoretically capable of delivering nuclear warheads across intercontinental distances. Furthermore, the American strike aircraft based in Japan and Western Europe (notably the F-111E and the A-7D) could reach targets in the Soviet Union without refuelling (in fact, these last two types compare favourably with Soviet medium bombers as far as range and payload are concerned). The United States has apparently included these forward-based systems (FBS) in calculating the strategic balance,[14] and so might find it hard to exclude them from consideration in future SALT talks.

One question, however, is how many of these aircraft one should count: all those possessed by the allies, only those operated by American forces, or only those American planes normally stationed within striking distance of the Soviet Union? A second is, how would one verify any controls over FBS, considering the numbers of such aircraft, the varying types and the multiplicity of bases? A third question is what, if anything, the West might be willing to see controlled in exchange for restrictions on forward-based systems: Soviet intercontinental delivery vehicles, which would be logical if one accepted the Soviet definition of 'strategic';[15] Soviet medium bombers, which

[13] The United States has begun to count the FB-111A as a 'long-range' bomber–perhaps to justify putting the *Backfire* in the same category. *Rumsfeld Report, 1976*, p. 44.

[14] News Conference of Dr Henry A. Kissinger, 27 May 1972, in *Weekly Compilation of Presidential Documents, op. cit.* in note 1, p. 934.

[15] The Soviet Union defined as 'strategic' any super-power weapons system capable of delivering nuclear warheads on the homeland of the other super-power, whereas the United States insisted that these have an

could reach the United States on one-way missions, but not otherwise (unless staged and refuelled in the Arctic); or Soviet MR/IRBM, which are strategic from a European, if not from an American, viewpoint? Here again, the technical difficulty of devising an 'equitable' solution suggests that one should choose the simplest measure acceptable to both sides—which might well be to designate some, but not all, of the American FBS as 'strategic' if this is essential for bargaining purposes.

Another type of weapon system left untouched by SALT I was the cruise missile. Although the United States has scrapped the last of her intercontinental cruise missiles, and the Soviet Union never developed one, the latter has armed both surface ships and submarines with other types of cruise missile, some of which have ranges as long as 450 statute miles. These, and particularly the ones carried by missile submarines, are capable of striking at targets in the United States, but the United States has assumed for years that they would be used primarily in ship-to-ship operations or directed against targets on the Eurasian land mass (an assumption not very comforting to Norway or France). Now, however, the United States is beginning to deploy surface-to-surface missiles on her own warships and has under development a submarine-launched cruise missile, fired through torpedo tubes, which 'would provide a desirable augmentation of our strategic capabilities and a unique potential for unambiguous, controlled single weapon response'.[16]

As far as surface ships are concerned, there is no real problem in instituting controls, since such missiles are easily identifiable and the number of ships mounting them seems to be known with a fair degree of accuracy. Controls on ship-borne missiles are, however, likely to operate to the disadvantage of the Soviet Union, whose navy has relied heavily on surface-to-surface missiles to replace heavy guns and partially offset the long-range strike capabilities of American carrier aviation. Moreover, surface ships of both super-powers would find it difficult to reach positions from which they could launch their missiles against targets on each other's territory, so that there is no particular reason for considering them 'strategic' or for attempting to extend controls to a whole new class of combat vehicles.

With respect to SLCM, the question becomes one of what kind of

[16] *Schlesinger Statement, 1975,* p. II–39.

---

effective range (or, in the case of aircraft, an effective combat radius, which would enable two-way missions) of 3,000 nautical miles. In practice neither party adhered strictly to its definition, since the Soviet Union did not count its SLCM and the United States tried at one point to include MR/IRBM in the category of 'strategic' weapons.

controls, and at what price. A freeze would obviously operate to the disadvantage of the United States; asymmetrical ceilings might alleviate this disadvantage to some degree but would scarcely seem worth haggling over; and very low ceilings, or significant reductions, could adversely affect the Soviet Union, which might demand compensating reductions in other American weapon systems. However, given the fact that the new American s l c m could turn every American (and allied) submarine into a platform for strategic launch vehicles, the Soviet Union might be willing to cut her s l c m force (and/or to reduce other elements of her strategic nuclear forces) in return for an American undertaking to forgo production of this new weapon. Whether the United States would do this is doubtful; whether any agreement could be enforced is even more doubtful, since the proposed missile will have a tactical (short-range) version as well as a strategic (long-range) one. Thus, despite the importance of constraining or reducing s l c m, this would not seem very feasible.[17]

Reduction in forces

S a l t i imposed no cuts in strategic offensive forces; in fact it permitted the Soviet Union to add to her operational i c b m force and to build more missile submarines, on the basis of a compromise between differing national estimates of what construction was actually under way.[18] Yet it is obvious that each of the super-powers has more than enough strategic nuclear delivery vehicles (s n d v) and warheads to destroy the other, if not enough for an all-out counterforce attack against missile silos, air bases and other military targets. Thus there would seem to be some reason (in terms of reducing costs, easing fears and stabilizing the strategic balance) to lower the levels of strategic nuclear forces on both sides – an endeavour to which the United States and the Soviet Union are committed by the Vladivostok Accord.

As far as costs are concerned, there are two major ways of achieving economies: phasing out existing weapons systems and reducing the procurement of new ones. Because they are costly both to provide and operate, bombers are obvious candidates for force reductions; for example, the 244 B-1 bombers the United States is considering buying would cost over $20 billion to produce and almost $2 billion a year to operate at current prices.[19] Missile submarines are even costlier to

[17] The United States has already agreed to count bomber-carrying air-launched cruise missiles (a l c m) with ranges of over 300 nm against the ceiling on m i r v vehicles established by the Vladivostok agreement.

[18] See the News Conference of Dr Henry A. Kissinger, 27 May 1972, *op. cit.* in note 1, p. 932.

[19] *Congressional Record*, 94th Congress, 1st Session, Vol. 121, No. 871, (5 June 1975), p. S9845.

build (with each *Trident* submarine estimated at $1.3 billion) but considerably less expensive to operate. As for ICBM, new systems would of course be extremely expensive (as the Soviet Union is finding out), but once installed their operating costs are comparatively low—in the case of the United States about $800 million a year compared to $1,300 million for the *Polaris-Poseidon* fleet and $3,500 million for bombers and tankers.[20]

If, however, one aims at easing fears rather than reducing costs, the picture looks very different. No one seems seriously worried about bombers, whose relatively slow time-to-target and comparative vulnerability to strategic defences make them poor counter-force weapons, even when equipped with 'smart' bombs. Nor, under present circumstances, are SLBM capable of effectively attacking hardened silos, since their comparatively small warheads, relatively low accuracy (due in part to their ballistic flight-path) and lack of a precise launch-point, mean that they have a poor kill probability.[21] For precisely the opposite reasons, ICBM are most effective in launching counter-force strikes, but they are also, unfortunately, most vulnerable to such strikes (at least as long as they are programmed to 'ride out' attacks rather than to fire on warning); bombers can take to the air and missile submarines can hide in the sea.

The asymmetries between Soviet and American strategic offensive forces suggest that agreements aimed at cutting strategic forces, whether designed to reduce costs or tensions, would be difficult to reach. For example, any significant cut in Soviet heavy bombers would leave little more than a token long-range force and, unless accompanied by equally significant cuts in medium bombers, would not achieve marked savings. Conversely, deep slashes in the American bomber fleet (or a cutback in the number of B-1s to be produced) would save money but could not be matched by similar Soviet reductions and, barring trade-offs for other Soviet intercontinental delivery vehicles, would leave the United States at a further numerical disadvantage. Reductions in missiles would do little to ease the threat to American land-based systems unless they focused on the two which have the greatest potential for counter-force operations, the SS-19 and the SS-18, Mod 2. However, the United States has no comparable weapons to trade (with the possible exception of the 54 *Titan* II ICBM); therefore, unless she could persuade the Soviet Union to give up those ICBM most likely to enhance its war-fighting capabilities, she

---

[20] Alton H. Quanbeck and Barry M. Blechman, *Strategic Forces, Issues for the Mid-Seventies* (Washington, DC: Brookings Insitution, 1973), Tables 3–1, p. 37; 3–2, p. 41; and 3–3, p. 45.

[21] Once TV-guided or image-imprinted re-entry vehicles are developed, this may change.

might have to offer something better than one-for-one reductions–
thereby further aggravating existing numerical imbalances.

As far as stabilizing the strategic balance is concerned, each side has
different perceptions of the existing balance and of the components
which enter into it: the Soviet Union, for example, attaching less
importance to bombers than the United States. Moreover, the perceived value of these components may vary not only with their cost
and survivability but also with their age, political utility (i.e., how
important they seem to the possessor country, its allies and adversaries) and the role they can play in waging nuclear war–which may
be why the Soviet Union has emphasized high-thrust ICBM. And
although formulae can be devised for equating some of the technical
capabilities of launch vehicles, it is difficult to take into account the
differing strategic doctrines of the United States and the Soviet
Union, their consequently different estimates of the value of particular
weapons systems, and the bureaucratic and service interests in those
weapons systems.

All these variables make it difficult to determine which forces will be
cut. They do, however, suggest that there are limits to symmetrical
reductions, and that trade-offs between different weapons systems
might be more acceptable to both sides. Without arguing that the list
below is exhaustive or that the trade-offs listed are likely:

1. American B-52 bombers could be bartered for obsolescent Soviet
   SS-7 and SS-8 ICBM, on some weighted basis–a move which would
   both preclude the further build-up of the Soviet SLBM fleet and
   reduce the number of ALCM the United States could deliver in case
   of war;
2. United States *Polaris* missile-submarines could be applied against
   unequal numbers of older Soviet submarines, most of which carry
   shorter-range SLBM and some of which are non-nuclear;
3. Soviet ICBM could be reduced in consonance with American reductions in Forward-Based Systems in Europe, perhaps in ratios
   favourable to the Soviet Union;
4. American (and possibly allied) medium bombers could be swapped
   for Soviet medium bombers or MR/IRBM.

In some instances these trade-offs could be tacit rather than formal,
with the Soviet Union replacing its ageing fleet of Tu-16 medium
bombers with smaller numbers of the newer and more versatile *Backfire*, even as the British phased out the last of their V-bombers. In any
case, the trade-offs are likely to be relatively small, partly because
of the obstacles to asymmetrical reductions, partly because of
concern over setting precedents for future agreements. In all
probability they will result in continued 'equality' between the

United States and the Soviet Union, even if that equality is more symbolic than real.

Qualitative improvements in weaponry

As many analysts have pointed out, SALT has so far dealt almost entirely with quantitative restraints on weapons; save for the restrictions placed on increasing the dimensions of silos, nothing was done to preclude the qualitative up-grading of weaponry. Yet, as shown in the chart below, there are a number of ways of adding significantly to

Chart 1: **Possible Improvements in Strategic Nuclear Delivery Vehicles**

For First Strike	For Second Strike
1 Greater accuracy	1 Increase in warhead yield
2 Improved reliability	2 Improved reliability
3 Increased availability	3 Increased availability
4 MIRV	4 Dispersal of launch vehicles
5 Manoeuvrable warheads	5 Various types of launch
6 Greater payload	vehicles
7 Non-optimum flight path	6 Concealment of launch vehicles
8 Increased penetrability	7 Mobility of launch vehicles
9 Ability to report success (for	8 Hardening of silos
diverting subsequent salvos)	9 Survivability of command
10 Rapid retargeting	and control
	10 Penetration aids
	11 Hardening of warheads
	12 Rapid retargeting

Adapted from W. F. Biddle, *Weapons Technology and Arms Control* (London: Pall Mall Press, 1973), Table 22, p. 242.

the capabilities of existing vehicles. Some at least of these could pose threats to the survivability of land-based strategic nuclear forces—and hence to the stability of the strategic balance. More would have psychological consequences which could stimulate offsetting reactions by other countries—or at least strengthen the arguments of those within these countries who would in any case endorse countermeasures. Since all these improvements would cost money, there may be valid reasons for attempting to head off or curb the up-grading of strategic weapons.

Unfortunately, it is extraordinarily difficult to do this. Some improvements, such as hardened warheads, better guidance systems and more reliable firing mechanisms, could not be detected without the most intensive and intrusive inspection. Others, such as quieter nuclear-powered submarines and faster aircraft, would be hard to preclude unless one were granted a veto over the design and production of these weapons systems–and even then advances in technology almost guarantee improvements in performance. Moreover, such improvements tend to occur incrementally, so that their impact is cumulative rather than singular, which makes them hard to detect. Only where weapons systems are entirely new, or so largely redesigned that old performance standards are inapplicable, can their development be detected, and then only at the stage when they are tested. This suggests that efforts to constrain qualitative improvements in weaponry will, of necessity, be concentrated in those few areas where these improvements promise to be significant, where detection prior to deployment is feasible, and where measures to control such improvements are both practicable and verifiable.

One such area is that of multiple independently targetable re-entry vehicles. The introduction of MIRV can enhance retaliatory capabilities by enabling attacks on more, and more rewarding targets, compensate for fewer delivery vehicles surviving, and require an adversary considering a first strike to achieve a very high degree of effectiveness. (For example, an attacker would have to destroy or neutralize 98.4 per cent of a fully MIRV-equipped American *Minuteman* force in order to preclude the launching of 50 warheads in a retaliatory strike –and he would have to accomplish this within a time-span short enough to prevent the launch of vehicles left undamaged by his initial salvo.) Conversely, MIRV enable an attacker to multiply the effects of a counter-force strike and make this more desirable–he may knock out two or more re-entry vehicles for the expenditure of one. Furthermore, once MIRV have been developed and tested, he can install them with little fear of detection, thereby secretly enhancing his strategic capabilities. For these reasons, and because of their potential effect on the arms race as well as on strategic stability, most analysts have argued in favour of curbing MIRV.

Unfortunately for those advocating curbs on MIRV, the programmes of the United States and the Soviet Union are out of phase, with the United States significantly ahead in the development of MIRV for both ICBM and SLBM.

Even more unfortunately, it would be difficult to verify either a complete or a partial ban on MIRV once these had been developed and tested. Only by removing the nose cones of missiles and inspecting the warheads (which would yield a good deal of useful technical information about fusing, hardening, etc.) could an inspection team satisfy itself that ICBM or SLBM were not carrying MIRV. Even then, a country determined to evade inspection could do so by producing MIRV-equipped re-entry vehicles, or even duplicate missiles armed with MIRV, which could be installed in large numbers at short notice. This suggests that once MIRV have been developed, one must rely on indirect, rather than direct, means of inhibiting deployment.

One way of doing this, as the United States has suggested, would be to count all missiles of a given type as MIRV-equipped, once that missile has been tested in a MIRV mode. This would obviously make verification simple – at least as long as test flights could be monitored successfully. It would, however, deprive the Soviet Union of flexibility in her ICBM deployment, since all of her new missiles could carry either single or multiple warheads, and the SS-18 has been tested in both variants.[22] Moreover, it would (if they accepted it) preclude their deploying any MIRV-equipped SLBM, since almost all of the 1,320 MIRV-equipped launchers authorized would be 'counted' against land-based missiles. Thus, this approach, while commendably simple, may be so one-sided in its application as to be unacceptable.[23]

Another way of inhibiting the deployment of MIRV would be to limit the number of test firings each side could hold. Since some such firings are required for confidence-testing of existing ICBM and SLBM, restrictions on them could handicap the design of new systems and retard progress towards greater accuracy – thereby making MIRV-equipped missiles less useful in counter-force attacks, and consequently less threatening. And although each side can conceal or degrade the data the other can obtain from test firings,[24] it would be hard to hide their occurrence, especially if they had to be conducted over prescribed ranges and announced in advance.

Despite the asymmetries just mentioned, and the difficulty of veri-

[22] *Rumsfeld Statement, 1976*, Chart 11B-1, p. 54.

[23] There are, however, hints that Moscow might agree to such a restriction as part of the final arrangements for SALT II. (The *New York Times*.)

[24] Apparently, the Soviet Union has shifted from the analogue to the digital system of transmitting signals from her test missiles, thereby making it much more difficult for the United States to determine the characteristics of these missiles – and especially of their warheads (Tad Szulc, 'Have We Been Had? Soviet Violation of the SALT Deals', 7 June 1975, reprinted in the *Congressional Digest*, 94th Congress, 1st Session, Vol. 121, No. 103 (26 June 1975), S 11 718). Although this is apparently not in violation of the Interim Agreement, other measures introduced by the Soviet Union (such as covering her mobile missile launchers with canvas) may be. More importantly, these moves, together with the (legal) introduction of larger missiles, have aroused concern both about Soviet good faith and about the skill of American negotiators – thereby ensuring that any new agreement will undergo a thorough screening by the Congress (see article by Bernard Gwertzman in the *New York Times*, 5 August 1975, p. 2).

fying restrictions on multiple warheads, there are several possible constraints which warrant consideration. One would be to allow MIRV development to proceed to the point where high accuracies can be anticipated, which would mean stopping or limiting American tests now and letting the Soviet Union continue for another year or two before curbs were imposed. Another would be to set ceilings on MIRV-equipped launch vehicles of a particular size or throw-weight which could constrain the deployment by the United States of *Minuteman* (now under development) and preclude the replacement of all Soviet SS-9 by the more modern and versatile SS-18. A third—though more difficult—measure would be to lower drastically the agreed ceiling of 1,320 MIRV-equipped delivery vehicles, thereby requiring changes in current US deployment patterns and inhibiting Soviet attainment of the capability for a partial disarming strike. Whether these or other limitations will be acceptable is perhaps another question.

There are also asymmetries between the two super-powers in the development of air-to-surface missiles (ASM). While both sides have them, the United States is proceeding further and faster than the Soviet Union in building lighter, longer-range and more accurate ASM; also, American bombers, with their greater payload, are able to carry more ASM than are their Soviet counterparts. Fortunately, these weapons are likely to be relatively unsuitable for first-strike counter-force attacks, partly because of the time required to deliver them on target and partly because of the uncertainties about the penetration ability of the bombers carrying them. Nevertheless, they will confer a significant advantage on the United States, unless they are in some way curbed or offset.[25]

The problem here is that it is almost impossible to preclude the development, testing and production of ASM suitable for intercontinental delivery vehicles, since very similar ASM can be carried by tactical aircraft. Moreover, ASM can be tested without detection by the other super-power and, once perfected, may be stored internally in aircraft, concealed from view. For these reasons it may be best to deal with ASM by limiting the numbers of bombers, by imposing restrictions on their size and gross take-off weight, or by establishing ceilings for those carrying ALCM, rather than by tackling the issue directly.

A third area, and one of greater concern, is that of improvements

[25] According to US Deputy Secretary of Defense William P. Clements, Jr, the medium-range ALCM, which is equipped with a warhead of approximately 200 KT, will have a highly accurate guidance system that will give it a counter-force capability against all but fully hardened military targets. Edgar Ulsamer, 'The Pentagon Looks at Strategic Options', *Air Force Magazine*, February 1974, p. 55.

in missile accuracy, which could greatly increase the counter-force capabilities of even small-yield warheads. It has been estimated that a combination of better geodetic knowledge, improved guidance systems, and homing devices (such as the image imprint, in which an RV automatically changes its flight-path so that a picture of the target on a television camera in its nose matches a picture previously taken from a satellite) could enable an attacker to achieve a CEP of 30 metres or less.[26] Such improvements in accuracy would enable either side to strike at military installations, such as the nuclear-separation plant at Oak Ridge, Tennessee, or at civilian facilities, such as the dam at Dnepropetrovsk in the Ukraine, without causing heavy collateral damage and massive casualties. Alternatively, a more accurate RV could be used to kill hard targets, such as missiles in super-hardened silos or submarines in concrete pens. At best, therefore, increased missile accuracies may add to concern about the vulnerability of land-based missile systems, and at worst they may introduce instabilities which could lead to intensification of the arms race, if not to pre-emptive strikes in times of crisis.

Here again, it would be possible to restrict improvements in missile accuracy by limiting and monitoring test firings. New boosters (designed to achieve increased accuracy) could be identified by their characteristic signatures as registered on forward-scatter over-the-horizon radar, and by satellite-borne, infra-red sensors.[27] Moreover, any appreciable change in the structure, size or weight of a re-entry vehicle could be detected directly or indirectly by ship-board sensors in the splashdown area. Thus it is not impossible to verify adherence to agreements which preclude or restrict increases in accuracy, assuming that such agreements can be reached.

This is also true of other improvements, such as the up-grading of launch vehicles. Available national means of monitoring missile test firings can not only determine with confidence the introduction of a new RV or booster but can give considerable information about changes in their size and configuration. They can differentiate between solid- and liquid-fuel rockets, determine alterations in the composition of fuel and enable reasonably accurate calculations to be made about the thrust and payload/range of a given missile. They can also, albeit with less confidence, detect changes in the launch method, such as a shift to a 'cold boost' technique employing gas or

[26] D. G. Hoag, 'Ballistic-missile Guidance', in Bernard T. Feld, et al. (eds.), *Impact of New Technologies on the Arms Race* (Cambridge, Massachusetts: M.I.T. Press, 1971), p. 100.
[27] Ted Greenwood, *Reconnaissance, Surveillance and Arms Control*, Adelphi Paper no. 88 (London: IISS, 1972), pp. 21-2.

compressed air. The question is not, therefore, whether prohibitions on such improvements can be verified, but whether the prohibitions are worth it.

Missiles are not, of course, the only new weapons that could arouse concern. The Russians are known to be working on many advanced weapons, such as an ABM interceptor with a loitering capability and exotic ballistic-missile defences; in fact, they refused to accept a formal ban on laser missile defences at the time of the SALT agreements.[28] While even laser missile defences might not degrade the American strategic deterrent, they could cause a psychological shock, could certainly spur the development of countervailing systems (such as nuclear-powered ram-jet low-altitude cruise missiles, whose development was stopped a decade ago) and could conceivably end the current agreements on the limitation of strategic armaments. Other weapons which could have similar–if lesser–effects include space-borne missile-control systems, which might enable much more effective counter-force attacks; mobile ICBM; highly effective airborne warning and control systems (AWACS), coupled with long-range fighter-interceptors; and even a significant up-grading of surface-to-air missiles, which might make them effective against incoming re-entry vehicles as well as bombers.

This ought to argue in favour of restrictions on research and development. In practice, however, the possibility of technological innovations is commonly cited as a reason to maintain freedom to conduct research, so that new weapons can be precluded or countered once they appear on the technological horizon.[29] More importantly, it is extremely difficult to constrain research and development short of the stage when weapons are tested–and hence can be detected by national means of verification. This suggests that future efforts to constrain R & D should follow the pattern set by the Treaty on the Limitation of Anti-Ballistic Missile Systems, which both sides agreed should come into force only 'after a component moves from the laboratory development and testing stage to the field testing stage, wherever performed'.[30] It also suggests that any such constraints

---

[28] The Agreed Interpretations [concerning the] ABM Treaty [and the] Interim Agreement, para. E, provide only for discussing specific limitation of ABM systems 'based on other physical principles ...': The *New York Times*, 14 June 1972, p. 18.

[29] *Statement of Secretary of Defense Elliot L. Richardson before the Senate Armed Services Committee on the FY 1974 Defense Budget and FY 1974–1978 Program, Wednesday 28 March 1973*, mimeograph, p. 14.

[30] US Congress, Senate Committee on Armed Services, *Hearing [on the] Military Implications of the Treaty on the Limitation of Anti-Ballistic Missile Systems and the Interim Agreement on the Limitation of Strategic Offensive Arms*,

should be imposed on a narrow basis, not an overall one, and should be limited to those weapons which could give one side a meaningful strategic advantage, rather than including all those which could cause minor perturbations in the strategic balance.

Constraints on defensive systems

If one looks at the three major types of defensive system, it would be easiest to place further curbs on anti-ballistic missile systems, partly because the precedent has already been set by the agreement not to build the second missile network authorized under the Treaty. Scrapping the two existing networks would not only save money but could head off efforts to improve ballistic missile defences to the degree where they would once again seem to be meaningful military options, for missile sites if not for cities. However, neither the United States nor the Soviet Union may be willing to scrap its network, pay the political costs of eliminating missile defences and rule out the possibility of extending these in the future, for protection against an Nth power.[31]

Super-power air defences are asymmetrical, so befitting the threat. As of mid-1976 the United States had only some 500–600 interceptor aircraft (and no surface-to-air missiles, as these were eliminated in 1974) for use against the 140 Soviet long-range bombers. Conversely, the Soviet Union maintained over 2,500 fighter/interceptors and some 10,000 SAM for defence against the much larger American bomber force, American carrier planes and ground-based strike aircraft and the aircraft of other members of the Western alliance. Even so, the prospects of precluding high levels of damage from bombing are not very good.

However, air defences do complicate the problem of launching an attack, do avoid giving an adversary a 'free ride' which could greatly increase his kill capabilities, and are potentially useful against third powers. For these reasons, it is unlikely that either side would be prepared to eliminate them, or that the Soviet Union, which seemingly attaches considerable importance to air defence, would be willing to cut them drastically. More significantly, air defences are useful against tactical fighter planes as well as against intercontinental bombers. It is almost impossible to differentiate between interceptors assigned to strategic air defences and those earmarked for the protection of troops; in fact, the same plane frequently serves

---

[31] The United States has shut down, though it has not dismantled, its ABM system in North Dakota.

92nd Congress, 2nd Session (Washington, DC: USGPO, 1972), p. 377 (hereafter cited as *Hearing on the Military Implications of SALT*).

both purposes. It is even harder to differentiate between strategic and tactical SAM—especially in the case of low-level semi-mobile weapons like the Soviet SAM-6 and the American SAM-D. And while early-warning radar and other fixed radar could be singled out for constraints, it is questionable whether the game is worth the candle.

To a large extent the same is true of anti-submarine warfare (ASW) forces, even though these might have a potentially more significant effect on the strategic deterrent. As re-entry vehicles increase in accuracy, land-based missiles will become increasingly vulnerable, with the result that this component of the strategic deterrent may be either eroded or replaced by sea-based missiles. If ASW operations improve in effectiveness to the degree where they could begin to threaten missile submarines, this could touch off another offensive–defensive interaction and provide a stimulus to the arms race. Moreover, ASW operations, already costly, are getting more so—with one marketing study suggesting that American expenditures under current programmes will rise from $2.5 billion in 1972 to $4.5 billion in 1975.[32]

If one chose to do so, there are ways of inhibiting improvements in ASW capabilities.[33] One would be to preclude further deployment of large-scale phased-array sonars which can detect (and perhaps locate) missile submarines.[34] A second would be to forbid the establishment of barrier zones (using sonobuoys, hunter-killer submarines equipped with active sonar, and other devices) through which submarines could not pass without being detected. A third would be to ban the tracking of missile submarines by surface ships or hunter-killer subs, while a fourth would be to establish sanctuaries, not too near the coasts of the super-powers, in which they would have freedom to deploy missile submarines but not ASW forces.

This latter approach, perhaps the most promising in terms of ensuring the invulnerability of missile submarines, is also perhaps the most difficult. For one thing, it would involve acceptance of the idea of

---

[32] The *New York Times*, 20 October 1972, p. 15. According to the Brookings Institution, this study understates current costs which, for all ASW programmes, amount to about $8 billion per year. Quanbeck and Blechman, *op. cit.* in note 20, p. 79.

[33] Kosta Tsipis, Anne H. Cahn and Bernard T. Feld (eds.), *The Future of the Sea-based Deterrent* (Cambridge, Mass: M.I.T. Press, 1973), pp. 79–169.

[34] See the articles by Richard Burt, 'Fight Jets Key to Arms-Talks Accord', *Christian Science Monitor* (Eastern Edition), 16 January 1973, p. 3, and Jerome Kahan, 'Where to For SALT II?', *Washington Post*, 19 November 1972, p. B-2.

sanctuaries for attacking submarines, which might be psychologically difficult. For another, it would presumably require some means of verifying that only missile submarines (and not hunter-killer subs) were entering the area: means such as their passage on the surface or the use of special marking devices. It might also be hard to allow SLBM in and keep SLCM out, yet the latter, designed for anti-shipping operations, could represent a threat to sea lanes of communication (in fact, even missile submarines could carry torpedoes for this purpose). Finally, both the establishment of sanctuaries and the problem of safeguarding the sea lanes through these sanctuaries would require co-ordination with both allies and neutrals, which might be difficult to obtain.

The difficulties of attempting to constrain ASW forces themselves are even greater, since they include a variety of elements—aeroplanes, ships, helicopters, shore installations—in a complex network of relationships.[35] Furthermore, some of these elements play a significant role in fleet anti-submarine warfare capabilities, so that to constrain them might be to downgrade the protection of surface vessels against submarine attack and to hamper both fleet operations and convoy escort. Additionally, some components of ASW forces have multiple uses—like helicopter-carriers and destroyers, which can be used in amphibious operations. Moreover, constraining ASW forces immediately involves one in questions concerning the effects of geographic asymmetries, the capabilities of detection devices, the relative utility of submarines as counter-force weapons, and a host of equally different issues. Finally, constraints on ASW forces would directly involve other countries, many of whom have navies designed to conduct anti-submarine warfare, and even more of whom depend on sea lines of communication which ASW forces are designed to protect.

One might perhaps be more inclined to push ahead with constraints on ASW forces, despite these difficulties, if the threat to the sea-borne component of the deterrent were really all that great. In practice, however, there are severe limitations to the potential effectiveness of all types of ASW measures; in fact, the former American Chief of Naval Operations, Admiral Elmo R. Zumwalt, Jr, testified that American missile submarines were completely invulnerable to Soviet ASW forces, and would remain so for some time to come.[36] Thus, for the moment at least, it is possible to avoid tackling the problem of constraining ASW forces.

[35] For an excellent discussion of the weapons, tactics and problems of anti-submarine warfare, see Richard L. Garwin, 'Anti-submarine Warfare and National Security', *Scientific American*, Volume 227, no. 11 (July 1972), pp. 14–25.

[36] *Hearing on the Military Implications of SALT*, p. 536.

SUPER-POWER INTERESTS IN STRATEGIC ARMS LIMITATIONS

Whether any of these measures for the limitation of strategic armaments—or others yet undreamt of—come into being depends not only on their military implications and their technical feasibility but also on the interests of the super-powers in adopting them. In general, the same factors which motivated the United States during the SALT I negotiations are still operative. These include:

1. A desire to avoid specific threats to the security of American strategic retaliatory forces, such as could develop from an enhanced Soviet capability to launch counter-force strikes.
2. A wish to reduce fears and ease tensions between the two super-powers, and to capitalize on the momentum already established towards the improvement of American–Soviet relations.
3. The hope that she can avoid an intensified arms race and a new cycle of American–Soviet interactions, and can reduce the economic and social costs of present strategic weapons programmes.[37]

Against these incentives to a new agreement one must set uncertainties about the Soviet force build-up, and especially Soviet research and development, which make the United States disinclined to accept curbs on improvements in her own weapons or to impose restraints on her own research. Furthermore, the United States is concerned about adverse allied reactions to particular kinds of strategic arms limitations, reactions which were strongly expressed during and after SALT I. Finally, there is a desire to maintain a 'strong' military posture because of the psychological impact this allegedly has upon the Soviet Union.

Although this skein of opposed interests and aims is hard to disentangle, it does shed some light on specific measures in which the United States has shown—or might be expected to show—interest in SALT negotiations. One of these would be to bring under control other weapons systems which could either affect 'essential equivalence' or could appear to tilt further the strategic balance in favour of the Soviet Union—as could the introduction in quantity of improved versions of the *Backfire* bomber. Another would be reductions in heavy ICBM, which would ease the threat to the survival of American land-based systems. Moreover, because she has few equivalents with which to bargain and because her fleet of B-52 bombers is ageing, the

[37] For further details see J. I. Coffey, 'American Interests in the Limitation of Strategic Armaments', in Kintner and Pfaltzgraff, *op. cit.* in Chap. 2, note 3, pp. 60–71.

United States might be willing to retire some bombers as part of a package deal. Certainly she is interested in overall reductions, which would obviate the necessity of having to build up to the 2,400 ceiling or SNDV set by the Vladivostok Accord in order to achieve 'equality'; in fact, the sentiment in favour of reductions in these very high force levels was so strong that the United States Government had to ask the Soviet Union to bring forward the period within which negotiations on reductions would begin.

The United States has also shown a willingness to accept some constraints on MIRV, though not at levels which would affect her ongoing programmes. She has so far rejected banning the flight-testing of particular types of MIRV, or putting ceilings on the number of tests allowed, as a way of slowing MIRV deployment and inhibiting increases in missile accuracy.[38] Moreover, she is seemingly unwilling to give up her own new weapons, such as the B-1 bomber, the *Trident* missile submarine and the Strategic Cruise Missile. Accordingly, it is questionable whether the United States will attempt to preclude the introduction by the Soviet Union of new missiles, better aircraft or lighter ASM, since she would presumably have to accept similar restrictions; in fact, the American–Soviet Agreement of 21 June, 1973 states specifically that 'the modernization and replacement of strategic offensive arms would be permitted under arms-control agreements to be concluded'.[39]

For her part, the Soviet Union seems interested in preserving the strategic parity she has so laboriously attained, avoiding destabilizing technological developments, and reducing the cost of present and future strategic weapons programmes. She may also be influenced in her future proposals by awareness of the shortcomings of some weapons, such as her ABM system, and by the technical problems attendant on modernizing and upgrading her strategic nuclear forces. Moreover, it may be, as Marshall Shulman suggests, that the Soviet leaders are aware of the decreasing political utility of strategic nuclear forces.[40]

In a larger sense, however, those leaders may be motivated more by a desire for political stability than by any concerns about the costs and difficulties of continuing the arms build-up. They certainly attached great importance to the *political* connotations of the Moscow Summit and to the opportunities to expand trade and to increase cultural exchanges, which, along with SALT, made up the overall

[38] The *New York Times*, 31 March 1974, p. 7.
[39] *The Times*, 22 June 1973, p. 7.
[40] Marshall D. Shulman, Comment [on an article by W. K. H. Panofsky], *Survey*, Vol. 19, No. 2 (Spring 1973), p. 176.

package of agreements signed at that Summit meeting. They may feel that good relations between the United States and the Soviet Union, to which arms-control arrangements could contribute, would preclude China from exploiting her *rapprochement* with the United States to the detriment of the Soviet Union, and would further the acceptance of their policies in and towards Western Europe.[41]

This does not necessarily mean that the Soviet leaders are prepared to scrap their strategic weapons programme in the interests of improving *détente*. They may judge that if they can weather the near-term future, in which the United States will have a significant advantage in deliverable warheads, then they can in turn achieve an edge—and possibly exploit it. (Not all members of the Soviet ruling group may believe that there is no political utility to strategic nuclear weapons—any more than do all Western analysts.) Moreover, the importance attached by the Soviet military to *waging* nuclear war should this prove necessary (and not just to deterring it) means that improvements in weaponry may be regarded as essential to the maintenance of Soviet security. In addition there are powerful elements in the Soviet Union which apparently favour continuation of Soviet weapons programmes on the grounds that these are the primary reason why the United States agreed to SALT I.[42] (Others than Americans may feel that there are advantages to 'negotiating from strength'.) Finally, the Soviet leaders cannot afford to ignore the military, the 'defence industry sector' and the other interest groups opposed to arms control whose influence will certainly be felt.[43]

This does not mean that the Kremlin is not interested in further moves towards arms control, only that there may be some limits to these interests—as there are in the White House. The Soviet Union

[41] In this connection see John Newhouse, *Cold Dawn: The Story of SALT* (New York: Holt, Rinehart & Winston, 1973), pp. 167–8, and the discussion of this subject at the Fifth International Arms Control Symposium, summarized in Kintner and Pfaltzgraff, *op. cit.* in Chap. 2, note 3, pp. 99–101.

[42] General Viktor G. Kulikov, Chief-of-Staff of the Soviet Armed Forces, quoted in an article by Victor Zorza, 'Moscow's Rampant Hawks', in the *Christian Science Monitor* (Eastern Edition) 15 September 1972, p. 16. *See also* the remarks by First Deputy Minister of Defence Admiral Sergei Gorshkov, quoted by Zorza, in the *Washington Post*, 20 September 1972, p. A 19. The veteran political leader Mikhail A. Suslov gave credit first of all to the success of Soviet foreign policy, but secondly to 'the growth of the power of the Soviet Union', *The Baltimore Sun*, 24 August 1972, p. A 1.

[43] For a discussion of the nature and extent of internal opposition to SALT I, see Thomas W. Wolfe, 'Soviet Interests in SALT', in Kintner and Pfaltzgraff, *op. cit.* in Chap. 2, note 3, pp. 34–8.

has evidenced a strong desire to bring under control weapons not covered in SALT, including both West European regional nuclear forces and American strike aircraft based in Europe and carrier-borne aviation. While she has also indicated a willingness to make reductions in her own forces,[44] she is not prepared to accept asymmetrical reductions—at least not to the extent necessary to reach current American nuclear force levels.

As for MIRV, the Soviet Union has (understandably) been unwilling to settle for less than equality with the United States; Soviet officials have reportedly argued that 'where you [Americans] are, we must be' and have stated that SALT II would succeed only if the Soviet Union had a demonstrated MIRV capability.[45] Nor have they been willing to curb others of their new weapons, such as the SS-16-X mobile ICBM and the large gas-ejected missiles which they have built, arguing instead that the United States should halt her programmes for the production of B-1 bombers, the construction of *Trident* missile submarines and the development of air-launched cruise missiles, which the Soviet Union apparently sees as part of an attempt to regain strategic superiority.[46]

Finally, the Soviet Union has expressed an interest in restricting ASW weapons and technology,[47] for very understandable reasons. These reasons have to do in part with the geographic disadvantage she suffers: most of her submarines must initially follow narrowly circumscribed routes when leaving their home ports, routes which are exposed to surveillance by allied ASW forces. Furthermore, these submarines must in many instances pass near American or NATO bases, from which aircraft and hunter-killer submarines can detect them, and between which barrier zones can be erected (as between Iceland and the Orkneys in the North Atlantic). This, coupled with the fact that Soviet subs are comparatively noisy, means that the

---

[44] Nixon–Brezhnev Agreement on the Prevention of Nuclear War, *op. cit.* in Chap. 1, note 11. She also undertook in the Vladivostok Accord to negotiate on force reductions, and acquiesced in the American suggestion that these be started as soon as the implementing agreements had been ratified, rather than in 1980–1, as initially provided.

[45] *The Washington Post*, 18 August 1973, p. 4.

[46] See article in *Pravda*, 7 April 1974, summarized in Hedrick Smith, 'Pravda Assails US Position on Arms', *New York Times*, 8 April 1974, p. 3, and the speech by the Chief-of-Staff of the Soviet Armed Forces, General Viktor G. Kulikov, reported in *Ibid.*, 10 May 1974, p. 12.

[47] *The Washington Post*, 19 November 1972, p. A 26. According to Joseph Kruzel, they also introduced the idea of establishing sanctuaries for missile submarines during SALT I. 'SALT II: The Search for a Follow-on Agreement', *Orbis* Vol. XVII, No. 2 (Summer 1973), p. 353.

Soviet Navy would find it harder than the American Navy to deploy for a surprise attack, and that in the event of war it might suffer heavy losses, even among those missile submarines already on station off the American coast.

Conversely, American submarines can reach vital targets in the Soviet Union from areas like the Indian Ocean, which the Soviet Union can never hope to secure. Additionally, its own ASW forces in the Mediterranean and the North Atlantic lack the forward bases and the air cover which could make them more effective than they now are. Thus, curbs on the extension of phased-array sonars, prohibitions on tracking, cutbacks in ASW forces, and even the creation of sanctuaries for missile submarines (if they were properly located), could all benefit the Soviet Union. If the wish is father to the proposal, therefore, one could expect the Soviet Union to advance some such measures as those during SALT III. Beyond this, little can be said.

EUROPEAN INTERESTS IN STRATEGIC ARMS LIMITATIONS

If direct information about Soviet interests in strategic arms limitations is scant, that about the interests of the countries of Europe is virtually non-existent. While there have been some generalized analyses of the effects of SALT, expectations about future arms negotiations, and the potential consequences of possible outcomes, there has been little or no public debate on the subject. However, European interests do exist, and may in some instances affect superpower acceptance of particular measures, as they did the American refusal to accept curbs on Forward Based Systems.

East European interests

In general, members of the Warsaw Treaty Organization welcomed SALT, as did the Soviet Union. This was mainly because they saw the agreements of Moscow and Vladivostok as setting limits to the strategic arms race between the two super-powers, reducing fears and tensions and making a start on the process of improving relations with the United States and the West at large. They, like their Soviet allies, tended to see the agreements as a consequence of increasing Soviet military power and the solidarity and achievements of the countries of the Socialist Commonwealth. They have not manifested any concern with the specific details of SALT, since they have neither forces which could be affected by particular understandings, nor interpretations (as do the British and the French), nor, as far as an outsider can judge, have they been heavily involved in the SALT negotiations.

As one looks towards SALT III and succeeding negotiations, it would seem that these attitudes are likely to persist. First of all, the countries of Eastern Europe would welcome the increased stability attendant on further limitations on strategic armaments, since this would ensure maintenance of the Soviet strategic deterrent (on which their security in some degree rests) and lessen the danger that war could occur as a result of one side or other believing it had secured an exploitable strategic advantage. They would probably prefer to see this stability achieved at lower levels of forces, because of the favourable psychological impact of reductions and because these would mark further progress towards the *détente* which is generally desired. It is questionable whether they would be concerned about the ways in which stability was achieved or the nature of reductions, neither of which would affect them directly. Nor, as far as one can see, are they likely to have much of a voice in future negotiations, partly because their level of knowledge would limit the contribution they could make and partly because of the apparent lack of a mechanism or process for consultation on strategic arms limitations within the Warsaw Treaty Organization. Thus the East Europeans, unlike their Western brethren, may have little to do with SALT.

West European interests

West European reactions to SALT were also generally favourable. The simple fact of agreement between the two super-powers on such an important matter seemed worth-while in itself, and promising for the future. The agreement curbed weapons programmes which might have given the Soviet Union a politically exploitable advantage or which could, at the very least, have intensified the strategic arms race, with accompanying increases in fears and tensions. Finally, the agreement blocked or limited programmes which could have adversely affected West European nuclear delivery capabilities, as could an extension or thickening of Soviet ballistic-missile defences.

At the same time, SALT raised in many minds a number of questions, both political and military. One set of questions concerned the effects on the credibility of the American deterrent of the formal ratifiction of strategic parity and, as a corollary, the implications for future Soviet behaviour, with some of the Allies worried lest the Soviet Union might feel freer to take actions carrying a higher risk of war. Another concerned the potential impact of SALT on NATO, with some West Europeans feeling that the United States might give priority to the maintenance of good relations with the Soviet Union and that, in the process, she might be prepared to accept some erosion of alliance solidarity and cohesion. And a third related to the possibility that future limitations on strategic armaments might affect West European security either directly, by hindering the modernization and growth of independent nuclear forces, or indirectly, by reducing or redeploying American forces and weapons systems deemed essential to the maintenance of a military balance in Europe. To some extent these questions were prompted by fears about the firmness of the American commitment to Europe and by concerns over the fixity of symbols of that commitment, such as American troop strength—matters which bear little relation to SALT. To some extent, however, they arose out of the difficulty of interjecting European views into the complicated negotiations on strategic arms limitations, negotiations whose course seems to have been determined as much by interactions among competing bureaus and interest-groups in Washington as by interchanges with the Western allies—or even with the Soviet Union.[48] To some extent also they probably reflected recognition that the strategic postures of the United States and her allies are so different, and their interests in SALT consequently so divergent, that the United States might be prepared to accept arrangements which could indirectly or directly affect West European military capabilities.

There are a number of areas in which SALT I did have an impact on these capabilities. For example, while the Treaty on the Limitation of Anti-Ballistic Missile Systems ruled out a Soviet build-up which could have largely nullified the effectiveness of British and French SLBM, it also sanctioned the maintenance and improvement of ballistic-missile defences around Moscow, a city which, for political and psychological reasons, is a high-priority target of those same British and French nuclear forces.[49] As one looks to the detailed implementation of SALT II, and even more to subsequent phases, it is apparent that there are a number of measures applicable to strategic nuclear forces which could further affect West European military capabilities for good or for ill.

(i) Bringing other weapons systems under control
To move from the general to the specific, the Allies would undoubtedly have mixed feelings about bringing other weapons under control in SALT. They would presumably like to see such controls extended to Soviet medium bombers (and MR/IRBM), partly for symbolic reasons and partly in the hope of reductions in these weapons, which enhance Soviet capabilities *vis-à-vis* Western Europe. However, these Soviet regional forces may seem less important now that the Soviet Union has developed weapons such as the Variable-Range Ballistic Missile (VRBM) and has greatly expanded her force of tactical

[48] For illustrations of this, *see* Newhouse, *op. cit.* in note 41, esp. pp. 148–53, 157–62, 176–82, and 221–31.
[49] Geoffrey Kemp and Ian Smart, *op. cit.* in Chap. 2, note 3, pp. 215–16.

nuclear-delivery vehicles. Moreover, attempts to control these Soviet launchers would immediately raise the question of controlling comparable Western weapons systems, such as the IRBM and *Mirage* IV light bombers in France and the V-bombers in Britain, even though Britain no longer counts the latter as part of her strategic nuclear forces. This does not mean that the Western allies would be uninterested in controls over, or cuts in, Soviet regional nuclear forces, but rather that the complexity of negotiations and the possibility that these may impinge on their own nuclear deterrents might incline them to leave sleeping missiles in their silos.

This judgment may also extend to Forward-Based Systems, which, as previously noted, are primarily intended for intra-theatre operations rather than strikes against the Soviet homeland. This is not because the West Europeans are concerned about the military effects of counting some FBS as 'strategic', since the numbers involved would be relatively small.[50] Rather, they might be concerned about the possible extension of controls to *their* nuclear-capable aircraft, which are perhaps twice as numerous as those manned by American pilots. They might well resent arrangements which would benefit the United States but leave untouched the regional (and tactical) nuclear forces which are threats to their security. They might also feel that American strike aircraft could be better used as bargaining counters in negotiations on mutual force reductions (and in any case, they would probably prefer negotiations on FBS to be conducted in a forum where their views could be presented, rather than one from which they were excluded, as they are from SALT). Thus the West Europeans would undoubtedly prefer the question of FBS to be left alone, although they might not object too strenuously to a partial extension of controls which would neither unduly inhibit the flexible deployment of American air power nor significantly affect the conventional balance in Europe.

(ii) Reductions in forces

The Allies would probably like to see reductions in strategic nuclear forces, since they could ratify progress towards *détente* and free

[50] If, as would be reasonable, one counted only those planes capable of carrying out two-way missions against the Soviet Union from present bases, this would total about 100 aircraft. The 72 F-111Es in Britain could, with minimum bomb-loads, reach Kaliningrad (old Königsberg) and adjacent regions in the western Soviet Union. The 30-odd carrier-based A-7Ds could hit at Soviet targets only when their ships were deployed in the Eastern Mediterranean. Other strike aircraft, such as the F-4 *Phantoms*, could not reach targets in the Soviet Union from the airfields in Western Europe on which they are normally based.

American defence resources for other purposes, such as the upkeep of troops in Europe. They would probably regard such reductions even more favourably if they succeeded in curbing Soviet counterforce capabilities, since West European analysts and officials are not only mindful of the Soviet potential for installing MIRV but also concerned about the psychological implications of an apparent Soviet strategic advantage. They would not, however, welcome measures which would preclude the United States from exploiting her technological advantages (as deep cuts in missile submarines might do) or which would weigh in the strategic balance their own regional nuclear forces, such as the Soviet Union tried to include during the first two phases of SALT.[51]

Ultimately, however, the allies will have to decide what to do about the congeries of aircraft, land-based missiles and SLBM which make up NATO and Warsaw Pact regional forces in Europe. One alternative would be to do nothing, on the ground that the issues are politically so difficult and technically so complex that attempts to deal with them may be counter-productive. Another alternative would be to build a European nuclear force which, because of its size and by virtue of the political unity of its creators, could constitute a significant and credible deterrent.

A third, and very different, alternative would be to bargain for some reduction of nuclear armaments in Europe. For example, selected elements of the American FBS, together with the British and French strategic nuclear forces, the Soviet MR/IRBM and medium bombers and perhaps the American FB-111A medium bombers, could be placed in a new category, for discussion outside SALT II. If the allies were willing to negotiate but unwilling to reduce their own forces (as they well might be), then offsetting reductions in American FBS and Soviet regional forces could be worked out, to the advantage of the West Europeans. If they were unwilling, for the moment, even to discuss reductions in American forces, then the Soviet Union would receive 'compensation' for the American FBS in the removal of 60–70

---

[51] In SALT I the Soviet Union claimed the right to increase the number of missile submarines she was allowed if the NATO allies should 'increase the numbers of submarines they would have operational or under construction on the date of signature of the agreement'–Unilateral Statement by the Delegation of the Soviet Union, the *New York Times*, 14 June, 1972, p. 18. The United States indicated that she did not accept this statement, which would permit the USSR additional submarines if France or Britain added to their fleets, or would have required the United States to give up the option of replacing her *Titan* II ICBM with SLBM. *See also* the Background Briefing by Dr Kissinger, *op. cit.* in note 8, p. 192, which indicates that the Soviet Union raised this issue again in SALT II.

FB-111As from the bargaining over intercontinental vehicles. And if either side increased its regional forces, presumably the other would be entitled to build up its own counterpart to those forces–a loophole which would enable the West Europeans either to match any expansion in Soviet delivery vehicles or, in the long run, to go ahead with creating some form of European nuclear force–an option which many would like to keep open, even if they would prefer not to exercise it.

(iii) Qualitative improvements in weaponry

In contrast to their interests in the nature of controls over strategic offensive systems and in the types and levels of reductions in strategic offensive forces, the West Europeans seem to have no direct concern about constraints on qualitative improvements, such as missile accuracy and reliability, the development of lighter air-to-surface missiles, and so on.

Their major interest would seem to be in barring technological advances which could threaten strategic stability, a task which they can leave to the United States. They may well be ambivalent about curbs on other qualitative improvements, such as MIRV. On the one hand, such curbs could enhance strategic stability and preclude the Soviet Union from achieving a seeming military advantage; on the other, no conceivable curb is likely to reduce the threat, since the Soviet Union already has enough weapons of the accuracy and yield required for counter-force strikes against all conceivable military targets in Western Europe–with enough left over to devastate the region should the course of any war so dictate. Furthermore, restrictions on MIRV could hamper the United States in maintaining of a capacity to launch counter-force strikes against Soviet MR/IRBM, VRBM and other delivery vehicles targeted on Western Europe–a capacity already diminished by the increase in the number of targets which must be destroyed in order to reduce prospective levels of damage to the United States.

Perhaps more importantly, constraints applied to the nations of Europe might significantly affect the future capabilities of British and French strategic nuclear forces. Although Britain has opted to retain *Polaris*, rather than buy *Poseidon*, she may yet decide to re-equip her submarines with MIRV missiles, a move which could multiply tenfold her ability to strike at targets in the Soviet Union; were she to be precluded from developing MIRV of her own, she would be even more dependent on United States sources for advanced SLBM. France, too, would undoubtedly oppose any measures which could inhibit her from upgrading her missile submarines, should she so desire.

The problem here is that the Soviet Union is not likely to acquiesce in a situation which permitted the NATO allies to multiply their strategic nuclear capabilities, at least not without obtaining compensating offsets. Moreover, unless constraints on research and development in general (and missile flight tests in particular) extend to France and Britain, these countries could be 'proving grounds' for innovations in American weaponry, thereby evading any agreed controls. Thus the Soviet Union might, as the price for constraints on upgrading weapons or curbs on new weapons, ask for the application of these restrictions to the countries of Western Europe and for limitations on the transfer of technology and/or the sale of advanced weapons to those countries, according to the precedent set by Article IX of the Treaty on the Limitation of Anti-Ballistic Missile Systems.[52]

This would pose a threefold problem for the Western allies. First of all, at least some of them depend on the United States for advanced weapons such as SLBM (for British nuclear submarines) and long-range strike aircraft (for the West German Air Force); curbs on the further development of particular weapons—such as the submarine-launched cruise missile—could affect the Allies' ability to modernize and upgrade their forces by buying such weapons from the United States. Secondly, the Allies depend even more on the flow of information, which covers a range of weapons and equipment relevant to both strategic nuclear forces and other components: aircraft, SAM, laser-guided bombs, and guidance and control radar, to mention just a few. Thirdly, if restrictions on the development of new weapons are to be fully effective, they may also have to apply to qualitative improvements carried out by Europeans on their own.

These and other restrictions, singly or in combination, could hit hardest at improvements in European nuclear forces, which are most likely to benefit from weapons transfers or flows of information. They could be critical if the West Europeans found it necessary to upgrade their retaliatory forces in order to offset Soviet innovations (such as the introduction of a ballistic missile interceptor with a capacity for loitering after launch) and were forced to undertake the slow and costly process of duplicating American developments. These restrictions could be crucial if the Europeans decided to build a truly independent nuclear force, with all that implies in the way of diversified delivery vehicles, advanced warhead design, secure communications, and other high-cost, high-technology measures. Already the sale or transfer of components of anti-ballistic missile systems is forbidden

[52] Perhaps with this in mind, the United States made a Unilateral Statement on the No-transfer Article of the ABM Treaty, indicating that this did not constitute a precedent for a treaty limiting strategic offensive armaments. The *New York Times*, 14 June 1972, p. 18.

by treaty, and although the United States has insisted that this restriction does not set a precedent for other areas, it may find it difficult (or undesirable) to maintain this position if the allies move towards the creation of an European Nuclear Force. Thus, it is not hard to understand why the West Europeans should look askance at measures aimed at certain kinds of constraints on improvements in weaponry.

(iv) Constraints on defensive systems

As indicated previously, constraints on strategic defensive systems could significantly affect European military capabilities, either for better or for worse. Their precise effects would depend on which systems were constrained, the nature of the constraints and whether they applied only on the territories of two super-powers, to their forces wherever deployed, or to particular geographic areas, such as Europe.

As far as ABM are concerned, scrapping the Moscow network would, of course, greatly improve the ability of the West Europeans to deliver nuclear strikes on politically important and industrially significant targets,[53] but it seems unlikely that the Soviet Union would help Britain and France to enhance their retaliatory capabilities. Thus the West Europeans may have to settle for measures which preclude the thickening of Soviet ballistic missile defences, their extension over the western part of the Soviet Union or their replacement by more advanced systems.

As far as the NATO allies are concerned, constraints on air defences would probably be acceptable if applied only to the United States and the Soviet Union, since they could increase the ability of French light bombers and German strike aircraft to penetrate Soviet air space. They might be viewed differently if they extended to American fighter planes and surface-to-air missiles deployed in Europe, since these not only protect military installations–airfields, depots, and so on–but are integrated into the NATO Air Defence System for area coverage of civilian targets. Constraints would also probably be regarded as undesirable if they extended to Europe at large, partly because some types of controls could affect the ability of the European allies to deal with attacks by tactical aircraft in either conventional or nuclear operations. However, since constraints on air defences seem unlikely, such judgments are perhaps irrelevant.

The reactions of the European allies to constraints on ASW forces are likely to be both mixed and contingent. On the one hand, Britain

[53] Ten of the 33 Soviet cities with over 500,000 inhabitants lie within a 500-mile radius of Moscow, i.e. within the maximum effective range of the present ballistic-missile defences.

and France could gain from measures which preserved the invulnerability of their missile submarines and gave greater freedom to deploy them off the coasts of the Soviet Union. However, it is not at all certain that they or other countries would look as favourably upon the establishment of sanctuaries for Soviet submarines off their own coasts (Norway, for example, is already concerned about preventing submarines from penetrating her fjords). Moreover, constraints which cut into the United States' ability to ensure the safety of the Atlantic Fleet, or to convoy shipping in time of war, might be regarded unfavourably, since these could affect American ability to dispatch reinforcements and supplies to Europe. This suggests that measures to reduce American and Soviet hunter-killer subs, bar the tracking of missile submarines and establish sanctuaries remote from the coast might be acceptable, as would restrictions upon phased-array sonar, which has little or no relevance to European defences. Conversely, establishment of sanctuaries near the coast of Europe, or attempts to limit numbers of patrol craft, helicopters, destroyer escorts and so on, would generate opposition, even if these cuts applied initially only to American forces.

(v) Understandings concerning the use of nuclear weapons
All the measures aimed at controlling weapons are, of course, potential rather than actual, and can only handicap the further development of West European forces, rather than affecting existing military capabilities. What could affect them, and also influence perceptions of security, would be the emergence of an understanding between the United States and the Soviet Union over the use of nuclear weapons. In fact, the American–Soviet pact on the prevention of nuclear war was interpreted by many West Europeans as signifying a greater American reluctance to protect European interests, and as foreshadowing a time when the West Europeans could not count on the protection at present afforded by the American deterrent.[54]

European fears concerning an American–Soviet understanding take a variety of forms, as previously noted. One is the fear that, in the interest of preserving peace and avoiding confrontations, the United States might allow West European positions to be eroded, in the case of the relations between West Germany and West Berlin, for example. Another is that, in seeking to avoid nuclear war, the United States might restructure her forces in Europe and reshape her strategy for

[54] *The Times*, 23 June 1973, p. 4, and 25 June 1973, pp. 5 and 13, the latter page containing an editorial on the subject. The point was remade by Michel Jobert, at that time French Foreign Minister, during the December 1973 meeting of NATO ministers. *The New York Times*, 11 December 1973, p. 1.

their employment in such a way as to weaken the credibility of the deterrent, thereby exposing her allies to Soviet pressures. There is also the fear that if war should break out the United States would employ her nuclear forces (and so constrain the use of nuclear weapons by her allies) to insulate American and Soviet strategic nuclear forces and confine any conflict to the continent of Europe; indeed the late President Georges Pompidou was only one of many who were apparently convinced that this was the United States' aim.[55]

One cannot deny that avoidance of military confrontation may at times require a settlement of disputes which is not wholly satisfactory to all parties involved; this has, however, been true of every settlement since time began. Nor can one deny that desire to avoid the outbreak of nuclear war may induce the United States to avoid deploying certain weapons (such as 'mini-nukes'), to exercise tight control over the use of aircraft and missiles now in Europe, and to seek to develop a strategy which would minimize the need for employment of nuclear weapons; this, in fact, has been American policy for at least ten years.[56] This is not to say, however, that such moves would weaken the deterrent and leave Europe unprotected. The American–Soviet agreement specifies, good relations between the two super-powers require, and the general course of Soviet foreign policy indicates that both parties will 'refrain from threat or use of force against the other party, against the allies of the other party and against other countries, in circumstances which may endanger international peace and security'[57]—a policy which, if implemented, will contribute more to peace and security in Europe than any given level of deterrent forces. Moreover, no effort to clarify the rules of engagement is going to remove all the ambiguities inherent in any use of nuclear weapons and all the uncertainties about the consequences of a particular decision to do so; indeed these ambiguities and uncertainties are so essential to deterrence between equals that they will undoubtedly influence the strategies of both super-powers.

---

[55] *Statement before the French National Assembly*, 13 April 1966, Speech and Press Conference No. 243 A, April 1966, p. 4. *See also* Wynfred Joshua and Walter F. Hahn, *Nuclear Politics: America, France, and Britain*, The Washington Papers, Vol. I, No. 9 (Beverly Hills, Calif.: Sage Publications, 1973), pp. 6–8. Meeting this concern may be one incentive to the development by the United States of 'limited strategic response options'– which could be exercised in the event of Soviet aggression in Europe as well as in the event of a disarming strike against American ICBM.

[56] See J. I. Coffey, 'Strategy, Alliance Policy and Nuclear Proliferation', in *Orbis*, Vol. XI, No. 4 (Winter 1968), esp. pp. 978–83.

[57] Article II, Nixon–Brezhnev Agreement on The Prevention of Nuclear War, *op. cit.* in Chap. 1, note 11.

Furthermore, rules of engagement may be to the Europeans' advantage. For example, the denuclearization of narrow zones, or the designation of strips along frontiers from which certain types of weapons would be barred, may avoid both provocation and the risk of inadvertent escalation without adversely affecting the ability to initiate nuclear strikes against targets in that zone, should the need arise. An understanding that nuclear weapons would initially be employed only against targets in one's own territory or (with their permission) that of one's allies could maintain the credibility of the deterrent with less risk than at present: it would reduce fears of a pre-emptive strike and hence the incentive to launch a nuclear *riposte* so intensive or extensive as to precipitate a large-scale exchange of nuclear weapons. Finally, limiting initial use to a narrow zone (and possibly to battlefield targets, such as troop concentrations, artillery positions, and so on) could achieve the political and psychological impact NATO seeks without the escalatory effects of attacks against the bridges across the Vistula or the airfields around Prague.[58]

All this is not to suggest that it will be easy to work out constraints on the use (or the threatened use) of force, as the participants in the Conference on Security and Co-operation in Europe have found. Nor is it to say that measures designed to preclude the outbreak of nuclear war will leave unchanged the weapons, forces and strategies–and the perceptions–of the members of the two alliances. It is to point out that understandings about the employment of nuclear weapons are essential if the members of the Atlantic Alliance are to achieve their twin goals of peace and security.

SALT : substance and process

So far as this analysis is valid it suggests that, as might be expected, most measures to limit strategic armaments will primarily affect the United States and the Soviet Union. Moreover, even if these powers agreed on measures which could impinge on West European forces, implementation would require the consent of the countries concerned –a consent which might not be easily obtainable. Thus, West European interests probably lie more in the direction of guarding against future developments which could adversely affect them than in blocking those likely to emerge from the next round of negotiations.

[58] There are, of course, counter-arguments: that short-range attacks do not so quickly and so irretrievably link the strategic deterrent to the defence of Europe; that limiting use initially to one's own territory penalizes the defender and rewards the aggressor, and so on. The purpose here is not to repeat all the arguments (for which see Chapter 5), but simply to point out that not all rules of engagement are necessarily detrimental to the security of the Atlantic Alliance.

One way of doing this would be to engage in the process of negotiation, both because European interests (some of which can be furthered by arms control) would be better served and because the super-powers could profit from the insights and the contributions of others. To this end the Europeans might consider establishing a discussion group on strategic arms limitations consisting of three of the NATO allies, two members of the Warsaw Treaty Organization and two representatives of the non-aligned countries. This could:

1. Study the effects of potential measures for the limitation of strategic armaments on their defence postures and interests.
2. Consider controls on other kinds of nuclear-delivery vehicles which could be employed in or against a European theatre of operations.
3. Devise rules of engagement which, in the spirit of the American– Soviet agreement on the prevention of nuclear war, could minimize the possible use of nuclear weapons in any conflict, or the likelihood of escalation if they were employed.
4. Report their findings to those negotiating strategic arms limitations, bargaining over mutual force reductions and implementing the confidence-building measures adopted by the Conference on European Security and Co-operation in Europe, leaving it to each group to deal with the recommendations in its own way.

Whether or not this approach is adopted, it is essential that there should be a European contribution to SALT. After all, these talks, like other negotiations on the control of armaments, are aimed at promoting peace and security on a global basis, not just on the territories of the United States and the Soviet Union. If this aim is to be achieved, the interests and views of others must be taken into account.

THE SAVOUR OF SALT

From what has been said, it is obvious that there will be difficulty in devising feasible controls over all areas which might be discussed in SALT, and even more in applying them so as not to adversely affect the military position of either super-power. Perhaps still harder will be reconciling the interests of the super-powers (which stem from political and economic as well as military and technical factors) with those of their allies, at least as far as the West Europeans are concerned. There do, however, seem to be a number of arms-control measures which, at least at first glance, offer promise, and which I would like to suggest for consideration.

The first would be to implement those reductions in strategic nuclear forces to which both super-powers are committed in principle. As suggested earlier, this could be done either by:

1. Arranging for specific trade-offs, as of B-52 bombers for Soviet ICBM, or *Polaris* submarines for older types of Soviet SLBM.
2. Lowering the ceiling on strategic delivery vehicles set at Vladivostok, leaving each side free to decide which weapons systems to phase down.

In either case, it would seem desirable to set sub-ceilings on particular categories of weapons (such as ICBM of more than 100 cubic metres in volume, or bombers of more than 200,000 lb gross weight when empty), in order to hamper the development of major capabilities to launch disarming strikes–to which bombers armed with ALCM can contribute, along with ICBM.

Still more desirable would be constraints on those improvements in weaponry which could generate fears of one side or the other acquiring a first-strike counter-force capability, or even the ability significantly to degrade the land-based components of strategic retaliatory forces. Unfortunately, the latter ability can be acquired in a variety of ways, some of which (like the development of terminal guidance systems for re-entry vehicles) are extraordinarily difficult to prevent. Even more unfortunately, the strategic doctrines of the two superpowers call for attacks upon each other's weapons sites, military installations and industrial facilities–attacks which may require sizeable numbers of accurate warheads.

Within the limits imposed by technology and doctrine there may, however, be measures worth considering. Among these are:

1. Curbs on the development of extremely accurate re-entry vehicles, to include a ban on manoeuvrable warheads and limitations on the number of missile flight tests authorized.
2. Constraints on the types as well as the numbers of weapons which could be MIRV-equipped.
3. Limitations on the payload carried by the strategic strike forces of both sides, bombers as well as missiles.[59]

---

[59] The inclusion of bombers seems necessary for two reasons. (1) As the Russians have pointed out, the Americans have a significant advantage in bomber payload, which more than offsets the larger payload of Soviet ICBM (see *The Military Balance 76–77*, p. 107). (2) The United States is developing a new medium-range air-to-surface missile with a 200 KT warhead and a highly accurate guidance system which will give it a counterforce capability against all but fully hardened military targets. Moreover, the Department of Defense proposes to produce several thousand of these ALCM which can be carried by all the types of bombers in the United States inventory. Ulsamer, 'The Pentagon Looks at Strategic Options', *op. cit.* in note 25, p. 55.

While these measures, singly or in combination, would not preclude improvements in war-fighting capabilities, they might limit them enough to alleviate fears of decisive advantages, particularly if imposed in conjunction with reductions in numbers of launch vehicles.

In conjunction with these measures it would also be desirable to place curbs on new and radically different weapons, in a fashion even more stringent than that now provided for exotic missile defences. Considering the effect that previous innovations, such as anti-ballistic missiles and MIRV, have had on arms build-ups, one ought seriously to consider whether new 'wonder weapons' (such as the strategic cruise missile launched from a standard torpedo tube from an aircraft, or even from a guide rail) should not be kept under wraps before they become operational, if not before they are tested. Although each side will undoubtedly want to take advantage of significant improvements being made in weaponry, and although there is no good way of preventing most improvements, it may be that discussion of the potential implications of new weapons–and of possible counters to them–could induce unilateral restraint in their deployment or lead to agreed constraints on differing, but equally destabilizing, weapons-systems. Indeed the monitoring of technological innovations and the promotion of limitations on their application might well be the most important task of the Standing Consultative Commission established by Article XIII of the Treaty on the Limitation of Anti-Ballistic Missile Systems.

As for constraints on defensive forces, those on anti-ballistic missiles would seem to matter little either way, in view of current restrictions on the levels and types of such missiles. Air defences, unfortunately, are almost impossible to handle, and, apart from attempting to constrain potentially worrying systems (such as a SAM which might readily be converted to an ABM), it would seem best to let time and cost take care of this problem in the Soviet Union, as it has in the United States.

ASW is a little different in that, while it would seem to present no immediate problem, concern over its potential capabilities could inhibit the restructuring of strategic offensive forces. Accordingly, it might be wise to head off efforts to improve detection capabilities, to limit tracking by surface ships or hunter-killer submarines, and perhaps to set some ceilings on this particular type of submarine. The establishment of sanctuaries, while perhaps useful, seems to raise so many questions that it might be better to defer action on this proposal. As for constraints on other elements of the operating forces, these would seem both unnecessary and impracticable–as well as potentially upsetting to the Western allies. If the situation changes so much that some constraints seem desirable, it would be better to attempt to set limits to increases in ASW carriers, frigates and patrol craft, rather than to opt for reductions in current forces.

Finally, there is the question of whether SALT II, III and subsequent stages in negotiations on strategic armaments should attempt to set rules for the use of nuclear weapons. To some extent, an *understanding* of rules is a *sine qua non* for agreement on arms limitations, since it enables each super-power to appreciate the value the other attaches to particular types and/or numbers of weapons. Many of the most important 'rules' have to do with the circumstances in which tactical nuclear weapons will be used and the targets against which they will be directed, rules which, besides being remote from the issues discussed at SALT, also touch closely on the concerns of Europeans, both East and West. Thus there is something to be said for focusing in SALT on measures dealing with accidental launches, avoiding inadverent war and inhibiting attempts to exploit strategic nuclear forces politically, leaving to other forums the even thornier problem of how to reduce the danger of escalation without simultaneously diminishing the credibility of the deterrent.

As far as the process of negotiation is concerned, SALT I lasted much too long in proportion to the results achieved, even if one assumes that it took a year to educate both participants in the negotiations. The same can be said of SALT II, even though the problems were technically more difficult than the issues dealt with in SALT I. Unfortunately, problems are outrunning time, as was true with the MIRV question during SALT I and may be true of the missile accuracy question during SALT II. A possible way of handling this may be to focus on a limited number of very urgent problems such as missile accuracy and manoeuvrable warheads, and reductions which could be made quickly and comparatively easily, such as trade-offs among ageing weapons systems. The time so gained could be used to determine more precisely which limitations on more modern systems would be feasible and acceptable to the super-powers and to decide when and how to introduce constraints on regional nuclear forces—a decision which would certainly need to be referred to a broader forum, possibly involving the People's Republic of China.

The impact of SALT on European security to date has not been great, largely because the measures adopted have simply ratified the existing strategic balances, intercontinental and regional. In fact the political and psychological effects of SALT have so far overshadowed the military ones. Unless future Strategic Arms Limitations produce results greater than those rather optimistically suggested, they, too, will have relatively little impact on the strategic balance and only marginal effects on the military balance in Europe. Only if the United States, as part of the price for any subsequent agreement, makes drastic reductions in FBS, accepts major constraints on the sale of new weapons, or restricts markedly the transfer of technology are NATO capabilities likely to be diminished disproportionately and West European fears aroused.

At some stage, however, American and West European interests in strategic arms limitations may diverge so markedly as to affect perceptions of security in Europe. This may happen if the United States accepts measures which would act against the improvement, enlargement and coalescence of existing British and French nuclear forces. It may occur if the net result of SALT is to reduce significantly the number of intercontinental delivery vehicles, leaving the Western allies to face vastly superior Soviet regional forces with (seemingly) diminished American support. And it may take place if the suspicion that the United States attaches more importance to agreements with the Soviet Union than to the preservation of ties with her European associates hardens into belief.

Obviously, developments outside SALT (patterns of super-power behaviour, success in promoting East–West co-operation, and so on) will also affect perceptions of security and West European attitudes towards SALT. Equally obviously, failure to negotiate further limitations on strategic armaments would affect these perceptions even more harmfully, since it would signal failure not just in one area but in the whole policy of *détente*. The issue confronting both Americans and West Europeans, therefore, is whether they are prepared to set aside some of their short-term concerns about relatively small perturbations in the military balance in order to try for longer-term and more important alterations in political relationships between East and West. At the moment, both the desire to improve these relations and the incentives for arms control seem to impel the West in the same direction: towards more comprehensive, but not yet universal, limitations of strategic armaments. One can only hope that the Soviet Union and her allies in Eastern Europe will move in the same direction–and for the same reasons.

Chapter 5

CONSTRAINTS ON TACTICAL NUCLEAR FORCES[1]

As indicated in the preceding chapter, strategic arms limitations impinge only peripherally and contingently upon European security. But restrictions on tactical nuclear forces will immediately and directly affect European security in a variety of ways. They could lead to the withdrawal or redeployment of American and Soviet tactical nuclear-delivery vehicles and/or nuclear warheads, thus altering the military capabilities of the two alliances. They could affect European nuclear delivery capabilities both present and future. They could affect the link between tactical operations and strategic nuclear war, and hence the credibility of the strategic deterrent—a matter of particular importance to the NATO allies. Finally, success or failure in imposing restrictions on particular types of weapons systems, such as Soviet SRBM (Short-Range Ballistic Missiles) and American strike aircraft, could alleviate or exacerbate concerns about the consequences of a conflict in Europe.

Before talking about possible restrictions, however, it may be

---

[1] As used here and hereafter the phrase 'tactical nuclear forces' (TNF) refers to those elements of the armed services designed and intended primarily for nuclear strikes against military targets in the theatre of operations targets such as troop concentrations, artillery positions, unit headquarters, supply points, air bases, and so on. Tactical nuclear forces can be further subdivided into:

(a) Tactical nuclear delivery vehicles (TNDV) such as artillery, rockets, strike aircraft and short-range missiles (including both land-based cruise missiles and those mounted on surface vessels or submarines).

(b) Defensive weapons suitable for use in tactical operations, such as anti-submarine rockets (ASROC) and low-level surface-to-air missiles.

(c) The nuclear warheads used by these various weapons systems.

To some extent these distinctions are arbitrary. The French *Mirage* IVA light bombers could presumably be directed against tactical targets instead of strategic targets in the Soviet Union, and ASROC against missile submarines, as well as against those attempting to lay mines. But at least my discussion should be clear.

desirable to set the stage with a discussion of the tactical uses of nuclear weapons[2] (with particular reference to the doctrines and concepts of NATO and the Warsaw Pact) and of the interests and concerns of the two alliances. We will then look briefly at the size, nature and deployment of tactical nuclear forces, before discussing the effects on the military balance of reductions in delivery vehicles and warheads, constraints on their deployment and restrictions on their use. Finally, this chapter will suggest measures which would pass the triple test of alleviating concerns, not eroding reassurances and ensuring 'undiminished security' for both NATO and the Warsaw Pact.

THE TACTICAL USES OF NUCLEAR WEAPONS

There are many kinds of tactical nuclear weapons systems, both offensive and defensive: artillery, rockets, missiles (including air-to-surface missiles, surface-to-surface missiles, and surface-to-air missiles), aircraft and ships (both surface vessels and submarines).[3] Nuclear warheads come in a multiplicity of types, suited to these launchers, and also in a variety of sizes, with yields ranging from some fraction of a kiloton to well over 100 KT.[4] This variety of launchers and warheads, and the effects that can be obtained from them, reflects the multiplicity of uses of nuclear forces and underlines their importance for both defence and deterrence.

One use to which nuclear weapons can be put is creating obstacles to an enemy advance either by blowing up bridges, blocking passes through rough terrain and otherwise destroying essential facilities or

[2] This is the phraseology used by NATO to take account of the fact that so-called strategic weapons, such as SLBM, may be employed against military targets outside the homelands of the super-powers, as in suppressive strikes on enemy airfields and missile sites. It is used here for the same purpose.

[3] For details concerning these weapons, see *The Military Balance, 1976–1977*, pp. 73–7.

[4] The nuclear shells for the dual-capable 155mm howitzer are supposedly in the lower sub-kiloton range (0.1 to 0.2KT). Some American officials have suggested the development of nuclear weapons of as little as 0.05KT, to be delivered within two or three feet of any target (*The Times*, 7 May 1973, p. 1). According to other reports, it should be possible not only to produce weapons of similar or smaller 'punch' but to vary their design, so that they could enhance the radiation, (facilitating their employment against troops in urban areas without destroying those areas in the process), suppress the radiation and increase the blast effects (improving their utility against relatively small hard targets) or induce radiation with a particular half-life (temporarily denying an area to an enemy without causing long-term contamination). *See* William Beecher, 'Over the Threshold', *Army*, July 1972, p. 18.

by establishing radioactive areas through which no enemy troops could pass, or in which only those heavily protected against radiation could hope to survive. Nuclear weapons can also be employed against units concentrating for an attack, their supporting artillery and other weapons and their local supply-dumps, with the idea of so weakening the enemy's forces and so disrupting his organization that he will be unable to launch his planned offensive. They can be used to block, canalize or destroy units which have penetrated the defender's front, or to inhibit reinforcement and resupply of such units (whatever the mobility and resistance to blast and radiation of armoured vehicles, this does not apply to truck-borne units and supplies, which are markedly more vulnerable). And, of course, the use of nuclear weapons can be extended to sea and air battles, with nuclear-tipped SAM especially effective against concentrations of enemy aircraft, and nuclear depth-charges lethal over a much greater radius than conventional ones.[5]

Nuclear weapons can also be used against targets behind the battle area, such as enemy missile-sites, air bases and communication centres. They can be directed against ports, rail centres, bridges and other choke-points in the lines of communication so as to delay the arrival of reinforcements and the movement of supplies. And they can be delivered on oil-storage tanks, depots, maintenance shops and other support facilities, disrupting the logistical back-up so essential to modern armies, navies and air forces.

This range of uses, the destructiveness of nuclear weapons and the speed with which they can be delivered, suggest that they could significantly affect the outcome of military operations if they were used. It also suggests that they may be used to deter aggression, by increasing an attacker's difficulties, multiplying his risks (both of failure and of escalation) and punishing his armed forces (and perhaps his civilian population). Indeed, using these weapons at any level and in any number would be such a radical departure from past practice that the mere threat of it may require a potential aggressor to reassess his situation and the action he proposes to take; as Bernard Brodie says, in such circumstances, 'face-saving, and even defeat, may not be as important as the avoidance of nuclear war'.[6]

But the possession of tactical nuclear weapons (TNW) is a two-edged sword. In Europe, at least, both sides have them. The deterrer must therefore also consider the potential costs associated with the use

[5] For a lucid description of battle tactics in nuclear war see Otto Heilbrunn, *Conventional Warfare in the Nuclear Age* (London: Allen and Unwin, 1965), pp. 50–9.

[6] Bernard Brodie, *Escalation and the Nuclear Option* (Princeton, New Jersey: Princeton University Press, 1966), p. 120.

of TNW, and whether he can reduce the attendant hazards to his own forces by limiting the scope and nature of his proposed operations without simultaneously reducing the effectiveness of his deterrent. Moreover, he must decide whether to launch his weapons at the first warning of an attack, thereby maintaining credibility at the possible risk of precipitating a nuclear war, or to give time for his threats to take effect and risk the aggressor achieving substantial gains through conventional assaults or delivering a pre-emptive strike which would seriously degrade the deterrer's tactical nuclear capabilities. Thus, deterrent policy may be neither clear nor cohesive.

NATO doctrine on tactical nuclear weapons

In the case of NATO, the words of the policy are clear but the music jangles, perhaps because too many of the chorus are singing in different keys. If, however, one considers not only what has been said but also what has been done (or not done) it is possible to detect a more coherent tune.[7] First of all, NATO intends to place difficulties in the way of any attack by maintaining conventional forces large enough for their defeat to require a significant military effort by the Warsaw Pact. It proposes to enhance the risks of any attempt to defeat these forces by an admixture of nuclear weapons which would be used on a small scale, should the situation so warrant, to demonstrate resolve and create uncertainties about the eventual nature and level of any conflict between East and West. If this does not incline the Warsaw Pact to cease military operations, NATO will employ larger numbers of nuclear weapons against military targets, in a war-fighting role, a measure which will produce heavy damage, if only as a side-effect. Finally, it will preserve the threat of strategic nuclear war as an ultimate sanction and to deter the Soviet Union from using the regional nuclear forces at its disposal.[8]

This doctrine, however, is unsatisfactory, in that it glosses over differences within the alliance about both the wording of the policy and its implementation. For one thing, there are divergent estimates of the ability of conventional forces to resist any large-scale assault, with most West Europeans less sanguine than most Americans about the length of time NATO can maintain an unbroken front.[9] There are

[7] For further details see J. I. Coffey, 'The United States and the Defense of Western Europe', *Revue Militaire Générale*, (December 1969), pp. 628–39 and (January 1970), pp. 47–65.

[8] Strategic nuclear weapons can also, of course, be used for bargaining and for war-fighting, which is why American officials have emphasized the desirability of options other than the launching of large-scale retaliatory strikes upon the Soviet Union.

[9] See the *Washington Post*, 1 June 1973, p. A20, reporting on the results

consequently also differences about the contribution of these conventional forces to deterrence, some people arguing that their purpose is mainly to check probes and lesser incursions, and that too great a conventional capability may weaken deterrence by encouraging the Warsaw Pact to believe it can launch sizeable attacks without fear of nuclear retaliation. Finally, the European members of NATO are more interested in deterring a war in Europe than fighting one, since even a successful conventional defence might cost as much, in terms of casualties and damage, as did World War II. To some extent these differences reflect similar differences over the utility of strategic nuclear forces in deterrence. (Many West Europeans hold that the threat of their use is essential to deterrence; many Americans argue that this threat is not credible, at least as an early and deliberate response to aggression, and that the members of the Alliance must develop and exercise other options.) They also reflect the geographical positions and interests of the several nations, with the Americans understandably reluctant to commit suicide by initiating a nuclear exchange, and West Europeans equally reluctant to be blasted by TNW—or stabbed by bayonets—while the Soviet Union (and the United States) remain unscathed. As one Frenchman put it: 'Europe is unwilling to become a new Vietnam, in which the super-powers can fight wars without risk to themselves.'

These differences are of more than theoretical importance, since, as we have seen, the United States possesses the bulk of the strategic nuclear forces and hence the major contribution to deterrence and bargaining in the context of a conflict in Europe. Furthermore, although the bulk of the tactical nuclear delivery systems are in the hands of her allies, the United States provides and controls most of the warheads for them.[10] Moreover, the United States has made strenuous efforts to control *all* decisions on the use of nuclear weapons within the Alliance, arguing that these weapons should be centrally directed

---

[10] With the possible exception of the *Buccaneer* squadron in West Germany, all British TNDV in Central Europe are equipped with American warheads, under American control—as are, presumably, all save the *Buccaneer* and *Vulcan* bombers in England. Although the French have atomic bombs for their *Mirage* fighter-bombers and are deploying *Pluton*, a short-range tactical nuclear missile, neither *Mirages* nor *Pluton* are based in West Germany. Thus, the British and French independent tactical nuclear forces are both few in number and not stationed in forward areas.

---

of a new Pentagon study of NATO conventional capabilities. *See also* the reaction to this article of, among others, Lord Chalfont (formerly Minister of State in charge of British arms-control policy) in *The Times*, 15 June 1973, p. 18.

and controlled, attempting to inhibit their independent development and, when this failed, offering advanced weapons under conditions calculated to reduce British (and French) ability to employ them independently.[11] The Allies have instituted joint targeting of American and British strategic nuclear forces, and have integrated into NATO strike plans those forces assigned to or earmarked for SACEUR and SACLANT, including the American missile submarines allocated to SACEUR. Moreover, they have agreed on procedures for authorizing the use of these and other forces available to NATO commanders, and on the principles which should govern their use (such as acquiescence by the country owning the TNDV, the country from whose territory they are launched, and, if they are used defensively, by the country on whose territory the targets may be found). However, decisions about the large-scale use of nuclear weapons must necessarily be made by the United States, whose President is in theory the only man able to authorize their use.[12]

The Warsaw Pact and nuclear war in Europe

The NATO doctrine is based on certain implicit assumptions about the behaviour of the members of the Warsaw Pact. It assumes, first of all, that they will not be deterred from using force by the risks and dangers attendant on that use: i.e. by the possibility of escalation. It further assumes that, having decided to use force, they will employ only their conventional components, leaving to NATO the option (or the onus) of being the first to use nuclear weapons. It also implies that, having once decided to use force, they will stop short without achieving their objectives and/or without using those elements which might help to secure them, notably their tactical and regional nuclear forces.

As suggested earlier, the latter supposition may be a reasonable one, partly because conflicts may start as a result of miscalculation rather than deliberate action, and partly because the first use of nuclear weapons may induce a reassessment of the situation. Other NATO suppositions about Pact behaviour may, perhaps, be more questionable. As far as deterrence is concerned, the Soviet Union is well aware of the potential costs of a nuclear exchange and the undesirability of

[11] See J. I. Coffey, *op. cit.* in Chap. 4, note 56, pp. 975–95.

[12] James S. Lowenstein and Richard M. Moose, *US Security Issues in Europe: Burden Sharing and Offset, MBFR and Nuclear Weapons*, September 1973, A Staff Report Prepared for the Use of the Subcommittee on US Security Agreements and Commitments Abroad of the Committee on Foreign Relations, United States Senate (Washington, DC: GPO, 1973), p. 20. This study will hereafter be cited as *US Security Issues in Europe*.

action which could lead to one.[13] And as far as the conduct of military operations is concerned, neither she nor her allies plan to fight a war in the way that NATO presumes they will.

For one thing, the members of the Warsaw Pact believe that a war in Europe will be started not by themselves but by NATO, probably as an outgrowth of instabilities in Europe or as a feedback from encounters outside Europe. Then, although they themselves do not intend to be first to use nuclear weapons, they doubt whether this war can be limited; the importance of the stakes would impel both sides to increase their efforts, and the strengths and armaments of the opposing forces would enable them to do so. Once the clash of arms is past the stage of a local incident, they foresee a strategic nuclear strike by the United States, accompanied (or followed almost immediately) by a mixed nuclear/conventional onslaught against the countries of the Warsaw Pact. In these circumstances, the role of the Soviet Union and her allies is to retaliate by launching strategic nuclear strikes, rebuff the NATO assault, counter-attack to complete the rout of the Western allies and bring the war to a successful conclusion by seizing key areas in Western Europe.[14]

Given these concepts, which envisage an all-out war by and against NATO, constraints on the conduct of military operations or the use of weapons seem unlikely. As the late Mr Khrushchev put it, neither side could be expected 'to concede defeat before resorting to the use of all weapons, even the most devastating ones'.[15] Specifically, the Soviet Union has tended to reject distinctions between tactical and strategic nuclear war (the former being regarded as essentially a part of, and an offshoot of, the latter) and to eschew concepts such as demonstration attacks, hard target options, intra-war deterrence, and so on.

Our purpose here is not, however, to assess in full doctrines for limited nuclear war, or even for deterrence, but to look at their implications for arms control and at the impact of possible arms-control measures on military capabilities, doctrinal concepts and other national policies and interests. The first step in this process will involve outlining these and other interests and concerns which may influence the acceptability of various arms limitations. The second will describe the numbers, types and deployment of tactical nuclear forces in Europe. The third will discuss the impact on these forces of three

[13] See, for example, G. A. Trofimenko, 'On a Pivotal Course', *World Economics and International Politics* (February 1975), translated and reprinted in *Strategic Review*, Vol. III, No. 3 (Summer 1975), esp. p. 105.

[14] Thomas W. Wolfe, *Soviet Power and Europe, 1945–1970* (Baltimore: Johns Hopkins Press, 1970), pp. 198–208 and 451–8; John Erickson, *op. cit.* in Chap. 2, note 5, pp. 65–73.

[15] *Pravda*, 8 March 1961, quoted in Wolfe, *op. cit.* in note 14, p. 211.

different types of constraints: on numbers and categories of weapons, on their deployment and on their possible uses. The aim is to try to determine which measures are likely to maintain the principle of 'undiminished security' and to alleviate old fears without arousing new ones.

Attitudes towards tactical nuclear weapons

As suggested above, the European members of NATO attach considerable importance to TNF which:

1. can enhance their war-fighting capabilities by denying areas to an adversary, by use on the battlefield, by interdiction of reinforcements and supplies, and, to a lesser extent, by suppressive attacks on Warsaw Pact tactical nuclear delivery vehicles;
2. can enlarge the risks attendant on aggressive action, create uncertainties about the outcome of those actions and, in the case of Eastern Europe at least, inflict some degree of punishment, thereby contributing to deterrence in their own right;
3. can form a link with the strategic deterrent and, in some sense and in some minds, bring this deterrent to bear on decisions about the initiation and conduct of military operations;
4. can improve the bargaining position of NATO members, both vis-à-vis the Soviet Union and within the Alliance.

The last two points are particularly important in that possession of nuclear hardware gives some entrée into nuclear decision-making. For example, while all members of NATO who choose to do so may sit on the Nuclear Defence Advisory Committee, which is the policy-making body at ministerial level, only those with nuclear-capable forces sit on the Nuclear Planning Group, which actually directs studies of nuclear operations and draws up detailed proposals for the use of nuclear weapons. This does not mean that all countries in NATO are unconcerned about TNW or would oppose constraints upon them. For one thing, there are the ambivalencies about current NATO doctrine mentioned earlier, with some seeking a lesser role for TNW. For another, most officials wish to avoid involuntary escalation, however brought about. Furthermore, the European allies are aware that the use of tactical weapons, even on a small scale, could be highly destructive, and that some uses could be completely devastating.[16]

[16] In 'Operation *Carte Blanche*', a 1955 exercise involving three NATO Army Corps, the 'use' of nuclear weapons within an area of some 10,000 square miles theoretically resulted in 1,700,000 'deaths' and 3,500,000 'injuries' among German civilians. Although NATO nuclear weapons have been upgraded since then they are not optimized for the conduct of limited nuclear war or for minimizing civilian casualties (General James

For these reasons, the Western allies may well support constraints on those NATO and Warsaw Pact nuclear delivery vehicles which are most difficult to control, notably the artillery pieces and rockets earmarked for use on the battlefield. They would probably like to see cutbacks in the Warsaw Pact's SRBM, nuclear-capable strike aircraft (and, even more, in Soviet regional nuclear forces) but would be unwilling to give up much in return, since they consider themselves out-gunned already. However, it is conceivable that they would accept reductions in TNDV, so long as these did not go as far as to deprive any NATO country of at least token hardware, end (or drastically decrease) American participation in NATO tactical nuclear forces, or significantly affect conventional war-fighting capabilities (as large cuts in strike aircraft might). At the moment there is no sign that they would agree on rules for the use of nuclear weapons, since these could interfere with the implementation of NATO strike plans, and there is little doubt that they would oppose any significant redeployment of nuclear delivery vehicles, especially if they were to be withdrawn from broad belts of territory.

The Soviet Union and her allies have somewhat different motives, which centre around eliminating, or at least drastically reducing, TNDV and tactical nuclear warheads in NATO Europe. Measures to this end would remove or greatly reduce the threat of tactical nuclear strikes against targets in Eastern Europe and/or the Soviet Union, and they would prevent (or at least greatly hamper) the acquisition of nuclear weapons by West Germany and, consequently, her meaningful association with an Allied or a European Nuclear Force, should either come into being. Moreover, such measures would place NATO at a disadvantage, both militarily and politically. If all or most TNW were removed from Central Europe, this would not affect the Soviet Union's regional nuclear forces, and she could readily redeploy warheads and light launchers in an emergency, thus maintaining a considerable military capability. While the option of redeployment would also be open to the Western allies, its implementation would depend on an American decision, which might not always be forthcoming. Thus the Soviet Union could hope to reduce NATO's confidence both in the effectiveness of its deterrent and in the Alliance's ability to resist pressures and (possibly even) threats of force.

Since these potential outcomes militate against NATO accepting the elimination of TNW, the Soviet Union and her allies may be willing to settle for less. Even the reduction of Forward-Based Systems would

H. Polk, 'The Realities of Tactical Nuclear Warfare', *Orbis*, Vol. XVII, No. 2 (Summer 1973), p. 441). *See also* Wynfred Joshua, 'A Strategic Concept for the Defense of Europe', *ibid.*, p. 458.

improve the Soviet military position and generate political advantages, particularly if the reduction extended to strike aircraft and missiles in the hands of West Germany and other allies, as well as to those operated by the United States. Similarly, narrow demilitarized zones might have political significance, as well as some military utility, and might therefore be acceptable.

What the members of the Warsaw Pact might give in return for partial limitations on nuclear weapons is also undetermined. The Soviet Union might find it easiest to trade strategic weapons for tactical ones by cutting back on obsolescent MR/IRBM (already phased down in recent years), and perhaps reducing her medium bomber force, where the Tu-16s and Tu-22s are being replaced by presumably smaller numbers of *Backfires*. Most difficult, given the extent to which they are integrated into military units, might be reductions in battlefield weapons such as *FROG* and *Scud*, and perhaps even in SRBM such as *Scaleboard*. It is not impossible, however, to visualize cuts in strike aircraft; these play a lesser role in Warsaw Pact tactical nuclear forces than rockets and missiles, offer an obvious parallel to NATO Forward-Based Systems and (in the case of Soviet units) might be redeployed to the Soviet Union rather than scrapped.

Before looking further at attitudes towards reductions, let us see what weapons are deployed in Europe and what the effects of particular cuts and restrictions might be.

Tactical nuclear forces

A wide variety of nuclear delivery vehicles are available to NATO and the Warsaw Pact. Their numbers are somewhat harder to determine, and their deployments even more so, but approximations are at least possible.

In the case of NATO, TNDV are in the hands of almost all countries belonging to the Alliance. As of 1976, two-thirds of the members had nuclear-capable 155mm self-propelled howitzers, either in their corps artillery, in their divisions or, in some instances, in units supporting their brigade groups. Almost as many also had the 203mm self-propelled howitzer, which is normally part of corps and army artillery. Most continental states had the *Honest John* free rocket, usually in separate supporting battalions, and some were buying the *Lance* missile, though only West Germany and the American forces in West Germany were equipped with the *Pershing* SRBM. Finally, eleven of the fifteen members had nuclear-capable aircraft, usually the F-104G or the F-4 *Phantom* at that time.

In short, both battlefield and interdictory weapons are widely distributed, though the bulk of the long-range strike aircraft are in West Germany, Britain (along with the British medium bombers) and with the American forces in Spain. All in all, there must be in NATO Europe almost 2,000 nuclear-capable artillery pieces, at least 300 rockets and missiles, and well over 1,000 nuclear-capable aircraft (see Table 2, p. 248). The nuclear warheads applicable to these weapons are widely distributed on their territories in time of peace, and with France maintaining her own nuclear stockpiles, but none under American control. The total number of warheads available, including atomic demolition munitions and air-defence weapons, is numbered in the thousands, but their precise disposition is unknown.[17]

There are also TNDV outside Europe, both in the United States and in other places where American forces are stationed. Each American aircraft-carrier has about 30 nuclear-capable strike aircraft, and six of these carriers could readily be deployed to European waters (two are normally on permanent station in the Mediterranean). There are also at least 1,000 other nuclear-capable tactical aircraft in the United States, some of which could be redeployed to Europe within hours, and others of which could follow shortly, along with any planes relocated from the Pacific. Finally, the US Army could fly in rockets and, given time and sea-transport, could redeploy missiles and nuclear-capable artillery. In a comparatively short time, therefore, NATO could add hundreds of TNDV to those already deployed in Europe, not counting any strategic nuclear-delivery vehicles diverted to tactical targets.

With or without these reinforcements, NATO nuclear forces could inflict heavy casualties in a first strike on an attacker, especially on the central front. They could block lines of communication passing through difficult terrain (such as those between the Soviet Union and North-Eastern Turkey) and could virtually obliterate the lines of communication into Central and South-East Europe, thus significantly affecting the land battle by reducing the Warsaw Pact capacity for reinforcement and resupply. They could probably knock out large numbers of Warsaw Pact nuclear delivery vehicles – although, given the number of vehicles, the extent to which the aircraft are protected by revetments, their dispersal and their deployment in depth, it is

---

[17] According to one estimate, the stockpile includes some 300 atomic mines, 3,000 artillery shells, 500 warheads for surface-to-surface missiles and 700 for SAM, 2,200 bombs and 380 nuclear depth-charges and torpedoes aboard land-based planes employed in ASW operations. George Sherman, 'Politics and the Nukes', *The Washington Star-News*, 13 May 1974, p. 14. This figure (which varies from year to year) did not include Strategic Air Command warheads, such as those stockpiled in Spain for use by US B-52 bombers, or those carried by both American and other NATO naval vessels. *US Security Issues in Europe*, pp. 13–14.

unlikely that NATO could destroy so many vehicles as to escape any retaliatory attack.

If the Warsaw Pact struck first, most of NATO's nuclear-capable artillery would probably survive, thanks to the number of guns, their distribution, and the fact that there are more lucrative targets for counter-force strikes. This would be true of rockets and missiles, but to a lesser extent (being less numerous and harder to hide and move, they are more vulnerable). Although NATO strike aircraft are deployed on fewer airfields than those of the Warsaw Pact and are less well protected against blast damage, they are also distributed widely and in depth—and Warsaw Pact tactical missiles and aircraft cannot reach bases in Britain or Spain. NATO second-strike capabilities would thus be reduced but not eliminated, the major problem being the maintenance of operational airfields from which either surviving aircraft or reinforcements could mount retaliatory strikes—if, indeed, these were either feasible or necessary in the kind of environment hypothesized, which presumably would bring into play strategic nuclear forces as well as tactical ones.

The Warsaw Pact relies on nuclear-capable artillery less than NATO, with only the 203mm howitzer earmarked for this role, comparatively small numbers of which are in the hands of Soviet forces only. Instead, it emphasizes rockets and missiles, with all Pact members having the *FROG* and the *Scud*; however, only Soviet troops operate the longer-range *Scaleboard* and *Shaddock* missiles. The same inequalities apply with strike aircraft, which only Poland and Czechoslovakia have in any number; in fact, the Soviet forces in Europe operate almost twice as many nuclear-capable aircraft as their six allies put together.

Overall, Warsaw Pact strike aircraft in Europe are somewhat less numerous than NATO's, a fact which in part reflects deployment patterns (most Soviet nuclear-capable aircraft are kept in the Soviet Union) but largely reflects the emphasis placed on rockets and missiles. Warsaw Pact forces in Europe have perhaps half again as many missiles and rockets as NATO; but their nuclear-capable artillery is small by comparison and may lack nuclear warheads.

As is true for the United States, the Soviet Union could redeploy, for operations against Western Europe, hundreds of nuclear-capable light bombers and fighter-bombers. If one counts the missiles and rockets organic to Soviet army units, and assumes that these are proportional to the number of divisions engaged, then the Soviet Union could readily double—and conceivably triple—the number of *FROG*, *Scud*, and *Scaleboard* in Eastern Europe; however, these weapons might be slow in arriving, like those from the United States. The SLCM and bombers of the Soviet Navy will not necessarily make up for any slow reinforcement, since they have special roles, and it is only when one turns to regional nuclear forces, and decides to include the medium bombers of the Long-Range Air Force, that Soviet reinforcement capacities begin to surpass those of the United States, and the number of nuclear delivery vehicles in the hands of the Warsaw Pact start to approach those available to NATO.

The launch vehicles deployed outside the Soviet Union are numerous enough to deliver in a first strike those shattering blows which are a hallmark of Soviet military doctrine, and to follow up with employment on the battlefield as required. They are, however, likely to be effective against orthodox military targets, such as troop concentrations and depots, and those NATO nuclear delivery vehicles deployed in forward areas, but they cannot reach the long-range strike aircraft in Britain and in Spain. Any attempt to neutralize the British, and perhaps French, regional nuclear forces would undoubtedly require assistance from the Navy, which could deploy SLCM; from the Long-Range Air Force, with its medium bombers, or from the Strategic Rocket Forces, whose IRBM and VRBM would be suited to this task.

In a second strike the Warsaw Pact would have more problems. Although most of its tactical aircraft would probably survive, thanks to their protection and dispersion, missiles such as *Shaddock*, *Scaleboard* and *Scud* would be more vulnerable. Moreover, since these missiles take about 30 minutes to launch, the Warsaw Pact's ability to mount a pre-emptive attack would be critically dependent on the degree of tactical warning received. Its small rockets and artillery pieces might also suffer losses, but are more numerous and harder to target. On balance, therefore, even an all-out NATO counter-force strike is unlikely seriously to degrade Warsaw Pact tactical nuclear forces, particularly since these could be reinforced from the Soviet Union, perhaps over a shorter time-span than would be required to re-deploy similar units from the United States.

This recital of numbers, deployments and capabilities of tactical nuclear forces does not, of course, exhaust all the possibilities open to either NATO or the Warsaw Pact—to do so would take more space than is available and more knowledge than any outsider is likely to possess. Moreover, it is in some sense isolated from other relevant capabilities, such as those of regional and intercontinental strategic forces.[18] It should, however, set the scene for discussion of various measures for the control and limitation of tactical nuclear weapons, to which we shall turn next.

[18] For example, the United States has placed under NATO command at least five missile submarines, with 80 launch vehicles.

ARMS CONTROL AND TACTICAL NUCLEAR WEAPONS

As suggested previously, several types of arms-control measures are applicable to tactical nuclear weapons: limitations on numbers, restrictions on deployment, controls over the introduction of new weapons, and constraints on use. Each measure will have a different effect on artillery, missiles, aircraft and other types of nuclear delivery vehicles, as well as on the warheads which they carry. Each will alter in varying degrees the uses to which TNF can be put in the event of war, such as blocking the advance of enemy forces, influencing the outcome of land, sea and air battles, interdicting enemy reinforcements and supplies, and suppressing that enemy's own air and missile forces. Moreover, each measure will have different implications for the military doctrines, perceptions of threat, and interests in arms control of the two alliances. I will try to explore more fully each range of arms-control measures and wind up with some which seem sufficiently attractive to be subjected to more detailed analysis.

Limitations on tactical nuclear weapons

In general, the effects of particular limitations will depend not only on their nature but also on the geographical areas to which they are applied. Given the asymmetrical deployments of the NATO and Warsaw Pact tactical nuclear forces, what may be feasible or desirable in Central Europe is not necessarily so on either of its flanks (see Table 2, p. 248). However, before discussing particular consequences, it may be desirable to examine the broad implications of various types of limitations.

A freeze on numbers of tactical nuclear delivery vehicles might be useful in ensuring that the MRCA on order by the West German Government are used to replace the F-104Gs now in inventory, rather than to increase the number of strike aircraft in the FRG or in other countries. As suggested by the illustration, however, such a freeze on TNDV would not preclude qualitative upgrading; nor would an overall freeze be very meaningful, partly because the number of TNDV is so large and partly because they could be transferred from one part of Europe to another. While a freeze on the numbers of each region would preclude that, it would also preclude any changes in present deployment patterns, leaving Norway, for example, unable to counter a new threat to her security by either permanent or temporary augmentation of her force of TNDV. Yet, some kind of freeze might please NATO, which at present has an advantage in numbers, by inhibiting a further build-up of Warsaw Pact nuclear forces. Whether it would be equally pleasing to the Warsaw Pact is another question, especially since it would not alleviate concern about these NATO advantages.

An alternative would be to impose ceilings on TNDV, either overall or by regions. If applied to total numbers of TNDV, they would permit a build-up by the Warsaw Pact, since NATO has many more nuclear delivery vehicles than the Warsaw Pact, thanks to its nuclear-capable artillery. On the other hand, if ceilings were imposed on each type of weapon, at the lowest level now extant, this would require NATO to scrap most of its medium artillery, and the Warsaw Pact to cut the number of rockets in its divisions by about two-thirds. If the ceilings were set at the highest extant level, this would allow (and, given the tendency to seek 'balance', almost require) increases in some categories of weapons which could be both expensive and disturbing: for example, NATO might not be very pleased if the Soviet Union, in an effort to match Western capabilities, developed and distributed nuclear shells for her 152mm gun/howitzers. It is, of course, possible that the two sides could agree on asymmetrical ceilings by types, reflecting trade-offs among the various kinds of delivery vehicle. Conceivably, these ceilings could be set low enough to cause reductions in some categories of delivery vehicle and enable less extensive build-ups in others. Certainly there could, and probably should, be different ceilings for the Northern, Central and Southern regions as well, as for types of weapons, thereby giving limited flexibility in redeployment. However, since the asymmetries in types of weapon and in their deployment are so great, and since the purposes for which these weapons are intended are so different, it might be extraordinarily difficult to reach agreement on any ceilings.

Another option would be to accept the present levels and make reductions from them, either overall or by type, and either symmetrically or asymmetrically. One immediate problem is that the two sides would have to agree on each other's current levels and on means to verify that these are in fact correct; if this were not done, either side could claim force-levels lower than actually existed, make smaller numerical reductions, and thereby gain an 'advantage'. The problem of verifying initial force-levels, thus preventing 'cheating' on percentage reductions, is one which plagued almost every arms-control conference during the 1950s. To some extent it may still be a problem with tactical nuclear delivery vehicles in Europe; however, these are (with some exceptions) rather difficult to hide, the numbers deployed seem to be fairly well known, and the intelligence nets of both sides are probably good enough to insure against gross violations of agreements. It may thus be possible to set aside the problem of verification and to turn to other problems connected with reductions in TNW.

The first of these is that symmetrical reductions will affect the very different forces of the two alliances unequally. To take just one illustration, equal numerical reductions in nuclear-capable artillery would denude the Soviet forces in Europe, while equal percentage reductions might require NATO to give up six pieces for every one the Soviet Army withdrew or scrapped. However, equal percentage reductions are probably the easiest to negotiate, and perhaps the fairest, in that effects on both sides will at least be proportional. Moreover, the asymmetries already mentioned may mean that unequal numerical cuts will in fact offset each other, thereby creating automatic trade-offs. Furthermore, equal percentage reductions in TNDV may keep pace with other reductions in military forces, thereby maintaining previous relationships between nuclear and conventional elements.[19]

Reductions on an overall basis have the advantages of preserving military flexibility and leaving to internal bargaining the issue of which weapons should be reduced, and whose they should be. On the other hand, there may be a tendency on both sides to keep the more powerful weapons and not to diminish those which seem particularly threatening, such as Forward-Based Systems. Moreover, verifying reductions on an overall basis may be difficult, even if both sides are explicit about the cuts they propose to make.

In contrast, reductions by type are simple, if rigid, and can be verified somewhat more easily, even in the case of seaborne delivery systems. They may, however, cause worries lest particular elements, such as the Turkish contingent of fighter-bombers, might be reduced below the level where they would constitute an effective military force. A possible compromise would be to cut back weapons on the basis of their uses. This would improve flexibility, in that both artillery and rockets (which are primarily suited for employment on the battlefield) could be lumped together, and might make the base forces on each side seem more equal. Moreover, one could meet different concerns about war-fighting capabilities by imposing different ceilings on classes of weapons by use, or by making different percentage reductions. A major problem here is that NATO and the Warsaw Pact employ their weapons systems so differently that it may be hard to reach agreement on the classes in which they should be placed. Thus reductions by type may after all be the only feasible approach.

As far as the areas to be covered are concerned, there are two subquestions:

1. Should reductions apply to Central Europe only, to Central Europe plus the Northern and/or Southern regions, to all Western

[19] See Chapter 6, pp. 159–61, 163–4.

Europe (including France, Britain, and other countries where NATO forces are based), to all of Europe plus the Soviet Union, or to all this area plus the United States, where reinforcing elements are stationed?

2. Should they apply universally to all weapons in an area, or on a selective basis; for example, if French territory is included, should the reductions affect the *Mirage* IVAs of the *force de frappe*, or only the *Jaguars* of the Tactical Air Force?

The major argument for looking primarily at Central Europe (the area receiving most attention at the moment) is that it is here the greatest number of weapons are deployed, including approximately half the American Forward-Based Systems in Europe. It is also the area about which the greatest concern is expressed, both in terms of potential damage resulting from a tactical nuclear war, and in terms of the possibility that some incident (such as West German access to nuclear weapons) may increase the likelihood of that war. However, measures focused on Central Europe would not alleviate concerns among the flank countries, some of which apparently feel equally threatened by other concentrations of nuclear delivery vehicles in, say, South-Eastern Europe.

While these concerns would logically argue for extending arms-control measures to the flanks, both the nuclear balances there and other relevant factors vary to such an extent that different measures would certainly be required. Moreover, even an extension of force reductions to the flanks would leave uncovered parts of Western Europe and all the Soviet Union, from which strikes could be launched against countries in the flanks such as Norway and Turkey. If one attempts to include these areas, however, other problems arise. In the case of Western Europe, the most significant is probably French opposition to any arms-control measures which could impinge on French forces, but even an extension of the controlled area to include Britain might create difficulties, first by involving the American and British aircraft now stationed there, and secondly by inhibiting the redeployment to Britain of any planes withdrawn from other parts of Europe. The Soviet Union has been notably sensitive about measures involving tactical nuclear forces within her borders (which include such diverse elements as rockets organic to tank divisions, missiles incorporated into army and front artillery brigades, light and medium bombers, naval vessels and submarines). While the failure to include the Soviet Union would give her advantages in terms of both ready forces and reinforcements, it is questionable whether she would in any case agree to reduce elements inside her frontiers, and certain that she would not do so unless the same reductions were applied in some way to the United States.[20]

So far we have been talking about limitations on nuclear launch vehicles, rather than on the warheads which they could deliver. Theoretically, cuts in warheads themselves could reduce fears of a nuclear attack and the destructiveness of such an attack. Whether they would do so in practice depends on the size of the cuts, what is done with the weapons, and what happens to weapons stored outside Europe.

As noted earlier, the Americans reportedly have about 7,000 warheads for land-based TNDV deployed in Western Europe, and the Russians about 3,500—which may not be in Eastern Europe. Obviously, reductions of 10 or 20 per cent in these stockpiles would make little difference; only when cuts reached 40 or 50 per cent would they begin to affect the ability of either side to maintain various types of warheads, allocate them to different purposes, and ensure that they were readily available to units which might need them in an emergency. Even then, reducing stockpiles in *Europe* would not be very meaningful, since either country could re-introduce warheads at short notice, either in preparation for an attack or in response to a crisis situation. Furthermore, while it would be comparatively easy to verify that weapons were being transferred out of an area, it would be more difficult to check on the stocks remaining (since this would require intrusive inspection), and virtually impossible to prevent weapons from being moved back again—at least across Western frontiers.[21]

If reductions in nuclear warheads are to be meaningful, therefore, they must provide for the destruction of any weapons taken from stockpiles in Europe. Even this would not markedly affect the military capabilities of the forces in Europe, since nuclear weapons from national stocks could be introduced in lieu of those removed; only if the destruction of nuclear warheads were part of an overall programme to cut down on these weapons could one expect it to produce

---

[20] This issue illuminates another: that reductions in tactical nuclear forces, even if extended to the Soviet Union, would not get at the Soviet regional nuclear forces which are of such concern to the West, nor at the British and French strategic nuclear forces (which are seen by some in the East as their counterpart). However, any attempt to include these in an agreement on the reduction of TNDV would raise a whole new set of problems as, regrettably, have efforts to deal with them in SALT. (See Chapter 4, pp. 85–6.)

[21] Office of National Security Studies, Bendix Aerospace Systems Division, *Verification of a Nuclear Freeze in Europe* (Ann Arbor, Michigan: 1965).

a significant result. And while the partial denuclearization of Europe could contribute to that process, it may not be the most feasible or the most desirable point at which to start it.

The problem of verifying ceilings on, or reductions in, TNW is one which extends beyond warheads. It will, of course, vary with particular weapons systems—missiles and rockets being large, single-purpose, cumbersome and easy to identify, while dual-purpose artillery pieces may be indistinguishable from others unless an inspector is allowed to look at the breech as well as the silhouette. Strike aircraft will present an even greater difficulty, since not all those which are nuclear-capable are actually allocated to a nuclear role; overall reductions in particular types may therefore not immediately affect the ability to launch nuclear strikes of a particular magnitude.

Fortunately, verification in Europe is relatively easy, mainly because the intelligence nets of both sides seem very efficient. It is, however, unlikely that political leaders will rely solely on their intelligence systems for verification. To some extent, observers or liaison officers monitoring mutual force reductions could verify constraints on TNF, but to do this effectively they would probably require a freedom of movement which they might not be granted. Alternatively, greater use could be made of limited overflights by aircraft and, perhaps, satellite reconnaissance, provided each of the super-powers (who have the most advanced systems) were able to work out arrangements with their allies that would satisfy them that they were receiving the data they needed. Finally, there is the possibility of setting up a system for providing reassuring information in response to questions about important discrepancies between what was supposed to be done and what various observation systems report has been done.

If constraints on tactical nuclear forces are to be meaningful, they must ultimately be extended over the whole of Europe and to parts at least of the Soviet Union, if not of the United States. They will probably have to include all types of delivery vehicles, and possibly extend to warheads. They will undoubtedly involve the kind of bargaining over trade-offs among different kinds of forces which alone can alleviate the fears of both sides without undermining their sense of security (trade-offs such as withdrawal of NATO tactical nuclear warheads in exchange for redeployment of Soviet tank divisions, or cuts in Soviet MRBM in exchange for an understanding that NATO will not introduce 'mini-nukes' into Europe).

In the short term, however, one must look to simpler and less extensive limitations, which can be more easily reached and more readily implemented. These could include :

1. Seeking 10–20 per cent reductions in tactical nuclear delivery vehicles by type–percentages large enough that the resulting cuts would be politically meaningful, and small enough that they would not be upsetting militarily (and hence unacceptable).
2. Applying these reductions to Northern, Central and Southern Europe, but not to France, Britain, the United States or the Soviet Union. Attempting to include these countries would make negotiations extremely difficult. Even if they were successful it might create more problems than it solved, by enormously increasing the requirements for verification and by introducing constraints on the forces of both sides which would handicap them in their efforts to maintain a military balance in Europe.
3. Applying such cuts as are made to Soviet and American forces individually, but to the other members of each alliance jointly, so that if Turkey wished to keep all her nuclear-capable fighter-bombers she could do so, providing Italy was willing to scrap more of hers.
4. Verifying these reductions by measures at the disposal of the two blocs.

Deployment restrictions

Restrictions on the deployment of TNW have purposes more or less similar to those which inspire limitations on them. One is to reduce the threat they might present by withdrawing them to rear areas, or by preventing nationals of particular countries from installing them on their territories. Another is to make them less usable for some purposes by increasing the distance between them and potential targets. A third is to make their presence or use less dangerous by establishing controls to prevent inadvertent escalation or by setting up denuclearized zones. And a fourth is to do all this in such a way as to maintain the level of reassurance that TNF at present provide–although, admittedly, assurances based on automaticity of escalation may decrease, just as those based on belief in the unlikelihood of war may increase.

There is a range of deployment restrictions which could be applied. One could, for example, exclude TNF from whole countries (such as Turkey), large areas (such as the Baltic), or from parts of countries (such as a strip along both sides of the West German–Czech frontier). One could restrict the deployment of all nuclear-capable weapons, or of some only. One could restrict the deployment of warheads along with delivery vehicles, or instead of restricting delivery vehicles (for example, East German troops could retain their *Scuds* and West German forces their *Lances*, but not the nuclear warheads for these missiles). And one could accompany restrictions on deployment of weapons with organizational changes, such as the removal of TNDV from smaller units and their allocation to a separate support command, which would make their involvement or use in the first stages of any conflict less likely. Alternatively, or additionally, one could establish control procedures, such as electronic locks on warheads or separate communications links from higher headquarters to those guarding nuclear warheads, which would inhibit the unrestricted use of TNW by military commanders.

Deployment restrictions applicable to whole countries or to other large areas could, it is argued, ameliorate threats, relieve tensions and perhaps create 'zones of peace'. They might also decrease the possibility that nuclear weapons would be directed against neighbouring countries, either in counter-force attacks or in retaliation for such attacks. And they could reduce the dangers and the risks of escalation arising out of either low-level decisions or misperceptions and misunderstandings by political leaders.

Unfortunately, deployment restrictions must be related to the ranges of the weapons which can be brought to bear: withdrawal of short-range *FROG* rockets from the Kola Peninsula will scarcely be meaningful to Norway if the *Scaleboard* SRBM remain behind. Moreover, establishment of restricted areas does not rule out the use of nuclear weapons against the countries in those areas, since longer-range weapons can be employed to shatter defences, block the dispatch of reinforcements and persuade a country that its only choice is to surrender. Furthermore, while restrictions of this kind may ameliorate threats to one side, they will not relieve tensions unless they apply to both. (For example, turning the Baltic into a 'sea of peace' by precluding the transit of nuclear-armed warships may appeal to the members of the Warsaw Pact, but it will scarcely appeal to Denmark unless restrictions are placed on Soviet destroyers armed with cruise missiles as well as on NATO submarines carrying atomic mines.) Finally, restrictions on the deployment of tactical nuclear weapons to particular areas, by reducing the ability of an alliance to respond to threats to the security of one of its members or to buttress that member against pressures backed by threats of force, may diminish deterrence.

From the perspective of a country which feels threatened, deployment restrictions should accomplish four things. They should:

1. Remove the most dangerous weapons (i.e., those which could launch counter-force strikes against the armed forces of the threatened country).
2. Eliminate the most destructive weapons, which could inflict damage upon its inhabited areas.

3. Deal particularly with long-range delivery vehicles, which can strike deep and, by virtue of their inaccuracy and the size of their warheads, could cause heavy collateral damage.
4. Re-deploy the least mobile weapons, such as SRBM, so that a neighbouring country's tactical nuclear delivery forces could not be built up quickly in the event of a crisis.

Unfortunately, these criteria do not all focus on a single type of weapons system. Strike aircraft are destructive (because of the bomb loads they can carry), dangerous (because of the accuracy with which 'smart bombs' can be delivered) and highly mobile, so that constraints on them may accomplish two aims but not a third. Even more unfortunately, a neighbouring country may rely heavily on the kinds of weapons that *do* pose a threat, precisely because they are seen as a threat to deterrence.

This suggests that attempts to work out trade-offs between the types of weapons which should be restricted and the areas from which they should be barred may founder. As we have already said, there are differences in the range, payload and accuracy, and hence in the military capability, of various types of weapon, and even of weapons of the same type: an Su-7 fighter-bomber cannot be compared to an F-4 *Phantom*. Moreover, asymmetries in numbers of delivery vehicles, both overall and by type, mean that constraints on one type of vehicle will have more significant implications than constraints on another. Furthermore, doctrine for the use of these weapons varies so greatly that even restrictions which might seem fair when measured by abstract criteria, such as payload and range, may be unacceptable to one side or another. Rarely will perceptions of threat bear any direct relationship to perceptions of military capabilities, so that agreement on measures applicable to wide areas may be hard to reach.

Restrictions applicable to smaller geographical areas or relatively narrow zones both promise less and risk less. They are likely to affect most significantly the very short-range TNDV particularly suited for battlefield use, rather than longer-range weapons. Their removal can be psychologically reassuring, both because it reduces particular military capabilities and because it lessens the possibility of inadvertent war; at the same time it may leave untouched the longer-range forces of both sides, which some see as linked more directly with deterrence. Conversely, narrow denuclearized zones may affect the ability to conduct a forward defence, because the shorter-range weapons most suited for that defence will not be available. An attacker could not only use longer-range weapons but, since he can choose the time and place of attack, could quickly reintroduce battlefield delivery vehicles at selected points. The absence of these weapons on the other side would reduce not only defensive capabilities but also the automaticity of escalation, which some see as an important contribution to deterrence.

The advantages of establishing narrow denuclearized zones could be enhanced by organizational changes in the opposing forces, such as the establishment of a separate Nuclear Support Command, and the reservation to higher levels of decisions about the use of this Command. One advantage of this is that it would facilitate the adjustment of military structure and doctrine to the existence of denuclearized zones, thereby creating fewer problems with the military. Another is that it would presumably facilitate control both over authorization to use TNDV and over the targets against which they might be used. It might also keep short-range nuclear vehicles out of areas where they would be subject to early capture or destruction, and hence inclined to fire in self-defence or as a way of justifying their existence.

However, this re-structuring–whether or not accompanied by the establishment of nuclear-free zones–would mean some loss of military readiness, because of the non-availability of TNDV and the time needed to get authorization for their use. This may lead the armed forces to increase their requirements for longer-range weapons, thereby re-establishing the threat which reorganization was supposed to remove. And in some cases (155mm artillery, for instance) it would be virtually impossible to remove nuclear-capable elements without drastically reducing the conventional fire-power of the remaining forces.

An alternative, which would minimize some of these disadvantages, would be to keep the weapons but not the warheads–i.e., to set up nuclear-free zones. Such an approach would preserve conventional capability, where this was important, but would eliminate the possibility of inadvertent escalation through decisions by lower unit commanders. Since nuclear warheads could be reintroduced rapidly (by helicopters if necessary), their peacetime absence should not drastically degrade the deterrent effect of TNDV, nor, unless an attack came without warning, their military capabilities. This is a double-edged advantage, however, in that the possibility of quick reintroduction of nuclear warheads makes their absence less reassuring than would otherwise be the case. Moreover, there are problems in determining that they are not in fact present in any nuclear-free zone, since this would require some technical knowledge of the procedures for supplying nuclear warheads and some intrusive inspection without advance notice, approval for which might not always be forthcoming.

All this suggests that restrictions on deployment of tactical nuclear warheads will be difficult to establish, and in some instances even more difficult to verify. Among the measures which could reduce the risk of inadvertent war and/or diminish perceptions of threat, however, there are several which seem potentially feasible:

1. The delineation of narrow zones along frontiers from which certain types of delivery vehicles, such as rockets or nuclear-capable artillery, would be barred.
2. The stationing of other delivery vehicles, such as *Pershing* and *Scaleboard* missiles, in rear areas, so that they could not strike at targets deep in the opponent's territory without moving forward. While such movement would not be precluded, notice could be required – and failure to give such notice would be significant in itself.
3. The redeployment of nuclear-capable aircraft to rear bases, which might increase response time but would also give additional protection against pre-emptive strikes.

Although it is conceivable that restrictions could be placed on other types of weapons, these are more likely either to take the form of trade-offs rather than symmetrical arrangements, or to result from negotiations on other issues; thus, restrictions on the deployment of nuclear-armed warships may come as part of overall limits on naval forces in the Mediterranean.[22] Given the complexity of negotiations or wider deployment restrictions, it may perhaps be best to leave these until later, since it is unlikely that they will be part of any first-stage agreement on TNW.

Controls on new weapons

The introduction of new nuclear delivery vehicles, improved warheads and up-graded tactical nuclear forces can have several consequences. One is that they can change the military capabilities of one side or the other, as would the introduction by the Warsaw Pact of quicker-reacting SRBM and longer-range strike aircraft. They can affect the survivability of tactical nuclear forces both favourably and unfavourably for the maintenance of a stable military environment: for instance, the quicker-firing missiles mentioned above would help the Warsaw Pact to weather a NATO first strike, and the longer-range aircraft would help it to launch its own. The introduction of new weapons, by thus affecting the war-fighting capabilities of the two sides, can also affect their perceptions of threat and their sense of reassurance. They can induce interactions between research and development and in procurement, like that between surface-to-air missiles and ground-hugging strike aircraft, and they can cause con-

[22] See Chapter 6, pp. 163–4.

cern about the modernization of an opponent's forces—NATO worrying lest the nuclear-capable MiG-21s replace the MiG-17s (which cannot carry atomic weapons) and the Warsaw Pact lest the MRCA scheduled to replace West Germany's F-104Gs markedly increase her ability to wage tactical nuclear war.

This does not mean that all technological innovations are bad. In one sense, low-yield warheads, more accurate delivery systems and better means of command and control can reduce both collateral damage and the danger that an adversary will escalate because the wrong target was attacked with the wrong-sized warhead. But it is difficult to get one side to accept improvements (such as 'smart' bombs or 'mini-nukes') in the other's arsenal, and it may be hard to persuade an adversary that he should introduce innovations which would enable him to fight a more controlled nuclear war, let alone limit himself to this sort of innovation.

Furthermore, controls over the introduction of new weapons are hard to establish. Given the tendency to make continuous improvements via newer models of the same weapon, or to upgrade those returned to depots for refurbishing, it is virtually impossible to prevent gradual alterations in weapons-systems. It is possible to inhibit the development of new weapons when they reach the test stage, by curbing tests or limiting the procurement, but it is hard to cover all the kinds of system, from destroyers to air-to-surface missiles, which play a nuclear role. Once weapons have been introduced into the inventory, it is possible to identify new types quite readily, but the multiple roles of some delivery vehicles, such as the *Buccaneer* and the Il-28 light bomber, means that one cannot restrict their deployment or numbers without the effects reaching far beyond the nuclear capabilities of the two alliances. Moreover, it would be hard to obtain agreement not to install new types in Europe—which, being the main area of confrontation between West and East, is the theatre in which each tends to deploy its newest and best weapons. Additionally, each side sees deficiencies in its own posture, and imbalances between the postures of the two sides, which new weapons would do something to rectify. And each may see modernization as an answer to the problem of ever-increasing costs : for example the *Lance* SRBM, which has replaced *Honest John* rockets and *Sergeant* missiles in the hands of American forces, not only requires smaller crews but is more effective,[23] so that replacements were not made on a one-for-one basis.

One could, of course, slow down the introduction of new weapons

[23] *Statement of Secretary of Defense Melvin R. Laird before the House Services Committee on the FY 1973 Defense Budget and FY 1973–1977 Program,* 17 February 1972, mimeograph, p. 80.

by prescribing a time-span for each system: for example, a new SRBM could be introduced only every so many years. Alternatively, one could specify a rate of introduction into the European theatre such that it would take, say, six years from introduction of the first new weapon to complete replacement of all the old ones. One could also conceivably agree to introduce new weapons first in rear areas, thereby reducing the stimulus to counter-action occasioned by their forward deployment. Such measures could be not only valid in themselves but could also be meaningful accompaniments to reductions in numbers of tactical nuclear delivery vehicles, the effects of which might otherwise be offset—or more than offset—by qualitative improvements in weaponry.

However, given the difficulties of verifying such arrangements, they must of necessity be limited to important, relatively scarce and highly visible weapons; checks on the yield or degree of radioactivity of nuclear warheads would be virtually impossible. Further, given the incentives to maintain flexibility and the complexities of working out controls on new weapons, it is probably desirable to avoid formal arrangements; instead, NATO and the Pact might exchange views about the kinds of improvements in weaponry which each finds disconcerting, and try to stimulate an awareness of their potential consequences so as to induce unilateral—but reciprocal—restraints on the introduction of new weapons.

Obviously, such measures would not significantly affect the military balance in Europe—which is perhaps one of their virtues. They could, though, affect perceptions of intent and thus enhance the sense of security of all Europeans. Equally importantly, they could contribute to that larger dialogue between East and West which is essential if peace is to be maintained—a dialogue which could have as one of its objectives further constraints on weaponry than seem either feasible or acceptable at this time.

Constraints on use

The purpose of constraints on the use of nuclear weapons would be to make the best of a situation in which continued reliance on nuclear weapons for deterrence precludes their removal from the theatre or drastic reductions in their numbers, and where their utility in crisis bargaining makes countries unwilling to accept restrictions inhibiting their rapid redeployment from one area to another. The idea would be to see whether other constraints can serve to maintain stability through deterrence and uphold interests in a crisis (or conflict) at less risk than is currently the case.

The kinds of constraints on the use of TNF which may be acceptable depend in part on estimates of the likely threat. If the threat is that of conventional assault, a country may hope to deter this without escalation by using nuclear weapons only on its own territory; if the threat is that of political pressure against an isolated area, such as West Berlin, that country may not wish to forgo the possibility of using nuclear weapons outside its frontiers. The acceptability of constraints will also depend on whether a country wants to prevent escalation or use it as a threat. In the former instance, it might be willing to accept restrictions even on the battlefield use of nuclear weapons; in the latter it would want to be able to attack targets deep in rear areas, with large weapons if necessary. The variables make it extremely difficult to analyse the utility of constraints on the use of TNF (let alone to select those which various countries might adopt) but the first is an essential prelude to the second.

One such constraint could be an agreement not to be the first to use nuclear weapons. It can be argued that a policy of No First Use does not weaken deterrence of nuclear aggression, since the policy no longer holds if the nuclear weapons are once employed. It has also been argued that such a policy would not necessarily erode deterrence of conventional aggression, partly because some forms of conventional attack will necessarily be met with conventional responses, and partly because a declaratory statement of No First Use can never be wholly credible (although this argument smacks of eating one's cake and having it too). If all major nuclear powers were to adopt such a policy—as China has already done and as the Soviet Union has from time to time suggested—nuclear blackmail would be impossible. Moreover, if a conventional attack should take place a policy of No First Use, giving the attacker no incentive to pre-empt, would minimize the danger of inadvertent escalation by the defender. Finally, it has been suggested that such a policy would reduce the value of nuclear weapons as crisis instruments and as status symbols, thereby discouraging proliferation.[24]

There are, however, equally powerful arguments against this policy, especially in a European context. One is that a declaratory ban would not preclude the use of nuclear weapons, since Warsaw Pact forces are geared to fight a nuclear rather than a conventional war, and would also certainly do so should war break out.[25] Even if this were not so, a country facing defeat might use nuclear weapons, since the consequences of defeat might be scarcely less frightful than

[24] For a further discussion of these points see Richard H. Ullmann, 'No First Use of Nuclear Weapons', Foreign Affairs, Vol. 50, No. 4, (July 1972), pp. 669–83.

[25] Thomas W. Wolfe, op. cit. in note 14, pp. 453–7. For a detailed account of Soviet doctrine see A. A. Sidorenko, op. cit. in Chap. 2, note 9, pp. 40–1 and 58–64.

those of nuclear war. Furthermore, a policy of No First Use would undoubtedly mean some reduction in the deterrent value of nuclear weapons (at least in the eyes of the NATO allies) in circumstances in which any increase in conventional forces is unlikely. More important, such a policy might not actually lead to any reductions in weaponry, since each side would still deem it necessary to maintain a deterrent to the employment of nuclear weapons by the other. For this reason, the policy might not reduce Soviet fears, which centre on the un-authorized use of nuclear weapons and on incidents leading to a situation in which the policy might be reversed.[26] For all these reasons, it might be preferable to look to policies for reducing the likelihood of conflict, rather than to those which would determine whether it were nuclear or conventional, and to examine other and more feasible constraints on tactical nuclear weapons.

One such constraint would be to use nuclear weapons only at high levels of conflict, thereby avoiding inadvertent escalation, making sure of enemy intentions and perhaps avoiding the need to use these weapons at all. This policy, which calls for the establishment of a virtually impassable 'firebreak' between conventional and nuclear war, is designed to minimize the dangers of escalation, but it may also reduce the utility of escalation in conveying to an adversary the intention of the defender to resist and his willingness to employ all measures essential to that resistance. Moreover, the firebreak concept is based on the assumption that parties who escalate through several levels of conventional conflict will stop short of using nuclear weapons, whatever the situation at the time that this seems to be the sole feasible option remaining. The concept is also potentially unstable in that setting the firebreak too high may open the way to all kinds of military adventures, whereas setting it too low could subject it to unsupportable pressures, which could result in its being breached at just the wrong time. The question is not whether one should be prudent in deciding whether to use nuclear weapons and restrained in their employment – that goes without saying. Rather, it is whether it is desirable to say in advance that there are circumstances under which one would not use those weapons, thereby sacrificing the bene-fits of uncertainty for the uncertain benefits of making a clear distinction between conventional and nuclear war.

A variant of the firebreak is the 'pause', in which the nuclear response to conventional aggression would be delayed, not until the

[26] Wolfgang Heisenberg argues that only a conventional balance between East and West would create a situation in which a No-First-Use agreement would assuage Soviet fears and have a stabilizing effect. *The Alliance and Europe: Part I: Crisis Stability in Europe and Theatre Nuclear Weapons*, Adelphi Paper No. 96 (London: IISS, Summer 1973), p. 27.

conflict had reached a particular level of intensity but rather for a given period of time. This pause would be used, first of all, to enable an aggressor to halt inadvertent or unauthorized incursions—if, indeed, assaults on such a scale as to penetrate the NATO or Warsaw Pact defences could be so described. It would give the defender time to communicate and bargain with his adversary, a process which would certainly involve the potential use of nuclear weapons if all other measures failed. It would also allow for consultation—and, one would hope, for consensus—among the countries involved in any decision to use nuclear weapons. In short, this concept would call for exploring every possible means of dampening a conflict before authorizing the use of weapons which could have potentially destructive consequences for both sides.

All these are advantages which reasonable men may be loth to forgo, which is why the pause is part of NATO doctrine for the defence of Western Europe. There are, unfortunately, some disadvantages to the concept. The pause may give an adversary time to complete a *coup de main* and confront the defender with the options of acquiescing, attempting the perhaps impossible task of ejecting the aggressor by conventional means, or employing TNW after all. Another snag is that the pause may be so prolonged—especially if the NATO allies attempt to reach agreement on the number, timing and targeting of any nuclear strikes—that the front may break; even if it does not, the aggressor may advance to positions where he is less vulnerable to the battlefield employment of nuclear weapons, or else achieve gains which would be useful 'bargaining chips' should he decide to seek a negotiated solution. Furthermore, the pause leaves to the aggressor the option of launching a nuclear first strike which, even against alert forces, may be meaningful. A final disadvantage is that even a pause may not enable the defender to keep control of the situation, since that depends on who uses what weapons against which targets.

Obviously, the tighter the control over warheads, targets and procedures for releasing nuclear weapons, the less the likelihood of *some* forms of unauthorized use, such as employment in self-defence by military commanders. If these controls extend also to the armed forces of allies who do not have nuclear weapons, they can also preclude unauthorized use by nationals of those countries, even if *their* political authorities give consent. For both these reasons the United States Government has established electronic locks and other safeguards over warheads supplied to both its allies and its own troops,[27] and has been

---

[27] According to press reports, these electronic locks will be improved and extended to all tactical nuclear warheads, some of which can now

insistent upon the direction and control of NATO nuclear operations by a single authority: the President of the United States. However, few control systems are tight enough to rule out all possibilities that junior officers may decide to employ nuclear weapons on their own, as would appear from the discussion of the control system employed in the French *force de frappe*.[28] Nor will they rule out misunderstandings and miscalculations by political leaders, whoever they may be. Thus, controls on the use of TNW provide a safeguard against some causes of inadvertent nuclear war—but not against all.

At least three reservations must be made about the effectiveness of controls in maintaining a stable military environment in Europe. One is that controls which are too tight and direction which is too centralized may somewhat degrade the deterrent effect of nuclear weapons, since an adversary's uncertainty about the decisions of several independent political authorities will always be greater than his uncertainty about the decision of one. Another is that centralized direction and control may to some extent erode the sense of security of allies not possessing nuclear weapons, who may be unwilling to entrust their national security in time of crisis to a foreigner, however sympathetic and however involved. A third reservation is that the usefulness of controls in dampening or de-escalating conflict depends not only on the effectiveness of the controls, but on the uses made of nuclear weapons once the choice has been exercised.

One approach would be to enhance the ability to fight a nuclear war at a relatively low level and within relatively restricted areas, thus climbing the 'escalation ladder' one or two rungs at a time. This approach would emphasize short-range weapons, such as artillery and rockets, rather than longer-range ones, such as missiles and strike aircraft. It would call for the use of delivery vehicles based within the area of the conflict, rather than outside it, so that an adversary would not be forced to extend the conflict if he tried to neutralize them; in this context, 155mm howitzers are preferable to *Pershing* SRBM, and *Pershings* to the F-111E fighter-bombers based in Britain. Furthermore, small-yield warheads delivered with great accuracy would be preferable to larger-yield ones, even though the latter might be more effective militarily. The aim in all cases would be to show determination to check any aggression and, equally, to avoid intensifying or

---

[28] *The International Herald Tribune*, 18 June 1973, p. 1. See also *US Security Issues in Europe*, p. 18, which implies that, once take-off was authorized, the pilots of Quick Reaction Alert aircraft could drop nuclear bombs whether or not the United States so wished.

---

be armed manually. The *New York Times*, 17 December 1973, p. 1. *See also* the *Rumsfeld Report*, 1976, p. 86.

extending the conflict (unless this were essential to check the aggression).

This approach also suggests restraint in the selection of targets. Attacks on military targets rather than civilian ones will help to indicate that the nuclear response is aimed at defeating an adversary, not punishing him, and strikes against advancing units rather than against supporting weapons would communicate a desire not to extend the conflict. So would the use of 'iron bombs' against air bases, missile sites and other places where TNDV are deployed: using nuclear weapons against them might lead that enemy to believe that a disarming strike was under way and that he should launch his own missiles. While there are some costs attached to forgoing the use of nuclear weapons in counter-force strikes and in interdictory operations, a large-scale tactical nuclear war in Europe could be so disastrous to both sides that it would be preferable to attempt to settle it by bargaining, rather than by a fight to the finish.

Part of this bargaining process also involves the areas within which nuclear weapons are used. As indicated earlier, attacks deep in an enemy's rear are more likely to escalate the conflict than shallow ones, both because of the kind of targets struck and because the purpose of the strikes may be misinterpreted. Possibly the best way of convincing an opponent that one would prefer not to escalate the conflict would be to use nuclear weapons only on one's own territory. This policy could combine a meaningful war-fighting capability with a comparatively low risk of escalation, especially if reliance were placed on purely defensive weapons, such as atomic demolitions. It could give enemy soldiers an incentive to 'lean forward in their fox-holes' rather than attack, since they would be safe from nuclear strikes until they crossed the border. It would avoid punishing innocent people, such as civilians in enemy territory, and could minimize collateral damage, both by providing an incentive to care in targeting and, possibly, by enabling the removal of one's own people before nuclear weapons were employed.

Unfortunately, restricting the use of nuclear weapons to one's own territory could create problems. One of them, which also applies to other restrictive measures, is that it would give an opponent the option of launching a first-strike counter-force attack–albeit against alert and dispersed tactical nuclear forces. In addition it would sacrifice the advantages of strikes against supporting weapons, such as artillery and missiles, and would reduce the effectiveness of interdictory and suppressive attacks, despite the accuracy offered by precision-guided munitions. There is also the psychological difficulty of detonating nuclear weapons on one's own territory (and probably against some of one's own people) without striking at the enemy's homeland.

Finally, such a policy may increase fears that nuclear war in Europe could become acceptable, at least to the super-powers, with the result that the strategic deterrent would lose much of its effectiveness in protecting interests and territories of Europeans.

In the light of this, a reasonable approach might be :

1. To minimize the use of nuclear weapons, relying on their functional utility when employed in small numbers to produce military results and on the fact of their use at all to shock an adversary into reassessing the situation.
2. To seek thus to restore the *status quo*, but not to attain exploitable political or military advantages, and certainly not to win (which is not possible in any meaningful sense).
3. To communicate to the adversary, prior to any conflict, one's intentions and aims with respect to the use of nuclear weapons, in the hope that these may influence his decisions in ways at least tolerable to both sides.

Whether or not war is too important to be left to generals, as Clemenceau once said, it is much too important to be left to improvisations, whether by generals or by their political superiors.

A FIRST STEP

The preceding discussion suggests that the asymmetries in force structures, military doctrines and the geographical positions of NATO and the Warsaw Pact will make it hard for them to reach agreement on measures for controlling TNF. Moreover, these forces are so important to both alliances that neither will readily accept curbs on its nuclear arsenal. In view of this, a case can be made for confining any initial measures to those which do not greatly alter the military balance and do not require extensive revisions of military doctrine. It also argues for postponing those kind of measures which, whatever their utility in promoting crisis stability or avoiding inadvertent war, may arouse fears about the intentions of other countries, whether allies or adversaries; on the contrary, the aim should be to alleviate fears, whether these derive from estimates of military capabilities or from forecasts of future behaviour. With this in mind, let us see whether we can steer between the Scylla of doing too little and the Charybdis of undertaking too much !

One of the things which could well be undertaken would be to begin discussions on the utility and the acceptability of limitations on the use of nuclear weapons. If nothing else, these might test the feasibility of the NATO concept of 'flexible response', a concept which is not only alien to Soviet doctrine but also appears to be viewed by the Warsaw Pact as infeasible, because of weaknesses in the conventional forces required to implement it.[29] Similar discussions could be held about the effects of introducing new weapons on perceptions of threat and estimates of intent, about the kinds of reassurance that might mitigate the consequences of deploying new weapons, and about unilateral practices that might bolster these reassurances. It may also be possible to introduce restrictions on the deployment of some types of TNDV:

1. in particular areas, such as the Norwegian Finnmark or Thrace, where this can easily be done with important political consequences but minimal military effects.
2. as part of broader restrictions on the deployment of forces, or as part of trade-offs between American FBS and Soviet regional nuclear forces.

Most significant, however, would be measures for reducing TNDV by type in each of the regions of Europe. The question of such reductions may be brought up in SALT II or the on-going negotiations on mutual force reductions, and in any case cannot be ignored forever. This measure may be worth examining on its own merits—a task to which we will proceed.

Effects of reduction in tactical nuclear delivery vehicles

Although there are many possible ways of reducing TNDV, the one which commends itself is to make cuts of, say, 20 per cent in the Northern Region, in Central Europe and in Southern Europe. Under this proposal, the United States and the Soviet Union would each have to withdraw 20 per cent of any TNDV in any of these areas and, if agreement on this point could be reached, to scrap all or some of them. The indigenous powers would also be required to scrap or to sell elsewhere a percentage of their TNDV, under somewhat less rigid arrangements. For instance the cuts could be allocated among the allies by region in accordance with intra-alliance agreement, thereby preserving some degree of flexibility. Or TNDV could be replaced by weapons of the same type which were not nuclear-capable: the F-104G *Starfighters* which six NATO members possess could be replaced by F-5Es, provided this were not precluded by agreements on the reduction of conventional forces.

Assuming that reductions such as this were put into effect, what would be their impact on the military capabilities of both sides on perceptions of security, and on stability in Europe? As far as the Northern Region is concerned (see Table 8, NATO and Pact Forces in Northern Europe, Mid-1976, p. 260), a 20 per cent reduction in

[29] Wolfe, *op. cit.* in note 14, pp. 451–8.

Danish and Norwegian weapons would not make any significant difference to their nuclear delivery capabilities (which are, in any case, largely symbolic), and if they affected their conventional capabilities, different models of artillery could replace them. Nor would such reductions be likely to affect Danish and Norwegian perceptions of security, which are based primarily on the cohesion of NATO and the willingness of other powers (especially the United States and Britain) to come to their support when necessary. They would certainly not affect stability; the Soviet Union is not more likely to attack because Denmark has given up a few artillery pieces. On the other hand, making reductions in the Northern Region would not have any effect on the Soviet Union, all of whose troops are stationed on home territory (see Table 8). Whether the resultant asymmetry is to be accepted, or whether the Soviet Union is to be asked to make 'voluntary' reductions in home-based weapons are matters of bargaining tactics; neither outcome will significantly affect the military balance in the region.

The nuclear-delivery vehicles on the Central Front fall essentially into two groups: very short-range weapons (10–150 miles) primarily suited for battlefield operations, and short-range weapons (200–600 miles) which are more suited for suppressive strikes and attacks on targets in rear areas. As far as battlefield nuclear weapons are concerned, if these reductions took place today, NATO would lose a few rockets, several hundred nuclear-capable artillery pieces and a handful of missiles under this proposal. (See Table 6, NATO and Pact Forces In Central Europe, Mid-1976, p. 256.) The Warsaw Pact would lose about 40 *FROG* rockets, approximately the same number of 203mm howitzers, and some 30 *Scud*. Cuts of this order require NATO to thin out its nuclear support across the Central Front, and might force the Warsaw Pact either to be more selective in its use of battlefield nuclear weapons or to reintroduce them secretly before an assault. In neither case, however, would these reductions significantly alter the situation; each side would have more than enough weapons to wage tactical nuclear war, should it choose to do so. And although the cut-back in dual-capable artillery might affect NATO's conventional capabilities, the M-109 self-propelled howitzer could be replaced by other models or offsetting cuts could be made in Warsaw Pact medium artillery under mutual force reductions; indeed, NATO might well achieve such a goal by delaying the drawdown of nuclear-capable artillery until agreement had been reached on cuts in conventional forces.

As far as weapons suited for interdictory and suppressive strikes are concerned, NATO would have to give up some two score *Pershings* and something over 100 strike aircraft–only slightly more than it has offered to trade for Warsaw Pact acceptance of common ceilings on ground forces,[30] and the Warsaw Pact a few *Scaleboard* SRBM and approximately 150 strike aircraft. Again, cuts of this magnitude would not make any difference to the nuclear capability of either side; since each would still have hundreds of weapons left, each could bring in reinforcements before or during the first stages of an attack, and each has other nuclear-delivery systems available (such as the British *Vulcan* and the Soviet Tu-16 bombers). The cuts in strike aircraft could to some extent affect capabilities for conventional conflict, but this could be minimized if American dual-capable aircraft were redeployed to Britain or Spain rather than the United States (a distance considerably greater than that by which Soviet planes would have to withdraw). Unless agreements to reduce conventional forces precluded this, the effects could also be offset by replacing indigenous nuclear-capable aircraft with those not able to deliver atomic bombs.

Overall, therefore, these reductions should not affect either the military balance or military stability in Central Europe. Perceptions of threat might in fact be reduced, the Warsaw Pact's because weapons that concern it were cut back, and NATO's because of the mere fact of Soviet cuts. Finally, perceptions of security should be maintained, in the case of the Warsaw Pact because its overall military power would not be significantly affected, and in the case of NATO because the link with the strategic deterrent would still remain.

NATO forces in Southern Europe would have to give up less than 100 pieces of artillery, a few *Honest John* rockets and perhaps 40 strike aircraft–plus a dozen nuclear-capable planes from the carriers of the Sixth Fleet. (See Table 7, NATO and Pact Forces in Southern Europe, Mid-1976, p. 258.) Warsaw Pact forces have almost no nuclear-capable artillery but would have to withdraw or scrap a score of *FROG*, a dozen *Scud*, about 40 strike aircraft (all Soviet) and possibly a few *Scaleboard* SRBM. Again, cuts of this magnitude would have no significant military effect in either nuclear or conventional war. They might slightly ameliorate Warsaw Pact perceptions of threat which, at least in the case of Rumania and Bulgaria, seem to centre around the presence of nuclear delivery vehicles in South-Eastern Europe, the Mediterranean and the Black Sea. Although they might also bolster slightly Yugoslavia's sense of security, they would probably not markedly affect NATO perceptions of threat, since the bulk of the Soviet nuclear delivery vehicles within range are stationed inside the Soviet Union. On balance, however, they should not affect stability, which will be determined by factors other than the presence or absence of a few TNDV in Southern Europe.

[30] *The Military Balance, 76–77*, p. 105.

To sum up, both alliances could significantly reduce their TNDV in Europe (perhaps by greater percentages than those suggested here) without reducing their military capabilities and without destabilizing consequences; in that sense, the common goal of undiminished security at lower cost may be attainable. Reductions such as those discussed should also favourably affect perceptions of security: those of the Warsaw Pact because they would begin the phase-down of weapon-systems with which they are concerned, those of NATO partly for this reason, and partly because *any* cuts may help to change estimates of Soviet intentions. They will not, however, affect those nuclear forces in the Soviet Union which pose particular (and possibly greater) military threats than TNDV in Europe, nor will they diminish the concern in many parts of NATO about the growing strength and continuing modernization of Soviet forces.

What is more, almost any measure (including the modest one just described) may create problems rather than solve them. Some people in Western Europe may look askance at *any* cuts in NATO nuclear forces, upon which they rely to offset Warsaw Pact superiority in conventional troops. Others may see arms-control agreements as giving the Soviet Union a voice in NATO decisions—a voice which would be even stronger if these arrangements extended to discussions of military doctrine and concepts for the employment of nuclear weapons. Still others may see these arrangements as foreclosing on the option of creating a *European* tactical nuclear force—as, indeed, the Russians would like to do. Accordingly, many in the West may resist controls on TNW, just as many in the East may resist adjustments in conventional forces. These attitudes reflect the common belief that one's own strength enhances security and promotes stability, while the power of an adversary represents a threat to the peace. (To paraphrase the old Biblical adage, men see the military motes in the eyes of their neighbours, but not the beams in their own.) These attitudes are also detrimental, in that they tend to perpetuate that reliance on armaments which makes a significant contribution to tensions between East and West and is a major cause of uneasiness in Europe.

For this reason one must begin modestly, with reductions which do not markedly alter military capabilities and with deployment restrictions which can convey reassurances disproportionate to their military implications. Only if such measures do in fact alleviate fears (and other circumstances are favourable) can one expect further progress towards the control of TNW. However, given the manifold concerns about these weapons, and the potential consequences of their use (or misuse), every effort should be made to progress further—that is, to impose constraints on the use of TNW, remove some or all of them from particularly sensitive areas, trade off weapons systems perceived as threatening (or substitute others which are less threatening) and curb the forces and the warheads deployed outside Europe.

One circumstance which will make such measures possible is, of course, a further improvement in East–West relations, an improvement which can come about only as each side perceives that the other is behaving circumspectly. Another may well be the adoption of measures to reduce conventional forces in Europe, and thus to assuage fears deriving from perceptions of present conventional postures; if agreements to this end are not reached, it is unlikely that agreements on TNW will be reached either. Thus the next step is to examine the prospects for mutual force reductions and the resulting implications for European security.

Chapter 6

MUTUAL FORCE REDUCTIONS

Ever since the end of World War II there has been a plethora of ideas for the disengagement of forces in Europe, the establishment of denuclearized or demilitarized zones, reductions in troop strengths and cutbacks in levels of weapons. What is perhaps new is that suggestions for arms control, which were previously given short shrift, are now commanding respectful attention.

The members of NATO see arms control in Europe as both reflecting some progress towards *détente* and facilitating the further improvement of relations between East and West; as permitting cuts in defence costs or compensating in part for the run-down caused by those cuts; as avoiding, delaying or at least limiting unilateral American reductions in European-based troops; and thus as contributing both directly and indirectly to the maintenance of a stable military environment. The countries of the Warsaw Pact may also see limitations on armaments as affording opportunities to promote *détente* and lighten the burdens of defence; alternatively, they might see them as a price they have to pay to secure other objectives (such as acceptance of the *status quo* in Europe) or as an instrument which can be used to weaken and divide the West. In any case, there is support for arms control in both West and East.

This support for arms control has manifested itself particularly in calls for cutbacks in those forces which confront each other in Central Europe.[1] The North Atlantic Council has suggested mutual and reciprocal reductions of both indigenous troops and those stationed in the area, carried out in such a way as to maintain the existing military balance and not to destabilize the situation.[2] For their part, the

---

[1] This includes on the Western side Belgium, the Netherlands, Luxembourg and the Federal Republic of Germany and, on the Eastern side, the German Democratic Republic, Poland and Czechoslovakia. It is sometimes referred to as the NATO Guidelines Area (NGA), i.e. the area to which NATO proposals for force reductions are to apply. The seven countries mentioned are, together with Britain, Canada, the United States and the Soviet Union, 'full participants' in the negotiations on Mutual Force Reductions in Vienna.

[2] 'Text of Communiqué of NATO Council Meeting [of June 1968]', *Department of State Bulletin*, LIX, No. 1516 (15 July 1968), p. 77; 'Text of

leaders of the Soviet Union have proposed 'reductions of forces and armaments in areas where military confrontation is especially dangerous, above all in Central Europe', a view endorsed by the Political Consultative Committee of the Warsaw Pact.[3] And members of both NATO and the Warsaw Pact have been negotiating since October 1973, on the mutual reduction of forces and armaments and associated measures in central Europe.

This support may insure that there will be negotiations but it does not guarantee there will be agreement. For one thing, it will be very difficult, given the asymmetries in the military postures, mobilization capabilities, and geographic positions of the two blocs, to work out reductions which will achieve the Soviet goal of 'equal security' or meet the NATO objective of 'maintaining the present degree of security at reduced cost'.[4] For another, the interests of various countries differ, as do their concepts of what the negotiations should achieve, and even how they should be undertaken. For a third, the success of any negotiations on force reductions in Europe is linked to other issues, such as the outcome of future talks on the limitation of strategic armaments (SALT) and the degree of progress towards the amelioration of political differences between East and West.[5]

This suggests that the implications of mutual force reductions (MFR) for European security should not be looked at in a narrow military sense, but rather in terms of the perceptions and concerns of the participants. Accordingly, I will attempt first of all in this chapter to look at the interests and goals of the major actors in any negotiations on arms limitation in Europe. Next I will outline various approaches to troop reductions and assess their technical feasibility and military implications. Finally, I will discuss the potential impact of some hypothetical reductions that seem both feasible and consistent with the interests of the protagonists.

[3] Leonid I. Brezhnev, 'Report of the Communist Party of the Soviet Union', at the XXIVth Party Congress, 30 March 1971, translated and reprinted in the *Current Digest of the Soviet Press*, No. 12, (20 April 1971), p. 13; Warsaw Pact Communiqué of 26 January 1972, reported in the *New York Times*, 27 January 1972, p. 3.

[4] 'Text of Communiqué of NATO Council Meeting [of June 1968]', *op. cit.* in note 2.

[5] For a comprehensive treatment of these and other factors influencing MFR, see Christoph Bertram's excellent study of *Mutual Force Reductions in Europe: The Political Aspects*, Adelphi Paper No. 84 (London: IISS, 1972), esp. pp. 15–17.

Communiqué of NATO Council Meeting [of May 1970]', *Ibid.*, LXII, No. 1617 (22 June 1970), p. 775.

INTERESTS AND GOALS OF THE MAJOR ACTORS

Attitudes within NATO

The members of NATO are conscious of the difficulty of reaching agreement on arms-control measures, a difficulty which derives in part from the variety of approaches which must be considered. It also derives from the problem of evaluating the military capabilities of various forces and weapons, not all of which lend themselves readily to comparison. It stems, too, from differing appreciations of the forces which should be involved, the areas which should be covered, the safeguards which should be adopted and the linkage (if any) between locally applicable measures and larger ones (such as freezes on budgets) and between conventional and nuclear-armed forces. As one American official involved in the process said, 'We must actually conduct three sets of negotiations: one with other elements in the United States Government, one with our allies, and one with the Russians—and the last is likely to be the easiest.'

This is true not just because of the nature of the problem but because of the issues underlying mutual force reductions. One is whether these will affect the size and capabilities of American troops in Europe, and hence the credibility of the American deterrent. Another is whether they may result simply in a shift of Pact forces from the Central Front to the flanks of NATO, enhancing German security at the expense of Greece and Norway. A third is whether the MFR talks may not require changes in NATO military doctrine and operational concepts, thereby resurrecting issues which, like Lazarus, had been consigned to the tomb.

Even if the military issues underlying various approaches to mutual force-reductions can be resolved, the attempt to do so may divide the alliance. Furthermore, certain kinds of agreements may impose legal restrictions on some members of NATO, but not on all, and almost any agreement would give the Soviet Union some degree of influence over NATO force postures and defence programmes. More importantly, arms control might erode NATO's sense of purpose and sap its already low vitality. Hence, some NATO countries are inclined to give a higher priority to maintaining alliance cohesion and freedom of action than to adopting measures for the control of armaments, however fruitful these may be.

Perhaps most importantly, many are worried lest mutual force reductions further tilt the military balance in favour of the Warsaw Pact, either by depriving the West of weapons which are deemed essential to its security or by so thinning Western defences that the armies of the Warsaw Pact could punch through them. Although they may deem war very unlikely, they cannot rule it out entirely, and hence must prepare to wage war if necessary. Moreover, they may fear the effect of a further weakening of Western defences on alliance cohesion and on the will to resist political pressures. Given these concerns, it is understandable that some officials should oppose force reductions of any kind, and that others should endorse only proposals so favourable to the West as to have little prospect of acceptance.[6]

Were this all, the prospects for force reductions in Europe would be bleak indeed. However, there are those among the allies who see arms control as a way of sanctioning those cuts in their own forces made necessary by political pressures and financial exigencies, cuts which have in some instances already been programmed.[7] There are others who view it as a meaningful way of easing tensions and as a contribution to *détente*. Thus, while some in NATO may deem arms control in Europe an evil, others may judge it a necessary evil, and still others consider it potentially good.

The Warsaw Pact

Superficially there is greater agreement within the Warsaw Pact than within NATO on the desirability of mutual force reductions. One reason is that defence costs in most Warsaw Pact countries are high, reaching 5·5 per cent of GNP in East Germany and perhaps 11–13 per cent in the Soviet Union.[8] Another is the desire of these countries to benefit technically and economically from more extensive exchanges with the West, to which agreements on arms control might

[6] For illustrations of such proposals *see* the Stockholm International Peace Research Institute, *Force Reductions in Europe*, a SIPRI Monograph (New York: Humanities Press, 1974), pp. 52–3.

[7] For example, West Germany proposes to cut back the active-duty strength of her armed forces from 495,000 to 465,000, a drop of about 12 per cent. She will compensate in part for this reduction by increasing the number of reservists on alert status and expanding refresher training for others. Federal Ministry of Defence, *White Paper 1973/1974: The Security of the Federal Republic of Germany and the Development of the Federal Armed Forces* (Bonn: Press and Information Office of the Government of the Federal Republic of Germany, 1974), p. 70. This will be cited as *German White Paper 1973/1974*.

[8] The Soviet defence budget of some 17 billion roubles ($19 billion at the official rate of conversion) understates Soviet defence expenditures which, according to Western estimates, amount to at least 50 billion roubles, or $55 billion (*The Military Balance, 1976–77*, pp. 109-110). According to other estimates, the Soviet Union may be spending as much as 75 billion roubles on defence, and some even go so far as to calculate a budget of $115–25 in equivalent dollar costs.

contribute. A third is their wish for improved relations with Western Europe, so long as this improvement does not threaten their domestic political stability. A fourth is that they have a common interest in reducing the 'threat' from NATO, and particularly in chipping away at West German power and influence and putting constraints on German military forces.

Equally, there are divergences of interest, as might be expected. Although many East Europeans may welcome force reductions as diminishing, however slightly, the pervasive Soviet presence, others—along with many Russians—oppose this as politically unsettling. While some may see arms control as facilitating a *rapprochement* with the West, others view it as providing an opportunity to exploit political differences among the Western allies. And while some may view with equanimity cuts in Warsaw Pact conventional forces, others (like their Western counterparts) may fear that this could weaken alliance defences.

On balance, however, Warsaw Pact interests may be better served by mutual force reductions than by standing pat. Reductions may ease the burden of defence, particularly heavy in the Soviet Union,[9] and they may achieve cut-backs in NATO tactical nuclear forces—which are regarded by many as *the* threat to the security of Eastern Europe.[10] They may move the Warsaw Pact closer to the abolition of blocs and the establishment of an overall system of European security, both of which are long-term objectives of Soviet and East European policy. Also, force reductions can probably be made without weakening Warsaw Pact defences, partly because only selected East European troops are earmarked for joint operations with Soviet units,[11] and partly because the Soviet Union would be able to reinforce those units from combat-ready forces inside her own territory.

The implications for mutual force reductions

It is apparent from what has been said that there are significant differences in the interest of various countries in mutual force reduc-

[9] These burdens derive in part from the effort to match the United States in strategic nuclear capabilities, and in part from the additional requirements for conventional forces resulting from Soviet embroilment with China. For example, during the period 1967–71 the Soviet Union increased from 15 to 44 the number of divisions deployed along her frontier with China and has more than doubled the overall troop strength in Central and Eastern Asia. *Strategic Survey 1971* (London: IISS, 1972), p. 54.
[10] See Chapter 2, pp. 44–5.
[11] See John Erickson, 'MBFR: Force Levels and Security Requirements', in *Strategic Review*, Vol. 1, No. 3 (Summer 1973), pp. 29–31.

tions; some are totally opposed, others are reluctant participants, and still others are hopeful, if not enthusiastic. It is also apparent that interests will vary with the types of forces to be limited (the Western allies being concerned primarily about conventionally armed ground troops, and members of the Warsaw Pact about tactical nuclear delivery vehicles). They will shift according to whether one is talking about small cuts or large ones, quick reductions or slow ones, measures applying only to stationed forces or those affecting all troops in a given area.

Nor is it only on substantive matters that the potential participants in MFR differ: the questions of which countries should have 'special', non-decision-making status at the Vienna Conference, and why, consumed perhaps as much time as any other issue.

The grudging accommodations which made possible the formal opening of 'Negotiations on the Mutual Reduction of Forces and Armaments and Associated Measures in Central Europe' suggest that these procedural differences may be surmountable, at least for the present. And the fact that both NATO and the Pact have introduced 'agreed' proposals at the negotiations in Vienna, indicates that more substantive differences within the alliances can be papered over. What is in doubt is whether the graver differences between the alliances can be resolved, at least without a greater spirit of accommodation than has yet been shown. This will require a change in the interests and policies of some of the participants, a re-examination of the attitudes which seem to persist on both sides (such as the Western belief that the Warsaw Pact is building up forces for a massive conventional attack, or the Eastern one that NATO is planning nuclear aggression). It will also require an appreciation of the various types of force reductions which could be undertaken and of their implications. To this we will turn next in the hope that it will lead us–and the countries concerned –to that re-examination of their attitudes and interests which alone will make possible meaningful force reductions in Europe.

APPROACHES TO MUTUAL FORCE REDUCTIONS

As shown in Chart 2, Decision Blocks for Force Reductions in Europe, there are an almost infinite number of ways of reducing, limiting or constraining conventional forces in Europe. Cuts could be made in manpower (on active duty, in the reserves and/or in paramilitary units, such as border guards), in combat units, such as infantry battalions and fighter-interceptor squadrons, or in various types of weapons, such as tanks, artillery, rocket-launchers, etc. They could take the form of equal or asymmetrical reductions, percentage cuts or ceilings set below present levels–again on either an equal or an

Chart 2: **Decision Blocks for Force Reductions in Europe***

Nationality of Force	Indigenous			Foreign (i.e. Stationed)	
Branch of Service	Army	Navy	Air Force	Other (Border Guards, etc.)	
Component	Active			Reserve	
Armaments	Conventional		Nuclear	Dual-capable	
Items to be Cut	Men	Weapons	Equipment (tanks, helicopters, etc.)	Units	
Bases for Cuts	Equal in number		Equal in percentage	Asymmetrical in number and/or percentage	
Application of Cuts	Proportional (to national share of Alliance forces)			Pooled (i.e. applicable to Alliance as a whole)	
Disposition of Men	Demobilize		Transfer to reserves	Transfer to active forces elsewhere	
Disposition of Weapons and/or Equipment	Destroy	Remove		Transfer to reserves	Leave in depots
Disposition of Units	Disband	Redeploy elsewhere		Return to country of origin	Transfer to reserves

* Adapted from 'Mutual Force Reductions in Europe: An Alternative Approach', by Richard Herrmann, Graduate School of Public and International Affairs, University of Pittsburgh, presented at the XVII Annual Convention of the International Studies Association, Toronto, Canada, 25–9 February 1976.

asymmetrical basis. They could hold equally for stationed and indigenous forces or vary with the country of origin. They could extend uniformly to all kinds of troops and weapons, or differ with respect to those particularly important to one side or other. The first step, therefore, is to assess the effects of various approaches on the military capabilities of NATO and the Warsaw Pact, in the hope of reducing a bewildering array of arms-control measures to a few which might be sufficiently attractive, singly or in combination, to warrant further consideration.

To this end it may be useful to recapitulate the overall balance of forces in Europe. As Table 3 (p. 250) shows, NATO (excluding Portugal) has about 2,900,000 men in Europe. Almost 1,500,000 of these— organized into about 77 division-equivalents with some 12,000 battle tanks—are combat and direct-support forces. Others fly the 3,400 combat aircraft available in Europe to the Western Alliance; and, just for the record, about 345,000 of these men operate the 252 major surface combat ships, the host of other naval vessels, and the approximately 500 naval aircraft, in the inventory of NATO forces in Europe as of July 1976.[12]

Table 3 additionally shows that the Warsaw Pact has deployed in Eastern Europe about 81 (smaller) division-equivalents, equipped with over 20,000 main battle-tanks and backed up by a total of almost 1 million combat and direct-support troops—about one-third fewer than NATO if French forces are not counted, and almost one-half smaller if they are. The Warsaw Pact maintains roughly 3,700 aircraft (excluding those based in the Soviet Union), over 800 more than are integrated into NATO defences, but only 700 more than are available to the Western Alliance as a whole. Again, to complete the picture, approximately 77,000 seamen man the 7 major surface combat ships and the other vessels of the East European navies, or serve aboard the Soviet Mediterranean squadron.

Obviously, these figures do not fairly represent the military potential which either side could bring to bear in a conflict, since they count some elements (such as the Italian Army) which would not be immediately available for combat, and overlook others which would, like the two Soviet motorized infantry divisions and the Naval Infantry Brigade deployed on the Kola Peninsula.[13] Equally

---

[12] Apparently reductions in naval forces (as distinct from a freeze on naval personnel) are not being considered at Vienna; neither will they be in this chapter. They are, however, discussed along with other types of constraints on naval forces, in Chapter 6, pp. 194–6

[13] These and other Soviet units in the far north, plus the ground divisions and air squadrons deployed in the western USSR, would add about 20 division-equivalents, 5,000 tanks and 1,300 aircraft to the Soviet

obviously, they do not, unless examined in greater detail, expose local imbalances such as that favouring the Warsaw Pact in the Far North (where 2⅓ divisions confront a single Norwegian brigade) or, in Thrace, where Greek and Turkish troops favouring NATO far out-number Bulgarian on the other side of the border. They do, however, show the importance attaching to including or excluding from MFR a particular area such as Western Europe, and of counting or not counting particular types of forces (naval personnel amount to about 12 per cent of NATO forces in Europe and only 6 per cent of those of the six East European members of the Warsaw Pact). And they should serve to illuminate the effects of various approaches to force reduction, which is, after all, the purpose of this section.

Cuts in personnel

Perhaps the most attractive approach would be to cut personnel. Reducing the number of men in the armed forces would have the great advantages of simplicity in negotiation and flexibility in application, the latter because cuts could be made in such a way as to ensure balanced forces or maintain a capacity for sustained military operations. This would lower costs, especially among the members of NATO, and release manpower for other pursuits, which could be a boon to most countries involved. Moreover, it could enable both sides to keep up their defensive capabilities by transferring to the reserves the men released from active duty, and by stockpiling equipment for those redeployed to their homelands—a measure of particular importance in the case of American forces.

The impact of cuts in personnel would depend on their nature and how they were applied. For example, identical ceilings on the number of men on active service would require a major cut in NATO troop strength, and equal ceilings on all military manpower in Central Europe would do NATO little good; only if these ceilings applied exclusively to ground troops—and particularly to combat and direct-support elements—would NATO benefit. If the ceilings applied separately to stationed and indigenous forces, the Soviet Union would have to withdraw almost 200,000 more soldiers and airmen from foreign soil than the United States, Britain, France and other allies, but the European members of NATO would have to cut their remaining forces drastically, while the East Europeans would need to do nothing. Thus attitudes towards troop ceilings, like those towards the equalization of wealth, depend on what you propose to equalize.

Similarly asymmetrical effects would result from equal cuts in

totals and increase the total manpower in combat and direct-support units to about 240,000 (*see* Table 3, p. 250).

numbers; the last American would have to leave Europe long before the last Russian and the last Pole would have to trade his rifle for a plough, while numerous Germans, Frenchmen and Turks continued to mould bullets. Once more, this approach would have uneven impacts in different regions, to include adverse consequences for the Warsaw Pact in Southern Europe and no consequences at all to Northern Europe, since all Soviet units there are within their own boundaries.

By default, then, equal percentage cuts may be best – although even these will have different military consequences, depending on how they are made.[14] They will also, of course, have different effects on different areas, and on different components of the armed forces. And they will, crucially, have different consequences according to whether they do or do not apply also to reserve forces.

Ceilings on, or cuts in, reserve forces would reduce mobilization capacities – a move of particular importance if extended to the United States and the Soviet Union, both of which plan to flesh out and deploy units now only partially manned or wholly inactive. They would make it difficult to maintain in a state of readiness units withdrawn from Europe or de-activated under mutual force reductions – at least without decreasing the flow of manpower to other elements of the reserves. They would restrict the use of logistic and administrative support elements drawn from civilian life, with very different consequences for, say, Britain and Poland. While such constraints might reduce offensive capabilities, they are even more likely to affect defensive deployments, a role for which reserves may be particularly well suited. Thus constraints on reserves, like those on active-duty personnel, could also have very uneven impacts on military capabilities.

Moreover, there are problems with measures which affect only military manpower. One is that limitations would be hard to verify, especially in the case of reserves. Another is that reductions could be largely offset, at least in Eastern Europe, by proportionately increasing the border troops or other militarized police. Moreover, cuts in military manpower could be partly nullified by having the demolilized soldiers sign up as 'civilian' workers (a move which would be difficult to check) and in any case would not necessarily affect military imbalances, such as the Warsaw Pact advantage in main battle-tanks or the NATO edge in long-range fighter-bombers. Thus, NATO might wish to freeze paramilitary as well as military units, and both sides might be interested in measures to ensure cutbacks in armaments as well as manpower.

[14] For a discussion of alternative ways of handling reductions on the central front, see pp. 155–6.

Cuts in units

One possibility would be to 'require' an across-the-board cut in combat units equal to the percentage reductions in military manpower; for instance, a 20 per cent cut would force the United States to remove one of the five divisions which she has currently in Germany. In some cases (warships, for instance) this is both a desirable and a feasible method of ensuring militarily meaningful reductions in forces; however, it can present the following problems.

Combat units may differ significantly in size, armament and capabilities for combat: an American armoured division having almost twice as many men as its Soviet counterpart and correspondingly stronger infantry, engineer and anti-tank elements. These units will contain varying percentages of logistic and administrative personnel, depending on their level and the service to which they belong. (Reductions in numbers of divisions could have very different consequences from reductions in numbers of battalions.) The choice of what units should be cut could affect not only the ability of the residual forces to engage immediately in combat but also their ability to absorb reinforcements—it being easier to reattach a company to a battalion or a battalion to a brigade than to reintroduce whole divisions into the theatre.

All this means that it will be very hard for negotiators to estimate the effects of trade-offs, much less to agree on them. For example, cuts in tank, infantry, artillery and engineer battalions could affect the ratio between combat and support forces to the detriment of NATO and the possible benefit of the Warsaw Pact, which could enhance the staying power of its remaining units. Cuts in numbers of divisions proportionate to reductions in manpower would have roughly comparable effects on immediate capabilities but could disproportionately affect reinforcement capacities, particularly if the equipment for these divisions had to be withdrawn or scrapped. Moreover, in neither instance would these cuts redress the imbalances between offensive and defensive forces which so trouble some in NATO.

This is particularly true since one or both sides could select for removal the more lightly armed units, keeping those with heavier guns and/or newer tanks. Alternatively (or in addition), either could change the tables of organization of the units remaining, to give them more weapons. Or it could produce and stockpile in the area additional sets of equipment, for personnel mobilized in time of crisis or flown in from overseas. Thus there are a variety of ways of offsetting the consequences of reductions in units, ways which both sides could be tempted to adopt to the detriment of any agreement which might be reached.

Cuts in weapons

An alternative would be to require cuts in weapons proportional to those made in manpower, thus requiring the Soviet Union to remove more tanks than the United States, but perhaps fewer anti-tank guns. Obviously, there are difficulties about cuts in weapons, one being that they can be applied only to larger and more readily verifiable weapons, another that the numbers of such weapons are not accurately known, and a third that these weapons are such a mixture of old and new, light and heavy, active and reserve, that assessment of the military implications of any cuts could be almost impossible. To some extent, these difficulties could be offset by establishing categories of weapons (such as light, medium and heavy tanks) within which reductions would have to be made, but even this would not prevent any party to the agreement destroying old equipment and keeping new, thereby enhancing his capabilities. Perhaps more importantly, percentage cuts in weapons equal to those in manpower would again cause the brunt of the reductions to fall on combat units, and would thereby aggravate NATO's problems in conducting a 'forward defence' of West Germany.

All this suggests that it may be desirable to concentrate on specific weapons, rather than on all categories of arms or on various types of combat troops. One criterion for selecting the weapons could be ease of verification, which would suggest removing artillery rather than mortars, and weapons in the hands of troops rather than those in storage. Another could be to choose particular weapons systems in which several parties have an interest; this could lead to a paring down of aircraft, missiles and other nuclear-capable delivery vehicles, along with those employable only in conventional operations. A third criterion could be a weapon's utility in offensive operations, which might mean reducing armoured vehicles instead of anti-tank guns.

Admittedly, there is no hard and fast distinction between offensive and defensive weapons, since tanks can be used to knock out other tanks, and anti-aircraft artillery to prepare the way for infantry assaults—as the famous German 88mm gun did during World War II. Nevertheless, it should be possible to define broad categories of weapons based on their primary roles—with tanks, armoured cars, armoured personnel-carriers, self-propelled artillery (except anti-tank and anti-aircraft guns), landing ships and craft and perhaps armed helicopters in one group,[15] and anti-tank guns, anti-aircraft

[15] Ideally, all helicopters and transport aircraft ought to be included, since they can carry airborne or air-transportable units; however, their

guns and missiles, and towed artillery in another—and to cut the former rather than the latter. The aim would be to reduce the ability of either side to launch offensive operations, while at the same time maintaining (or increasing) its ability to conduct defensive ones. While there may be difficulties in distinguishing between supporting artillery and self-propelled anti-tank guns, these can be resolved by setting limits on the size of the weapon to be restricted, if not by measuring its trajectory.

The same can be said of ground-based nuclear delivery vehicles, in the reduction of which some on both sides are interested. All the nuclear-capable missiles and rockets are so large as to be readily distinguishable from those used only for conventional fire support, and those used in air-defence roles are so different from the surface-to-surface missiles that a distinction can be drawn even here. At the moment, this is equally true of tube artillery, in that only weapons of 155mm or larger (203mm on the part of the Warsaw Pact) are armed with nuclear-tipped shells. If and as 'mini-nukes' are developed, or weapons like the *Davy Crockett* mortar re-introduced, it may be harder to draw such distinctions, but at the moment it is possible to distinguish nuclear-capable offensive weapons from those designed for 'defensive' use and from those equipped solely with conventional munitions.

Differentiation is not so simple in the case of aircraft. Many warplanes of both sides can carry out multiple missions (the MiG-17, for instance, serves as an interceptor, ground-attack and reconnaissance aircraft). Moreover, some of these planes are 'dual-capable'—i.e., can carry either nuclear or conventional armaments—and others can be adapted to become so. Thus, it may be necessary to resort both to some arbitrary definitions and to some close inspection if one is to categorize NATO and Warsaw Pact aircraft by type and classify some of them as nuclear-capable. This is, however, probably essential, since otherwise the Warsaw Pact could concentrate any cuts on its relatively low-performance interceptor aircraft, thus enhancing the quality of its numerically superior air forces *vis-à-vis* those of NATO. Moreover, both sides might wish to apply differential reductions to various types of aircraft, within an overall number or a given ceiling, or to arrange for possible exchanges among types along the lines authorized in

---

roles are so varied that it was thought best to ignore for the time being those not armed. Even then, some might ask whether one should not try to differentiate between those equipped with anti-tank weapons and those otherwise armed. The answer was given by fourteenth-century philosopher William of Occam: entities ought not to be multiplied except from necessity. So let us take the simplest solution and limit both.

SALT I for ICBM and SLBM. Finally, the Warsaw Pact seems to be more interested in reducing NATO nuclear-capable aircraft than other types, and may insist on restrictions applicable directly to these aircraft.

The actual effect of any reductions will, of course, depend on how deep they go, as well as on whether they are applied across the board or differ by type of aircraft. As with manpower, cuts of 5–10 per cent in aircraft are likely to be of psychological rather than military importance; only when they reach 20–25 per cent are they likely to have a significant impact (see Table 3). Even at that level, cuts in indigenous aircraft are likely to be more effective than cuts in stationed ones, since the latter could readily be reintroduced in a crisis or in preparation for an attack.[16] Numerically equal cuts, overall or by type, would adversely affect NATO, whose forces are slightly smaller but whose planes are qualitatively superior. Equal percentage reductions by type might (by increasing the ability of fewer NATO strike aircraft to penetrate weakened Warsaw Pact air defences) have roughly equal effects on capabilities. Conversely, reductions centred on strike aircraft (such as the Warsaw Pact might advocate) would diminish the ability of NATO to gain air superiority or interdict Soviet troop reinforcements during the crucial first days of any conventional conflict.[17] Hence we may expect either hard bargaining over trade-offs or relatively slight reductions in tactical aircraft, at least during the first stage of MFR.

[16] Newhouse and his associates calculate that the Pact forces could increase their numerical advantage from 1.8:1 to 2.0:1 by M + 30, even after French aircraft are added to NATO totals. See John Newhouse, et al., US Troops in Europe: Issues, Costs and Choices (Washington, DC: The Brookings Institution, 1971), p. 59. These ratios, however, are obtained by including Soviet aircraft in the western Soviet Union, and by assuming 50 per cent increases on each side between M-Day and M + 30; they may, therefore, be high. Former Secretary of Defense McNamara estimated that 'NATO tactical aircraft reinforcements would about equal the Pact's in the early stages of mobilization, after which we could add considerably more aircraft than the Pact' (op. cit. in Chap. 2, note 16, p. 81). Along with most Western analysts, he stressed that NATO aircraft were qualitatively superior to those of the Warsaw Pact by margins of almost 2:1. (In connection with the latter point see the New York Times, 5 May 1974, p. 5, which reports that NATO officials believe their qualitative advantages would give them air superiority on the central front.)

[17] Note that to the Western allies these aircraft are important to the nuclear deterrent; they should either be left untouched, or traded off only for reductions in Soviet intra-continental strategic launch vehicles.

THE CURRENT SITUATION

NATO Preferences

In general, NATO would like to see significant reductions of Soviet troops in Eastern Europe, wherever they are stationed, and is less concerned about cuts in the forces of other Warsaw Pact members. It would also like to see asymmetrical reductions in Warsaw Pact ground and air forces, especially in units such as tank divisions and amphibious brigades, which are particularly suited for offensive operations. Thus it would presumably favour ceilings on certain components of the armed forces, such as ground combat and direct-support troops, with Warsaw Pact reductions taking the form of de-activating or withdrawing entire divisions or tank armies. NATO will probably concentrate for the most part on central Europe, which is both the source of the greatest 'threat' and the one region where these kinds of ceiling would work to its advantage. And it will undoubtedly seek assurances that Soviet units withdrawn from Eastern Europe will not be moved to other areas (such as the Kola Peninsula) from which they could threaten NATO's flanks; that they be either dissolved or stationed deep in the interior of the Soviet Union; and that restrictions be placed on their redeployment to the European theatre.

NATO would prefer that there should be only small cuts in American (and other) stationed forces, and that these should not preclude their ability to return to the European theatre in fighting trim—which suggests cuts in manpower rather than organized units, and retention rather than removal of equipment now in Europe. The Western allies might accept somewhat larger reductions in indigenous forces (albeit with more readiness on the Central Front than on the southern flank, where the political opposition is greater), but they would not want them to apply to reserve units, upon which they rely heavily to match the reinforcements available from within the Soviet Union. And they would certainly want to preserve freedom of movement for their forces within NATO territory, both as a hedge against political pressures and as a contribution towards the creation of a joint European Defence Force. Thus what is sauce for the Siberian goose is not necessarily sauce for the West European gander.

Warsaw Pact preferences

The Warsaw Pact may well seek sizeable withdrawals of American forces and significant cuts in those of West Germany, but is not as interested in reductions in other NATO troops. It would be more interested in cutting NATO tactical nuclear forces than conventional ones and in constraining highly mobile elements (such as fighter-bombers) than comparatively static ones. And, given its own estimates of the global balance of power, it might insist that any units affected by MFR–especially American ones–should be dissolved rather than kept on the military roster.

It might in return acquiesce in low to medium reductions of Soviet troops (perhaps 10–20 per cent over a protracted first stage) and even higher cuts in other East European armies and air forces, but not on an asymmetrical basis. As one Soviet writer has pointed out, asymmetries in the force structures of the two alliances do not necessarily generate advantages but simply reflect differences in military doctrine, alliance relations and capacity to produce weapons.[18] Thus the Soviet Union and her allies might hold out for more or less equal percentage cuts in manpower, weapons and/or units (which would implement the principle of 'undiminished security') or might seek trade-offs, reflecting their greater concern about TNW–in either case putting forward measures opposed to those favoured by NATO.[19]

Furthermore, although the Soviet Union agreed with other participants in the CSCE to give advance notification of military manoeuvres, she seems to be unwilling to extend this to troop movements, much less to accept constraints on them. While she might finesse this issue by insisting that all American and Soviet units withdrawn from Europe should be disbanded, she is unlikely to give firm assurances that she will never strengthen her garrisons in Eastern Europe or redeploy the divisions now stationed there from one country to another. And she certainly would not do so without similar commitments by the Western allies.

Mutual force reductions in Central Europe

All this indicates why those conferring in Vienna have had great difficulty in agreeing on arms-control measures applicable to Central Europe. Indeed, the preliminary positions taken in the negotiations followed a predictable pattern, with NATO and Warsaw Pact proposals almost diametrically opposed.

The Soviet Union initially proposed (and its fellow participants from the Warsaw Pact endorsed) measures which would affect both super-power and other forces on a proportional basis, with reductions of 20,000 men each in NATO and Warsaw Pact ground and air forces

[18] Y. Kostko, 'Mutual Force Reductions in Europe', *World Economics and International Politics*, June 1972, translated and reprinted in *Survival*, Vol. XIV, No. 5 (September/October 1972), pp. 236–8.

[19] For an excellent analysis of Soviet incentives for, and objects in, mutual force reductions, see David Holloway, *The Soviet Approach to MBFR*, The Waverley Papers, Series 1, Occasional Paper 5 (Edinburgh: University of Edinburgh, March 1973), esp. pp. 27–9.

in 1975, to be followed in subsequent years by cuts of 5 per cent and 10 per cent respectively.[20] These percentage reductions would apply also to significant weapons such as tanks, aircraft, rocket launchers, etc., and cuts in both men and weapons would be effected 'in the form of comparable military units'. So far, however, the Warsaw Pact has given no indication as to whether these units would be small ones, such as battalions and air squadrons, or large ones, such as divisions and air wings.

Given the existing military balance in Central Europe (for which see Table 6), the numbers of airmen and soldiers to be demobilized or withdrawn under the initial Warsaw Pact proposal would equal about 170,000 for NATO and about 185,000 for the Pact.[21] If one defined tactical nuclear delivery vehicles in a limited way, cut-backs by both sides would be about equal; if one included nuclear-capable artillery, however, NATO would have to dispose of a further two hundred TNDV. While the Warsaw Pact would presumably scrap or retire more conventional weapons, it would still retain its present advantages of almost 2 : 1 in aircraft and tanks, upon which it relies to offset other NATO advantages, thereby observing the principle of 'undiminished security'.

This is not, of course, the Western view. As mentioned previously, NATO sees itself faced on the central front by Warsaw Pact ground and air forces which are superior in numbers of tanks, planes and guns, if not in overall combat capabilities. NATO therefore has proffered a package to achieve balanced, i.e., equal, ground forces in Central Europe.[22] This would be done in two stages, the first involving

[20] O. Khlestov, 'Mutual Force Reductions in Europe', *World Economics and International Relations*, No. 6, 1974, in translation in *Survival*, November/December 1974, especially p. 294. This has subsequently been modified to provide that only US and Soviet forces would be cut initially, that this be done in numbers proportional to troop strength on each side and that the second stage reduction be on the basis of agreed percentages. Aleksy Petrov, Tass 13 May 1976, translated and reported in FBIS, Soviet Union, 13 May 1976, Vol. iii, no. 94.

[21] If, that is, one uses Western figures for the number of men on the Central Front (see Table 6, p. 256). If, however, one bases these calculations on the figure of 805,000 WTO ground force personnel which the members of the Warsaw Pact reportedly stated that they maintain in Central Europe (the *Daily Telegraph*, 5 October 1976, p. 10), rather than on the 899,000 which the West claims they have, the reductions would be virtually identical.

[22] See the opening statement by the head of the US delegation to the Vienna talks, Ambassador Stanley R. Resor, Public Information Press Release 73–9, United States Arms Control and Disarmament Agency, 31 October 1973, mimeograph, pp. 6–7.

the withdrawal of approximately 16 per cent of American and Soviet stationed forces, the latter including tank divisions and possibly an entire tank army.[23] Since there are only half as many Americans in Central Europe as there are Russians, this would result in asymmetrical cuts in manpower, the figures commonly cited being 28,500 American soldiers and 3,000 airmen compared to 67,500 Soviet servicemen.[24] This first stage would not only (it is hoped) satisfy those still pressing for American troop withdrawals but partially achieve other NATO goals of cutting back Soviet troops and redressing existing 'imbalances'.

The second stage would go even further in these directions by establishing ceilings of 700,000 men on the ground forces of both sides, which would require NATO to eliminate another 60,000 men and the Warsaw Pact to reduce by over almost twice as many.[25] Even if reductions in weaponry were only proportionate to those in manpower, the Warsaw Pact would again lose more tanks, guns and armoured personnel-carriers, thus further diminishing its ability to conduct mobile operations. Since cuts in both manpower and drawdowns in weapons would affect the Warsaw Pact disproportionately, NATO might not only eliminate the disparities in combat manpower and in the character of the ground forces of the two sides which it considers disadvantageous, but might also partially offset the geographical asymmetries which allegedly favour the Soviet Union.[26] And since it would retain most, if not all, the dual-capable delivery systems on which it relies so heavily,[27] NATO might indeed feel more secure.

[23] The *New York Times*, 16 September 1973, p. 4.

[24] *Ibid.* A more official but less informative statement of the NATO proposal will be found in the US Department of State, Bureau of Public Affairs, *Foreign Policy Outlines*, May 1974, 'Europe: Mutual and Balanced Force Reductions'.

[25] This assumes that NATO 'counts' the 58,000 French troops in West Germany as of July 1976, even though the French have indicated that they will neither be bound by nor affected by the outcome of the Vienna Conference. If NATO is not counting the French in its proposal for a common ceiling, it would have to cut only a handful of men (see Table 6, p. 256).

[26] For a discussion of these disadvantages, and an argument that the NATO package will both enhance stability and maintain 'undiminished security', *see* Ambassador Resor's statement, *op. cit.* in note 22, pp. 5–6.

[27] In December 1975, a modified NATO proposal was offered which featured reductions in the number of tactical nuclear warheads, nuclear-capable fighter-bombers and *Pershing* ballistic missiles in the first stage withdrawal of American and Soviet forces. This proposal also called for ceilings for these weapons and for air forces in the central European area—an idea subsequently adopted by the Warsaw Pact. It was, however,

Whether the Warsaw Pact will be persuaded that this is equally true in its case is perhaps debatable; Pact spokesmen have already charged that the Western proposals would alter the balance of power in Central Europe and contradict the principle of undiminished security for both sides.[28] As of mid-1976, therefore, the negotiations at Vienna were seemingly deadlocked. As both negotiators and their observers know, initial proposals by opposing sides are seldom acceptable and almost never remain unchanged. The aim of all negotiators is to achieve an acceptable compromise. The aim of this observer is to suggest ways of achieving it. In the present instance, one could attempt this by devising hypothetical fall-back positions or by looking at possible trade-offs between various elements of NATO and Warsaw Pact forces, the process which has been followed by the negotiators at Vienna. This would, however, be both highly speculative and necessarily exhaustive – as well as exhausting. Instead, I propose to suggest some measures which might assuage the fears and appeal to the interests of both sides, in an effort to outline a basis for agreement.

One measure would be a cut in manpower of, say, 10–20 per cent,[29] which could apply:

1. Only to stationed forces; i.e., the Soviet Union on the one hand and Britain, Canada, France and the United States on the other would have to remove from the area 20 per cent of their men in uniform: Army, Navy and Air Force.

2. Equally to indigenous forces, so that the other countries involved would have to demobilize 10–20 per cent of their soldiers, sailors and airmen.

In either case these reductions could be pooled, so that France (for example) could withdraw fewer troops (or none) and the United States more, and that Czechoslovakia could disband more units and Poland fewer. This would help to lessen differences within the alliances over reductions and transfer bargaining over differences to

---

[28] Khlestov, *op. cit.* in note 20, p. 294. In their turn, the negotiators for the Warsaw Pact have borrowed a leaf from NATO's book, by offering to withdraw missiles and strike aircraft equal in number to those withdrawn by the United States – *if* the US and its allies will accept the Pact proposals. The *Financial Times*, 27 February 1976, p. 6.

[29] This range of figures was chosen deliberately, in that cuts of less than 10 per cent would have very little military significance and cuts of more than 20 per cent could adversely affect NATO's strategy of 'forward defence'. The analysis will focus on the upper figure, as the more significant of the two.

---

continent on Pact acceptance of common ceilings on ground forces. See *NATO Review*, Vol. 24, No. 3 (June 1976), pp. 30–1.

intra-pact forums, a move which might make East–West negotiations somewhat easier.

There are, however, two *caveats* to this suggestion. One is that if either side chooses to pool its cuts it should pay a penalty for so doing, in the form of additional reductions of 1 or 2 per cent. The other is that ceilings should be imposed on the forces which could be kept in the area by *any* state, indigenous or foreign. These ceilings would serve two purposes: to limit the size of the West German contingent in NATO (or parts of it) and to insure disproportionate reductions in Soviet forces, which are the largest of all.

Such a measure should be attractive to the Warsaw Pact, since it not only upholds the principle of proportionability but also applies to ground and air (and naval)[30] forces rather than to ground troops alone. For the same reasons, it might not appeal to NATO, even though it is flexible–both with respect to types of forces and their nationalities –and even though it would require disproportionate cuts in Soviet troop strength, which is one of the objectives of NATO. Before dismissing equal percentage reductions out of hand, it might, however, be worth assessing their potential implications.

As one looks at the present military balance, it is apparent that neither side could absorb a 20 per cent cut in stationed forces solely by abolishing headquarters, replacing base maintenance repairmen by civilian workers, and so on. Even if it were possible to absorb half the cut in that fashion–which is a very optimistic assumption for the Western allies and quite impossible for the Soviet Union–NATO would have to take elements from the ten American, British, Canadian (and French)[31] division-equivalents on the central front, and the Warsaw Pact would have to eat into the Soviet divisions in East Germany, Poland and Czechoslovakia. The consequent impact on the military balance depends, however, on what forces are cut and how the cuts are made.

Broadly speaking, NATO could cut stationed forces in one of two

[30] The inclusion of naval personnel serves two purposes: it allows greater flexibility in making cuts (albeit they must be somewhat deeper) and it precludes an off-setting build-up of naval aviation, marines, logistic support units, etc. Alternatively, naval manpower could be frozen at present levels and lessen cuts made in ground and air forces.

[31] As mentioned previously, the French have indicated that they will not apply to their troops in West Germany any reductions agreed upon at the Vienna Conference–which is one reason for recommending that cuts in personnel be probed. However, the French are reportedly withdrawing some artillery regiments (for re-equipment with *Pluton*) and will presumably phase down the elements remaining as they reorganize into smaller divisions. See *The Military Balance, 75–76*, p. 21, (footnote).

ways: by reducing the manning levels in units (from, say, 95 per cent of strength to 75 per cent), or by taking out units. If it chose the latter option it could either take out large units, as the United States did when it withdrew two brigades of the First Infantry Division (Mechanized), or small ones, as Britain did in removing the fourth company from the infantry battalions of the British Army of the Rhine. And it could make these cuts across the board, thereby presumably maintaining 'balanced' forces, or could make disproportionate reductions in service elements.[32]

The first approach, that of maintaining the overall structure but reducing the number of men per unit, is the one currently employed by most NATO nations. Its great advantage is that it maintains intact a command system and logistic base which could be fleshed out quickly in an emergency, in the case of stationed forces by airlifting individual replacements, or in the case of indigenous ones by mobilizing men from civilian life. Its major disadvantage is that it sharply reduces combat readiness, and hence increases reliance on warning of attack; it causes disproportionate reductions in riflemen, gunners, mechanics and other non-headquarters personnel who are crucial only in combat, and it may cause a temporary loss of efficiency in units which suddenly have to absorb large numbers of new men on mobilization. Although there are ways of alleviating the latter problem (through the periodic return of these replacements to their units), this may be difficult in practice, especially for stationed forces.

Under these circumstances, the alternative of keeping combat and support units at operating levels but reducing the number of units has much to commend it. Units withdrawn but retained in active status could be attached to other headquarters in their homelands but returned periodically for orientation or manoeuvres, as is now done with the dual-based infantry brigades and tactical air squadrons assigned to the American forces in Europe. Those deactivated but incorporated in the reserve could be recalled for refresher training with the organizations to which they would belong in time of war. Thus, the members of the Western alliance could keep both a reasonable capacity for immediate combat and the capability to add to this in an emergency.

The effects of this alternative would vary somewhat with the units chosen for withdrawal. If small units, such as companies, were removed or retired, the administrative structure might still be disproportionately large – especially if it had to provide logistic support for

---

[32] It could also, of course, make smaller percentage reductions in ground troops than in air and naval forces, particularly the last, a step which would fit with the 'short war' concept, which is receiving increasing attention in NATO.

those elements returning. Larger units, like battalions or brigades, which are more self-sufficient logistically and administratively, might place fewer demands on the residual forces, but could be harder to re-integrate – at least in the opinion of one authority.[33] However, only if one begins to remove quite large units, such as divisions, is one likely to maintain the balance between combat and support troops which was the avowed aim of this approach. Moreover, it is an approach that may commend itself both to the United States and the Soviet Union – particularly if the latter is asked to withdraw divisions of her own.

As Brigadier Hunt points out, the withdrawal of one American division (and supporting forces) would not necessarily weaken overall defences on the Central Front, since the southern sector (where the Americans are stationed) is perhaps the strongest militarily[34] as well as the least exposed geographically. Moreover, the French troops in Germany are deployed behind those of the United States, and it is at least conceivable that France may again co-operate militarily with NATO, and very likely that she would be involved if the Soviet Union launched an attack. And since the Soviet Union would have to remove even larger numbers of combat units, it is unlikely that the return home of one American division would be militarily harmful; in fact, the real question is whether it may not be in the European (as well as the American) interest, for the United States to absorb the cuts which otherwise would have to be made in the thinly stretched British and French forces in Central Europe.

This could probably be done without withdrawing more than one American division, by cutting support units. This is particularly feasible in the case of American forces, which, despite the recent formation of two additional brigades from support personnel, still have greater logistic capabilities and hence larger 'division slices' than their NATO allies, and which rely less on local labour than do, for instance, the British. This option could maintain the capability of the US Seventh Army for immediate combat, at the expense of its ability to mount operations of longer than 90 days duration.[35] Whether this is

[33] Kenneth Hunt, *The Alliance and Europe, Part II, Defence with Fewer Men*, Adelphi Paper No. 98 (London: IISS, 1973), pp. 29–30.

[34] *Ibid.*, p. 35.

[35] It has been estimated that an American Army division of approximately 16,000 men could, with an additional increment of 16,000 men, wage war for 90 days, but would require another 16,000 men for sustained support over an extended period of time. Morton H. Halperin, 'The Good, the Bad and the Wasteful', *Foreign Policy* No. 6 (Spring 1972), p. 77. *See also* the remarks of Senator Edward Kennedy, in the *Congressional Record, Senate*, 23 November 1971, p. S. 19513.

a serious defect depends largely on one's estimate of the durability of Western defences. If these crumbled in the south, the Americans might have to abandon their depots anyway; if the line were pierced elsewhere, the allies might have to resort to nuclear weapons long before the 90 days were up; and if some of these allies lacked ammunition even for 90 days' combat, the ability of American forces to carry on longer might be irrelevant.

The Soviet Union could not reduce her forces in Central Europe by 20 per cent without facing the same dilemma as the United States: either to skeletonize units and reduce their capability for immediate action, or to eliminate units and maintain balanced forces of smaller size. Since the manning levels of her divisions in Central Europe are above 75 per cent, she could reduce these somewhat without crippling effects. If she did this, she would retain a formidable capacity for short, sharp actions, but her ability to follow up initial thrusts would be even more dependent on the dispatch of reinforcements than it is now. Alternatively, she could keep 20–22 of her 27 divisions in a high state of readiness, and redeploy the others. Even then, however, the remaining units' capability for sustained action would not be as great as that of their NATO counterparts, since the Soviet Army draws much of its logistical support from the civilian sector of the economy, from whence it must be mobilized.

Therefore, a 20 per cent phase-down of stationed forces might not be militarily disadvantageous to NATO. Although it would lose about 75,000 American (or other) stationed troops, the Warsaw Pact would lose over 100,000 Soviet soldiers and airmen. While NATO could thin out a portion of the front where it is strong, the Warsaw Pact would, with smaller forces, still have to overcome defences elsewhere which would be largely unchanged. And while the United States could maintain her present strength virtually intact by cutting support units, the Soviet Union could not do so. Thus only if there is a sustained conflict, in which Soviet reinforcements gradually overpower NATO resistance, is the lack of American staying power likely to be felt.

If one also negotiated 20 per cent reductions in indigenous forces, the picture would not be quite as favourable for NATO. Although the number of men demobilized would then be approximately the same, over two-thirds of those in the West would probably have to come from the well-trained and well-equipped West German forces. This loss could perhaps be slightly diminished by making larger cuts in Belgian or Dutch troops, but the possibilities are limited both by the size of these countries' armies and by the probable reluctance of almost every nation involved to see West German strength increase in relation to that of its neighbours. Furthermore, West Germany could not cut 50–60,000 men from her army (the minimum cut she would have to make, even after pruning her air force and navy) without inactivating at least two of its twelve divisions or relying even more heavily on the mobilization of reserves than is now the case. Thus some might be worried lest this diminish the ability of NATO to resist a sudden Soviet thrust, and perhaps its ability to stem an attack by all the states of the 'Northern Tier'.

Against this must be set the fact that East Germany would probably have to drop one division-equivalent, Czechoslovakia two and Poland three. Admittedly, these may not be of comparable calibre to West German forces, and in the case of Poland they do not pose an immediate threat. However, it should also be noted that the Soviet Union would have to give up five to seven division-equivalents, as against one, or perhaps two, for NATO stationed forces. The balance in ground-combat capabilities may therefore not be as disadvantageous to NATO as it would seem at first glance.

Moreover, there are ways of stabilizing that balance further, by ensuring that weapons are cut back in proportion to troop strength, and seeing that this is done on a basis which favours the defender. Following up the suggestion made earlier, consideration might be given to 10–20 per cent reductions in:

1. tanks, self-propelled guns and armoured personnel-carriers, which are most useful in offensive (or in counter-offensive) operations;
2. surface-to-surface missiles, rockets and all artillery pieces of six inches (152mm)[36] or more in diameter, since these are capable of delivering nuclear weapons;
3. tactical aircraft, by type.
4. armed helicopters.

As before, these reductions could apply separately to stationed and indigenous forces, or to both together, and could be pooled among the different categories of forces, the only new proviso being that weapons in the hands of Soviet, Canadian, British, French and/or American troops would have to be withdrawn from the area, and that their removal should be subject to verification.

If this were done, NATO would have to retire or withdraw somewhat larger numbers of armoured personnel-carriers than would the Warsaw Pact, which has fewer (if larger) vehicles. It would also have to withdraw more self-propelled artillery (of which it has a much

---

[36] Technically, six inches equates to 155mm. Since, however, the Warsaw Pact armies have 152mm howitzers, it was felt that equality of sacrifice required that these be included. Moreover, the Soviet Union could develop nuclear-tipped shells for these artillery pieces, even though she has apparently not done so to date.

higher percentage) and perhaps more guns, since although the Warsaw Pact has a larger number of artillery tubes in Central Europe, it still relies heavily on smaller-calibre pieces, such as the 122mm gun-howitzer. However, the Warsaw Pact would have to dispense with over 3,000 medium tanks, compared with approximately 1,200 for NATO;[37] if only stationed forces were involved, the Soviet Union would have to pull out some 1,600 tanks in organized units as against 375–550 for the United States.[38] While such cuts would reduce NATO's ability to conduct a flexible defence, they would reduce Warsaw Pact offensive capabilities even more, partly because NATO's quantitative and qualitative advantage in anti-tank guns would become more meaningful. On the other hand, tanks which the Soviet Union withdrew could be reintroduced within a few days, whereas those taken out by the United States could not; hence, the Warsaw Pact could speedily return to the *status quo* should the need arise. Although this could place NATO at a further disadvantage during a competitive mobilization, existing Soviet capabilities for introducing armoured vehicles into Eastern Europe are so great that the incremental improvement would be marginal. Moreover, any potential disadvantage could be partly offset by more rapid manning of the tanks held in reserve (which would be left untouched) or by other defensive measures, such as the laying of minefields in time of crisis. Thus, even symmetrical reductions in armoured vehicles–at this level anyway–should improve NATO's defensive posture.

It is unlikely that the proposed cuts of 20 per cent in medium artillery would affect relative capabilities for conventional combat. For one thing, guns of this size constitute only a small percentage of those used by Warsaw Pact forces (for example, all 66 field pieces in an American mechanized division are 155mm or larger, while only 18 of the 72 howitzers in a Soviet motorized rifle division are of comparable size). For another, most of the NATO reductions will already have been made, by virtue of the cuts in self-propelled artillery accompanying reductions in other TNDV; in fact, the cuts in towed artillery should slightly improve NATO's posture. And in any case, each side has other weapons which would remain untouched, such as mortars (in which NATO has an edge) and multiple rocket-launchers, of which the Warsaw Pact has more.

Nor is it likely that the proposed reductions in medium artillery,

[37] These are tanks in organized units; if stockpiled tanks are included, the NATO figures would increase by about 200 on each side.

[38] The difference in figures depends on whether the United States withdraws 20 per cent of her own 1,350 tanks in active service or whether she also absorbs cuts which would otherwise have to be made in British and French armoured vehicles (See Table 6, p. 256).

rockets and missiles would hamper the ability to wage tactical nuclear war. NATO would still have almost 1,000 nuclear-capable guns and several hundred *Honest John, Sergeant, Lance* and *Pershing,* while the Warsaw Pact would have almost 200 *FROG* rockets and over 100 *Scud* and *Scaleboard* missiles, to say nothing of other nuclear delivery vehicles inside and outside Central Europe. Thus, cuts of 20 per cent in ground-based nuclear delivery systems would be largely of symbolic importance.[39]

Aircraft are perhaps more of a problem. As indicated previously, NATO strike aircraft are not only qualitatively superior to those of the Warsaw Pact but also are programmed for long-range interdiction and air-superiority missions, successful execution of which may be crucial to the defence of Western Europe. Moreover, NATO relies more heavily upon strike aircraft for nuclear fire support than does the Warsaw Pact—even though the latter has more nuclear-capable aircraft deployed in Central Europe (see Table 6, p. 256). If they are looked at together, these factors indicate that symmetrical reductions in fighter-bombers on any significant scale might cause a disproportionate decline in NATO capabilities. To offset this, the Warsaw Pact would be asked to scrap or to remove about twice as many planes (see Table 6); and indeed, this is why the proposed reductions applied also to interceptors, which might be considered 'defensive weapons'. Any resulting imbalance in either direction could be remedied in time of crisis, by redeploying planes from elsewhere. In fact, given the numbers of reinforcing aircraft available, the effects of 20 per cent reductions in war-planes now deployed in Central Europe might be more apparent than real, which would make it easier for both sides to accept the consequences of cuts in tactical aircraft.

As for armed helicopters, NATO—and especially the United States —makes more use of them than does the Warsaw Pact. However, those given 'tank-busting' roles can be replaced in part by ground-based anti-tank weapons, new models of which are being deployed in substantial numbers. Those intended to support ground operations with rockets and machine-gun fire are, unfortunately, less easy to replace; however, it is precisely these characteristics—and the possibility of employing armed helicopters offensively—which induced a call for cut-backs in the number deployed.[40] Though this cannot be said with certainty, it is probably true here also that the effects of such cuts might be more apparent than real.

[39] See Chapter 5, pp. 132–3.

[40] Another factor was that disproportionate reductions in NATO armed helicopters might recompense the Warsaw Pact for disproportionate reductions in fighter-interceptors.

Mutual force reductions in Southern Europe

The situation in Southern Europe (which includes Italy, the Balkans, Turkey in Asia, the Black Sea and the Mediterranean) is very different from that in Central Europe. In the first place, NATO forces are numerically stronger in this area than those of the Warsaw Pact, even after one counts those troops inside the Soviet Union which might be immediately available for combat (see Table 7, p. 258). While the Warsaw Pact has more tanks in the area, and both sides have about equal numbers of ground-based aircraft, NATO has more ships and more naval aircraft, which form an important component of military power in the region, especially for limited operations. For another, Italy is geographically isolated from its allies in Southern Europe, at least as far as ground forces are concerned, and cannot be involved in land operations unless Yugoslavia either sides with the Warsaw Pact or is overrun by Warsaw Pact forces. And for a third, Yugoslavia herself is an important military power, whose adherence (or opposition) to either alliance could affect the local balance of ground forces and the strategic positions of the two alliances for conventional operations.

In the Mediterranean the two alliances interact not only with one another but also with other states in the area. These include the countries of the Levant (Israel and her immediate neighbours), the states of the North African littoral—especially Libya, with its sizeable and important output of oil—and other non-aligned states, such as Malta and Spain. The nature of the interactions is such that military force—and especially naval power—is regarded as an important instrument for advancing national interests and maintaining national positions. Thus any force reductions in Southern Europe must take into account the ways in which the United States might try to uphold Israel in a future conflict, the possibility that the Soviet Union might feel impelled to support Syria against real or imagined threats to her security, and even the contingency that Greek and Turkish forces may clash over Cyprus or over the possession of the newly discovered oilfields in the Aegean Sea.

All this suggests that force reductions in that area will be slower in coming, different in nature and smaller in extent than those in Central Europe. They may also be asymmetrical, in that equal reductions in numbers would be disadvantageous to the Warsaw Pact (at least in terms of ready forces) and equal percentage reductions would be disastrous for NATO, especially as they would not affect the troops and aircraft in the Soviet Union. While it is conceivable that NATO may ultimately wish to bargain for reductions in forces inside the Soviet Union, or to trade off some of its advantages in manpower for disproportionate cuts in Warsaw Pact tank strength, this does not seem likely at the moment. And while the Warsaw Pact may wish to adhere to the principle of equality, it is conceivable that it would accept an application of that principle somewhere between equal numerical reductions and equal percentage cuts. Accordingly, one might imagine as first-stage reductions in Southern Europe:

1. Cuts of 15 per cent in Warsaw Pact personnel in the area, and of 10 per cent in NATO personnel, with provisions for dividing unequally any cuts in indigenous forces by paying a penalty of one or two per cent in additional reductions.
2. Similar percentage reductions in offensive ground-weapons, as defined for Central Europe, and in all types of aircraft.
3. Cuts of 20 per cent in all TNDV, including both ground-based and carrier-borne strike aircraft.
4. A freeze on the total number of naval vessels, by types, in the Black Sea and the Mediterranean, with allowance for offsetting increases if: (a) non-signatories such as France, Spain or Egypt add permanently to their fleets in the Mediterranean, or (b) the involved powers (which means mainly the United States, Britain and the Soviet Union) move in ships from elsewhere.
5. The redeployment from the Eastern Mediterranean of 10 per cent of the American and Soviet major surface combat units normally in those waters, leaving open the option of moving these to the Black Sea, the Western Mediterranean or elsewhere outside Europe (for instance, to the Far East).[41]

A set of measures such as these would bring about some reductions in tactical nuclear delivery systems, as desired by the Warsaw Pact. In addition to dual-capable artillery and *Honest John* rockets, the Greek, Turkish and Italian forces also muster about 200 dual-capable strike aircraft, which would be subject to 20 per cent reductions—with the option of replacing half of them with other strike aircraft which could not carry nuclear weapons, since the required cut-back in this type is only 10 per cent. A few additional planes could be involved if these reductions extended also to carrier-borne aviation, and the A-7Ds were either withdrawn or replaced. Since the Soviet Union has no nuclear-capable ship-borne aircraft, it is not unreasonable that she should be asked in return to withdraw one of the missile cruisers and escorts which normally form part of the Mediterranean

---

[41] The problem of how to compensate for overall increases in naval force will have to be dealt with separately, perhaps as part of an agreement covering world-wide deployments, and in another time-frame. See Chapter 6, pp. 194–6 and 200–4.

squadron and which, unlike their Western namesakes, carry surface-to-surface missiles as well as SAM or anti-submarine rockets. Thus, the reduction in nuclear-capable weapons systems would be large enough to be perceptible, if small enough to be largely symbolic.

To some extent this would be true of naval forces in general, at least as far as the United States and the Soviet Union are concerned, since each would have to redeploy only two major surface combat ships in other areas. However, Italy, Greece and Turkey, whose naval manpower amounts to better than 10 per cent of the men under arms, might also choose to make reductions which would lead to the deactivation of major surface combat ships, and certainly would have to cut somewhere in their navies. Given that NATO warships in the Mediterranean are five times as numerous as those of the Soviet Union, and that the American contingent, at least, could be returned rapidly to the Eastern Mediterranean, none of these changes will alter the naval balance, but they may impinge on the consciousness of the countries in the area.

The impact on immediately available air forces will be considerably greater, with NATO giving up almost 100 planes and the Warsaw Pact somewhat more (see Table 7, p. 258). Since almost half the NATO aircraft are fighter-bombers, however, compared to about one-third of Pact aircraft in the area, strike capabilities will be reduced further than mere numerical comparisons might suggest. This is one reason for seeking asymmetrical percentage reductions in air forces, another being that no cuts would be made in the Soviet Naval Air Force or in those regiments of the Tactical Air Force stationed within the Soviet Union—which could, of course, intervene rapidly in any conflict in Southern Europe.

The three NATO countries most concerned have slightly over 1 million men under arms; 10 per cent reductions would therefore have a greater effect than the proposed 15 per cent cuts in the considerably smaller Warsaw Pact forces. In fact they would mean dropping about 100,000 NATO soldiers, sailors and airmen compared to approximately 75,000 from the Warsaw Treaty Organization (see Table 7, p. 258). If the NATO reductions fell most heavily on Italy (which would accord with the wishes of Greece and Turkey) the ground forces of the last two would be only marginally affected. Since it is these which are in direct contact not only with Bulgarian troops but also those of the Soviet Union, this is perhaps prudent, as well as politically desirable. Perhaps more important is the fact that the measures proposed would bring about significantly larger reductions in Warsaw Pact tank strength (of the order of two to one). Even though this will not help those Turkish units facing Soviet troops in the Trans-Caucasus Military District, it should reduce the odds against their brethren (and their Greek counterparts) in Thrace, which is much more suitable for armoured operations. Moreover, since the South European members of NATO have proportionately less self-propelled artillery than their fellows in Central Europe, they may lose little from a 10 per cent cut in offensive weapons: since the 105mm howitzer is still the mainstay of their artillery, they may have to retire fewer guns of 152mm or over than would the more heavily equipped armies of other NATO members. In brief, the defensive capabilities of NATO should remain largely unchanged, partly because of the asymmetrical reductions in Warsaw Pact offensive weapons, partly because Yugoslavia will still remain as a buffer between Italy and the Warsaw Pact.

The defensive capabilities of the Warsaw Pact will also be little changed–although, admittedly, the sizeable cut in arms projected may force a change in plans for coping with any NATO attack in Southern Europe. While the heavier cuts in aircraft may seem disadvantageous, NATO will actually lose about twice as many strike aircraft (counting carrier-borne planes) and should therefore be less able either to blast a path for its own advancing units or to interdict reinforcements moving from, say Rumania, to the area endangered by a NATO attack. More importantly, the Pact will have made at least a beginning on reducing NATO nuclear-capable forces, which are the prime military (and psychological) threat to the members of the 'Southern Tier'.

These judgments apply, of course, to forces in being rather than those which can be mobilized or transferred from other theatres. Here also, however, the effect should be minimal, especially if both sides are permitted to (and choose to) maintain organized reserve units rather than discharging the personnel affected by mutual force reductions. Whether this is for good or ill, given the estimates mentioned earlier, may be a matter of dispute; what is clear is that mobilization capabilities in Southern Europe, as on the Central Front, will not be significantly affected unless and until one begins to deal with the forces inside the United States and the Soviet Union.

Whether these assessments are accurate is one thing; whether, even if they are, they will be acceptable, is another. The measures proposed do represent an effort to maintain 'undiminished security' by focusing on those elements which each side perceives as threatening and on those weapons most useful in offensive operations. They also represent an effort to balance quantity against quality, as in the provision for larger reductions of the less versatile and more lightly armed Warsaw Pact airplanes. Unfortunately, they also represent a reversal of the principle that the side with the bigger forces makes the bigger cuts–a principle which NATO has strongly endorsed (albeit on a selective basis) and which is implicit in the Warsaw Pact call for virtually identical percentage reductions by each alliance. Whether principle will stand in the way of practice cannot be determined unless and until negotiators at Vienna consider areas other than Central Europe.

Mutual force reductions in Northern Europe

As might be expected, the situation in Northern Europe differs markedly from that in either the Southern or Central regions. NATO ground forces are small, scattered and to some extent intermingled with those in Central Europe; for instance, the West German division north of the Elbe has as its primary mission the defence of Jutland, with elements of the Danish Army and of the Danish Home Guard. Similarly, Pact forces available for operations in this region are either deployed in Central Europe, like the Polish amphibious division and those Soviet tank and motorized infantry divisions which might attempt to seize southern Denmark, or stationed within the Soviet homeland, like the $2\frac{1}{3}$ divisions on the Kola Peninsula and their potential reinforcements from elsewhere in the Leningrad Military District (see Table 8, p. 260). The most significant components of both NATO and Warsaw Pact forces in the area are probably the navies. Although the Danish Navy operates primarily in the Baltic and the Norwegian Navy is small, the presence close by of the British Fleet means that NATO has immediately available on the northern flank a somewhat larger number of major surface combat ships, whereas the Warsaw Treaty Organization has more submarines and naval aircraft.[42] In time, the overall balance could be tipped further to NATO's advantage by the arrival of American and Canadian submarines and surface ships (including aircraft-carriers), with the Pact retaining superiority only in terms of submarines and of small surface ships.

The immediately available tactical nuclear delivery capabilities of the two adversaries are comparatively small, partly because the Soviet Union has not allocated many aircraft to the theatre, partly because the Norwegian and Danish air forces are not very strong. Moreover, the policy of these two countries precludes the introduction on to their territory in peacetime of nuclear warheads for their aircraft and other nuclear-capable weapons, which means that NATO would be compelled to rely initially on carrier-borne aircraft and/or on long-range elements of the land-based air forces in Britain, such as the F-111Es stationed there. While the Soviet Union does have naval vessels armed with surface-to-surface missiles which could deliver nuclear warheads against shore-based targets, these are more likely to be employed against shipping or against other naval vessels, as are Soviet naval aircraft.

---

[42] See Table 4, p. 251, which sets out naval forces by areas of operations.

Geographically, the NATO position is not dissimilar to that in Southern Europe, with one country (Denmark) largely isolated by water from potential attacking forces, and another (Norway) partly protected by the non-aligned buffer states of Sweden and Finland. These two non-aligned states, the two members of NATO and the Soviet Union, are all favourably inclined towards arms control, but such specific utterances as there have been relate largely to the establishment of a Scandinavian nuclear-free zone and to the conversion of the Baltic into a 'sea of peace', both of which were endorsed by the Soviet Union.

The military, geographical and political peculiarities of the region suggest that efforts at arms control concentrate on redeployments and assurances, rather than on reductions in forces–although it would help if East Germany deactivated its amphibious regiment as part of any arrangements affecting Central Europe, and Poland chose at least to reduce its amphibious division. As far as redeployments are concerned, these might take four forms:

1. The movement of any remaining East German and Polish amphibious elements, and of the Soviet Naval Infantry Brigade on the Kola Peninsula, to rear bases–or at least to areas some distance from the ships which would transport them in any amphibious assault.
2. The withdrawal from a Soviet–Norwegian border zone, say 25 kilometres deep on each side, of all weapons larger than machine-guns, mortars, and man-portable anti-tank weapons.
3. The delineation of restrictive zones in the Western Baltic and the Norwegian Sea within which only limited numbers of NATO and Warsaw Pact surface ships would normally be deployed.[43]
4. The removal of strike aircraft from northern Norway and from the Kola Peninsula, leaving only interceptors and other air defence forces–plus, presumably, the specialized light bombers, torpedo planes and reconnaissance planes of the Soviet Naval Air Force.

As far as reassuring measures are concerned, these could consist of:

1. Agreement to give warning of changes in deployment patterns, the conduct of manoeuvres, and other alterations in the basing of forces within 100 kilometres of the Soviet–Norwegian frontier.

---

[43] This would be easier if it were accompanied by restrictions on the deployment of missile submarines, which would obviate the necessity for the Soviet Northern Fleet to take advanced positions west of the Scandinavian Peninsula or to maintain sizeable forces at sea at all times. Whether the United States–and, even more, Britain and France–can be persuaded that this wine is worth tasting is perhaps another question.

2. An understanding that manoeuvres should not be held close to frontiers, or in positions from which amphibious assaults or tactical air strikes could readily be launched.

3. Acceptance of the principle that national means of verification can be employed without hindrance along frontiers and over demilitarized or restricted zones.

4. Arrangements for establishing observation posts in these frontier areas and demilitarized zones, the exchange of liaison missions, and other means of verifying reasonable compliance with deployment restrictions.

5. Recognition by each side that it must hand out information needed to satisfy the other that it is not violating the restrictions imposed —information such as the location of units which may be called into question, the types of aircraft in a selected air regiment, and so on.

The implications of first-stage force reductions

Militarily, the measures which have been suggested for Northern Europe would primarily affect the ability of either side to conduct small-scale offensive operations, such as an amphibious assault against northern Norway, or to launch a local surprise attack. They would not affect the ability of NATO or the Warsaw Pact to conduct large-scale operations, either with their existing forces or after mobilization. They could, however, reassure all states in the area about the intentions of their neighbours—and thus be even more valuable than changes in the military balance.

The measures proposed for Southern Europe would have a more significant impact on ground-offensive capabilities, partly because of the reductions in personnel and partly because of the corresponding cuts in offensive weapons. These reductions, coupled with reassuring measures such as limitations on manoeuvres, advance notification of troop movements, and so on, should make both allies and neutrals less concerned about probes, *coups de main*, intervention proceeding from disguised manoeuvres, or the massing of troops for political purposes. They should not, however, markedly affect defensive capabilities—nor the post-mobilization capacity of either side. In the case of air forces, the proposed reductions would cut current capabilities for both conventional and tactical nuclear war but would not markedly affect the balance following reinforcement by both sides. As for naval forces, the cuts would not have a significant impact on either current or post-reinforcement capabilities; their main effect would be primarily psychological.

The measures proposed for Central Europe would be more significant in terms of reductions in numbers, equipment and combat capabilities—but not in terms of the impact on the military balance.

What NATO might lose through cuts in stationed forces would be more than offset by the reduction in Soviet manpower, with the difference that the American Seventh Army could adjust to such reductions better than the Soviet Army Group in East Germany. The only problem is that reductions in indigenous forces, which are necessary to equalize the overall changes in military manpower, would impinge heavily on front-line NATO units, notably those of West Germany. And although the demobilized men could be added to the reserves, the loss of two or three German divisions might leave gaps in the front, especially since Dutch and Belgian forces would have to move forward into position after an attack had started.

To a large extent this potential weakening of NATO defences would be offset by the disproportionate cuts in Warsaw Pact offensive ground weapons, especially tanks. It could be further reduced by the additional warning time deriving from constraints on Warsaw Pact manoeuvre areas, from limitations on deployments in border zones and from other reassuring measures, should these be adopted. And it could in any case be minimized by measures to improve NATO forward defences, should the threat be deemed great enough to consider building strongpoints for militia, laying out minefields and taking similar steps.

As far as the Warsaw Pact is concerned, cuts in American and West German forces would markedly reduce both the ability of NATO to launch offensive operations and Communist concern that it might do so. Although the proposed reductions in tracked vehicles would disproportionately affect Warsaw Pact forces, which place greater emphasis on tanks, they would certainly not alter their *defensive* capabilities against NATO units, which would lose more self-propelled guns and armoured personnel-carriers. Moreover, even if Warsaw Pact members should choose to reduce the manning levels and readiness of their divisions, they could certainly block any assault by NATO units; in fact, since war is unlikely to come as a surprise, they could if necessary call up reserves and bring all divisions to full strength. If they chose to keep a lesser number of divisions at combat strength, they could still activate reserve units if necessary—minus the equipment withdrawn by the Soviet Union. And since both Czechoslovakia and East Germany have sizeable Workers' Militias, they need not fear that cuts of 20 per cent in their (or Soviet) troops would leave their regimes vulnerable to internal disorder.

The relatively equal impact of these reductions on active-duty forces in Central Europe does not, of course, mean that they would have an equal effect on mobilization capabilities. In general, the rate of build-up of the air forces of both sides would be unaffected, save for a slight further delay caused by the need to move back into

Central Europe those units withdrawn earlier. And even if one assumes that European members of NATO will improve the readiness of their reserve units, this would not in itself suffice to offset the advantages possessed by the Warsaw Pact, advantages which may be enhanced by the fact that Soviet troops need withdraw only across the Dnieper, while American soldiers would have to cross the Atlantic. Thus, should the Warsaw Pact choose to do so, it could outmatch the West in a build-up of conventional forces—just as it can now.[44]

It does not, however, follow that the mobilization and redeployment of Warsaw Pact forces would give its members an exploitable military advantage, even in a conventional conflict; as already mentioned, numbers are at best crude—and sometimes misleading—indicators of combat effectiveness. Moreover, no conflict in Europe will necessarily *stay* conventional, especially not one preceded by a massive build-up by the Soviet Union and sparked off by a large-scale assault. Hence, the fact that proposed reductions in conventional forces do not redress existing imbalances in mobilization capacities does not mean that they weaken the West militarily.

These cuts do not reduce—and may in some instances enhance—the ability of NATO to deal with *likely* threats to the security of Western Europe. Although NATO devotes most of its time and resources to coping with the *official* threat, that of a massive Warsaw Pact conventional assault, this is apparently not the most salient one—in fact, most West European officials and analysts seem more worried about invasions, probes and tests of will than about large-scale military operations in Europe.[45] The NATO forces in Southern and Central Europe would certainly be as capable of coping with lesser threats as

[44] There are some indications that the ability of the Warsaw Pact to do this may have been overstated. The former US Secretary of Defense, Dr James Schlesinger, testified that 'with our [US] aircraft capabilities, we are able to redeploy combat troops very quickly, in fact more quickly in a number of respects than the Soviets can in [*sic*] a location closer at hand . . . The difficulties of redeployment may be less for us than they are for our possible opponents'. US Congress, Senate, Committee on Armed Services, *Hearing* [*on the*] *Nomination of James R. Schlesinger to be Secretary of Defense*, 93rd Congress, 1st Session, 18 June 1973 (Washington; USGPO, 1973), pp. 6–7. Although Dr Schlesinger's statement must be considered in the context of a particular scenario and a given time-frame, it probably does hold good for the early stages of any competitive mobilization. And in the longer run, the Soviet Union might encounter difficulties in moving all her Category I divisions, providing Category II and III units with essential transport and logistic support, and maintaining the (frequently obsolescent) equipment now stockpiled for the use of these lower-grade divisions.

[45] See Chapter 2, pp. 40–2.

they are now–and those in Northern Europe more so, since Soviet strike aircraft would have been withdrawn from the northern part of the Kola Peninsula, and Polish and East German amphibious units reduced and/or redeployed. Moreover, the measures for establishing partially demilitarized zones along the Soviet–Norwegian frontier (and perhaps in Thrace), for limiting the use of manoeuvre areas near borders, for giving notice of major troop-movements, and so on, should all enhance military security as well as conveying reassurance about intentions as to the use of force.

These judgments about the military implications of particular arms-control measures are, of course, simply judgments–with which others may differ. Moreover, the effects of reductions in these (and any other) forces depend upon the perceptions of the countries involved. Those countries which are worried about their defences, fearful lest an opponent transmute a military edge into a political advantage, or concerned about the support they can expect from their allies in time of crisis, are naturally going to cling to the *status quo*; as the old saying has it, 'Better the devil one knows . . .'

Furthermore, some who might not worry about the consequences of first-stage reductions could be fearful of an uncertain future. One fear in NATO is that any reductions made under MFR may, by suggesting that the threat has lessened, lead to unilateral cuts in West European forces and/or the demobilization of American units withdrawn from Europe. Another is that the process of American withdrawals, once begun, might not stop short of complete disengagement, or at least of a cutback to levels which would lose all their military and most of their political significance. A third is that the Warsaw Pact may enhance its existing advantages by procuring better equipment, increasing the number of weapons stockpiled for emergency use, adopting of longer terms of service (which would improve the quality of its armed services) and by other measures which are easier for the Pact to take than for members of NATO.

Finally, some in NATO may be concerned lest growing Soviet military power should encourage more aggressive behaviour by the Soviet Union and weaken the will of the West to resist political pressures. This concern has become more pronounced since the recent build-up of Soviet strategic nuclear forces to rough equality with those of the United States. It has been sharpened by the growth of the Soviet Northern Fleet and by the presence in the Mediterranean of a Soviet squadron, which marks the extension of Soviet power and influence into an area which for long was a Western preserve. It has been enhanced by the continuous modernization of Warsaw Pact ground and air forces in Eastern Europe, since such measures threaten to tilt the conventional balance markedly against the Western countries, and may be further enhanced if this process continues. Thus, the members of NATO are concerned not only about direct military threats but about the indirect uses of military power to cover Soviet encroachments on vital Western interests, to overcome Western opposition to Soviet moves, and to discourage measures for Western political and military integration.[46]

On the other hand, the measures proposed would seem to contribute to the sense of security of the members of the Warsaw Pact, first by ensuring sizeable cuts in NATO forces (especially those of West Germany and the United States), and second, by inducing reductions in tensions. The comparable cuts in Warsaw Pact troops are not likely to be regarded as detrimental, especially since the Soviet Union would still maintain powerful forces in Eastern Europe. Although their concern about nuclear war might not be markedly alleviated by the marginal reductions in ground-based and airborne TNDV which were proposed earlier, the East Europeans would at least be no worse off. And they would still have the possibility of making further progress in subsequent stages of MFR, or, if the Soviet Union were willing, in separate negotiations on regional strategic forces.

ARMS AND SECURITY IN EUROPE

As suggested previously, no foreseeable outcome to the negotiations on mutual force reduction is likely to satisfy the Western allies. These may, therefore, be tempted to turn to other ways of ensuring their security: through rationalization of force postures, through the introduction of new technology and perhaps through the integration of their defence establishments. All these are feasible in some degree and some (such as the incorporation of precision-guided munitions into NATO arsenals) might even improve defence capabilities without unduly alarming the members of the Warsaw Pact. However, each of these has associated costs, economic, social, and in many instances political.

The probable difficulties and the potential costs of attempting to improve West Europe's sense of security by major alterations in force postures suggest that NATO should look instead at arms-control measures which could conceivably complement, or even substitute for, permissible increases in weaponry. One such measure would be a further reduction of offensive weapons in the hands of troops on both sides, including both deeper cuts in the categories already described and the extension of the restrictions to other types of weapon, such as self-propelled anti-tank guns above a certain calibre and fighter aircraft above a fixed weight. In addition, NATO might want to consider

46 See Chapter 2, pp. 42-3.

further limitations on the deployment of particular types of weapon in border areas or restricted waters, additional constraints on the conduct of manoeuvres, and other measures which would reduce the possibility of surprise attack. It might also want to consider agreements covering those weapons and facilities which could make possible a quick increase in forces, either for launching an attack or for exerting political pressure. For example, reductions in the number of airfields kept in permanent operating condition, as against those which are completely inactive or on a limited stand-by basis, would make the rapid deployment of additional combat aircraft more difficult. Similarly, cuts in tanks and other tracked vehicles in reserve would inhibit a speedy build-up of offensively oriented ground forces. Although such reductions would require limited monitoring of production facilities in at least Central and Southern Europe, and some transfer of reassuring information about stockpiles, this might be acceptable to both sides—particularly since ceilings on these weapons would be less asymmetrical than ceilings on those in the hands of troops.[47]

Ultimately, however, it may be necessary for NATO to consider global measures for the control of armaments. For one thing, these are the only means of dealing with some issues (like what to do with warships redeployed from European waters). They may also be the only way of alleviating concerns about the general modernization and improvement of Warsaw Pact forces—albeit at a cost, which no one in Western Europe has yet shown a willingness to pay, of imposing similar constraints on NATO forces. Thirdly, such measures offer one way of persuading the Soviet Union, as part of a package deal, to make reductions in, and accept restrictions on, forces based inside her homeland.

Fortunately, there is some prospect that the Soviet Union and her allies may be willing to make further cuts in their forces—and even to impose constraints on components of those forces untouched by any measure proposed so far. They themselves are affected by the interactions between the defence programmes of the two alliances and the resultant costs and by the implications of cuts for the improvement of political relations. They may also seek further reductions in weapons deployed in Europe, albeit of a different kind, and may be willing to trade off some of their advantages in conventional forces for cutbacks in, or redeployments of, NATO tactical nuclear delivery

---

[47] According to one source, the ratio of tanks in the hands of units in Northern, Central and Southern Europe favours the Warsaw Pact by more than 2:1 (18,450 to 8,250), whereas if those held in reserve by both sides are counted in, the ratio drops to about 3:2 (23,850 to 14,500). SIPRI, op. cit. in note 6), Appendix A, Table A 3, p. 83.

vehicles and/or nuclear warheads. Moreover, they are as much concerned with the global balance as with the regional one, and may realize that some important elements of NATO forces will escape control, unless this control is extended beyond the continent of Europe.

Whether these presumed interests will in fact lead to overall restrictions on armaments and armed forces is perhaps another question, the answer to which will be affected by even more difficult assessments of military capabilities, even more varied bureaucratic interests and even more diverse perceptions of security than the restriction of Europe-based forces. Although the answer is admittedly difficult, the question is so important that I will try to tackle it in the next chapter.

Chapter 7

OVERALL RESTRICTIONS ON ARMAMENTS

In the preceding chapters we have looked largely at arms-control measures which would immediately and directly affect armed forces raised or deployed in Europe, measures such as reductions in conventional forces and constraints on tactical nuclear weapons. It was, however, obvious from the start that European security could be affected by the strategic nuclear forces of the two super-powers, and hence that arms control aimed at enhancing that security would have to extend to these forces. It became equally obvious as the analysis continued that, unless limitations were also imposed on other super-power weapons and forces, Europe would remain insecure.

One reason is that actions taken outside Europe could directly affect the vital interests of the countries of Europe (as could the interdiction of sea traffic). Another is that super-power conflicts or confrontations anywhere in the world could spill back into Europe, thereby increasing the likelihood of war. A third is that a continuation of the process whereby the armed forces of the United States and the Soviet Union were left untouched (save for limitations on strategic weapons) while those of the countries of Europe were reduced would leave the latter in an even less favourable military position than at present.

This in turn could enhance European concerns lest military imbalances between their own and the super-powers' forces should make possible—or even incite—the exercise of political pressures. It could strengthen the belief that Europeans do not count for much in the eyes of the super-powers, that their interests can be disregarded with impunity. And it could exacerbate the feeling (clearly evident during the discussion of the Treaty on the Non-Proliferation of Nuclear Weapons) that the smaller powers are being asked to make all the sacrifices, while the super-powers go their own military ways.

One possibility would be to try to assuage these fears and alleviate these concerns by imposing overall restrictions on the armaments of countries belonging to the Western Alliance or to the Warsaw Pact. These could ameliorate both direct and indirect threats to European security, they could complement the kinds of measures previously discussed (which affect only some kinds of weapons and some types of forces), and they could conceivably also set the stage for controls on the armaments and military establishments of non-European powers—controls which must at some stage be adopted if their counterparts in Europe are to continue in effect.

The purpose of this chapter is to develop this idea further, by looking at:

1. Limitations on the size and the capabilities of NATO and Warsaw Pact forces which could alleviate concerns about military imbalances, both quantitative and qualitative.
2. Restrictions on the deployment of at least some components of these forces which could make more difficult the kinds of actions that might threaten European security.
3. Constraints on the employment of force, which might both reinforce deployment restrictions and minimize the likelihood of super-power conflicts and confrontations outside Europe.

LIMITATIONS ON THE SIZE AND CAPABILITIES OF ARMED FORCES

Overall limitations on armed forces may afford the best—if not the only—way of precluding worrisome improvements in an opponent's defence establishment. They may also be more flexible in their application, and hence more acceptable to the countries concerned, than specific restrictions on particular forces and weapons. They may have an impact on the military capabilities of the super-powers which could not be achieved by regional arms-control measures and, even if they do not, may erode the political utility of those capabilities by placing limits on the numbers of guns, ships and other symbols of power.

There are a number of ways of holding down the size of armed forces and constraining their capabilities, including limiting the number of men under arms, imposing ceilings on classes of weapons, restricting the amounts which can be spent for defence and controlling certain important activities, such as research and development. Each has its merits and its difficulties; each will apply unequally (and perhaps inequitably) to different countries; and each will be viewed differently by those countries. We will look first at the feasibility of each type of measure (i.e., its advantages and disadvantages), leaving its acceptability—and hence its implications—for later consideration.

The establishment of force levels

In the discussions on general and complete disarmament, which took place in the late 1940s and the early 1950s, each side put forward a seemingly endless series of proposals and counter-proposals for limitations on the number of men under arms. The initial concept took the form of proposals for percentage reductions in the existing forces, but it foundered over the question of verifying existing force levels as a prelude to making reductions–a procedure which the Soviet Union described as 'inspection without disarmament'. This led to suggestions for force ceilings which would be lowered during successive stages of disarmament until each state was left with only those forces required to maintain internal security.[1]

There is an aura of attractiveness about proposals to set force levels. They impose constraints on a highly visible and very important component of military power–the number of men under arms–and force levels are apparently simple and clear-cut. Moreover, such proposals seem equitable, gradations in power being accompanied by differences in force levels, and they allow flexibility in the allocation of manpower to different components of the armed forces.

In practice, however, many of these advantages turn out to be illusory. Force levels are by no means simple and clear-cut but give rise to an apparently endless series of questions. Should these levels apply only to members of the armed forces or to all militarized units, like the CRS (*Compagnies Républicaines de Sécurité*) of France or the Border Guards of Czechoslovakia? Should one count only men on active duty or those in the reserves as well? Should one count only men in uniform, ignoring civilian workers, civilian contractors and civilians employed in aircraft factories and other facilities? Moreover, how does one count all these various components? Should they be counted on an equal basis or on a sliding scale?

If ceilings on force levels do not apply to border guards and similar para-military formations, which are commonly equipped with light infantry weapons and frequently trained for combat rather than police missions, countries having such units would gain an advantage which could in some cases be significant: for example the East German Border Guards and Security Troops are four times more numerous than those of West Germany and equal almost a quarter of the strength of the West German Army. In addition, unless ceilings were applied to such para-military units, they could be strengthened to a degree which could largely offset reductions in military manpower. On the other hand, ceilings which did include para-military forces would penalize countries possessing them, since, whatever their utility in combat, it is not likely to approach that of trained soldiers or experienced seamen. In any case, such ceilings would be difficult to

---

[1] See, for example, the statement of principles of the Soviet bloc submitted to the Ten-Power Disarmament Committee on 8 April 1960, and that of the Western powers, submitted on 26 April 1960, cited in Bernhard G. Bechhoefer, *Postwar Negotiations for Arms Control* (Washington, DC: The Brookings Institution, 1961), pp. 541–3.

define (how should one count the Danish Home Guard and the Hungarian Workers' Militia?), hard to verify and virtually impossible to enforce. The best answer would probably be to settle for unilateral restraints on the size and equipment of para-military units, leaving each country free to adjust to changes in the forces of others.

As far as reserves are concerned, these can add considerably to the military capabilities of a country. Some states, like Switzerland and Sweden, design their armed forces around reservists. Some, like the United States, supplement their active duty forces with whole divisions drawn from the organized reserve, while others rely heavily on reservists to fill out units kept at cadre strength, as does the Soviet Union. Still others use them as West Germany does, to secure rear areas against raiders and saboteurs, or to replace men who may fall in combat. In general, reservists will be less well-trained than men on active duty and less ready for employment—which means they may be better suited to defensive rather than offensive operations—but differences in prescribed roles, levels of training and stockpiles of equipment will make some countries' reservists much more effective than others. Moreover, geography and communications nets will affect the speed with which they can be deployed, a factor of considerable importance in any confrontation in Europe.

Counting reservists would therefore impose severe constraints on some countries; not counting them would give considerable advantages to others; while counting them only in part would lead to endless arguments, as was the case during the disarmament negotiations of 1928–32. These considerations, plus the difficulty of verifying numbers of reservists, argue for leaving them untouched, at least for the present.

An even greater difficulty with curbs on military manpower is the fact that civilians can substitute for soldiers in a variety of roles, from barber to weapons artificer, and can perform almost every administrative task required for the armed services; in fact when the allies limited the *Reichswehr* to 100,000 men, at the Treaty of Versailles, they included in that figure civilian administrators, who were an integral part of the German logistic system. Attempting to count civilians does, however, considerably complicate the problem of verifying levels of manpower and could also cause inequities, because of the budgeting and personnel practices of the various countries (for instance, civilian teachers in schools for American children in West Germany are carried on the Department of Defense payroll). Moreover, counting those civilians on the payroll would not rule out other means of substituting for men in uniform. For instance, services for military establishments may be sub-contracted, either because it is cheaper or because it enables the mobilization of skills and resources not otherwise available (the radar research station at Orfordness, in England, was manned by American and British employees of the Radio Corporation of America under contract to the United States Air Force). It is questionable whether one could control this and other means of substituting civilians for soldiers without intrusive inspection, almost complete access to records and an impartial tribunal to hear complaints–none of which seems likely in the near future. Even then, one would not touch the vast industrial enterprises which carry on research and development, conduct tests, manufacture equipment, maintain and upgrade weapons and otherwise perform the functions which in an earlier and simpler age were carried out by military arsenals.

All this means that prescribing levels of men under arms is not simple and may not be effective in precluding the development of military capabilities. Moreover, force ceilings could create inequities, with advanced nations better able to shift to civilian support than underdeveloped ones, and totalitarian societies better able to do so clandestinely (e.g., by detailing tractor repairmen to work on tanks or providing laboratory facilities for military research). Further inequities may arise from disparities between the status of a state (and hence the force levels it is allocated) and the size of the territory it must defend, others from a state's geographic position between two hostile powers (like those of Poland in the eighteenth century, Germany in the latter part of the nineteenth century and the Soviet Union in the twentieth century). Furthermore, various states may combine in alliances, thereby aggregating their manpower totals, and presumably their military capabilities–for example, until 1949 the troop strengths of Britain, France and (possibly) of Nationalist China could be reckoned with those of the United States, whereas the Soviet Union stood virtually alone. A further inequity may stem from the fact that some powers will have more responsibilities than others, arising either from the retention of territories in various parts of the globe or (as in the case of France) from special relationships with former colonial states. And while one may argue that all forces in former colonial areas should be brought home, this is not like to happen soon.

The fact that inequities result from the establishment of symmetrical force levels suggests a considerable amount of bargaining before any ceilings on forces, equal or unequal, are accepted–if they ever are. But this does not mean that their imposition would not be useful. Force ceilings could have considerable symbolic importance, particularly if set below present levels; they could head off build-ups in armed forces by countries whose military strength is comparatively low; and they could affect the cutting edge of military capabilities (i.e., those men armed, organized and trained for employment in combat). They could also be accompanied by other measures—such as ceilings on classes of weapons—which could offset some of the disadvantages and make some of the constraints resulting from ceilings on forces more meaningful.

Ceilings on classes of weapons

Rather than attempting to control military capabilities indirectly—by establishing force levels, imposing budgetary restrictions and so on—one could move directly to set ceilings on types of weapons. This was the method used in the Interim Agreement on the Limitation of Strategic Offensive Arms, which, together with the Agreed Interpretations and Unilateral Statements of both sides, prescribed the total number of intercontinental launchers the United States and the Soviet Union could have, how many could be light and how many heavy, the circumstances under which ICBM could be converted to SLBM, and so on.[2]

Interested powers could similarly restrict tanks, planes, warships and other kinds of weapons. There are, however, greater difficulties here. Most of these weapons, unlike ICBM and SLBM, have multiple roles—the same basic aircraft serving as interceptor, fighter-bomber and reconnaissance plane. Moreover, qualitative differences in other kinds of weaponry may be even greater than qualitative differences among missiles: the capabilities of destroyers, for instance, vary not only with size but also with age, armament, electronic equipment, and so on. Also, while missiles are highly visible and easy to count, other weapons systems—particularly smaller and more mobile weapons, such as tank and artillery pieces—are not. Finally, tanks and aircraft, unlike ICBM, may be found not only in active units but also in the hands of reserve forces, in storage and in the process of production—so that cut-off points are much more difficult to determine.

Furthermore, attempts to impose ceilings on non-strategic weapons may encounter some of the same difficulties that marked the SALT talks, perhaps in exaggerated form. Although the number of ICBM at hand may be more than sufficient to carry out their wartime missions, the same cannot be said of the numbers of tanks, planes or guns, and ceilings on these kinds of weapon may induce (as the limitations on

---

[2] The Interim Agreement between the Union of Soviet Socialist Republics and the United States of America on Certain Measures with Respect to the Limitation of Strategic Offensive Arms, 26 May 1972, will be found cited in Chapter 4, note 1. Details concerning the numbers of missiles authorized will be found in Dr Kissinger's news conference of 27 May 1972 (*ibid.*), while the Agreed Interpretations and Unilateral Statements are cited in Chapter 4, note 2.

strategic armaments did) a shift to qualitative improvements, which might be even more meaningful in the case of conventional weapons than in that of nuclear ones. Since such ceilings would strike at many more elements of the armed services and their associated interest groups than did limitations on strategic armaments, they might also be correspondingly more difficult to introduce.

Nevertheless, increases in numbers of weapons can be perceived as threatening, as evidenced by the West German reaction to the introduction of some one thousand additional Soviet tanks into East Germany in 1973.[3] Moreover, in circumstances such as limited conventional operations numerical advantages could make a difference to the outcome and may be pursued for this reason. Such pursuit could be costly and could induce counter-actions by potential adversaries, thereby generating new tensions. There is thus reason for attempting to head off arms build-ups and to inhibit shifts in regional or local military balances.

Unfortunately, some weapons which are viewed as threatening, or which figure heavily in regional balances, are hard to control. For example, verification of ceilings on tanks would require some means of ascertaining with reasonable accuracy not only those weapons in the hands of both active and reserve units but also those in repair shops, depots and factories producing them. It would also require fair knowledge of both the capacity of these factories and the percentage of this capacity being utilized – otherwise production could be stepped up both quickly and with little evidence that this was taking place. It might mean concentrating production in designated plants. Certainly it would require some means of tracing the movements of the tanks produced and, more importantly, some indication of what was done with existing tanks – which could be retained in units, stockpiled for use in replacing combat losses, shipped overseas or scrapped, all with varying effects on weapons ceilings, military capabilities and political influence. Moreover, while normal sources of intelligence and (expanded) satellite reconnaissance could provide some insight into what was happening, it is questionable whether they would satisfy everyone that the prescribed ceilings were being honoured, and even more questionable whether they would provide evidence strong enough to support a charge that the ceilings were being violated.

In varying degrees this is also true of other weapons systems which are viewed as 'threatening'. Rockets and short-range missiles are larger, less numerous and presumably produced in fewer factories, and so somewhat easier to verify. However, even here the number

---

[3] These reactions were observed by the author, who in May 1973 was interviewing Federal Government officials in Bonn.

allocated to reserve units or in stockpiles may not be known with any precision, and the possibilities of exceeding ceilings without being detected—or (worse) leading opponents to believe that ceilings are exceeded when in fact they are not—may be quite high. Aircraft are obviously easier to monitor, despite their mobility, but may be more difficult to differentiate by type and armament, the problem here being not so much one of numbers as of capabilities. (For instance, conversion of the Soviet Air Defence Force's fighter-interceptor aircraft to multi-purpose planes could have the effect of increasing the combat potential of the Soviet Tactical Air Force by 60 per cent.) Thus, unless and until some forms of inspection are accepted, or extensive measures for providing reassuring information are adopted, the number of weapons systems on which ceilings can be placed will be relatively small.

One possibility would be to start with naval forces. In general these take a long time to build and are hard to conceal, and for both these reasons are relatively easy to control. They are useful militarily and also for the exercise of political pressures in what has come to be called 'gunboat diplomacy'. Additionally, many of the current concerns of NATO and the Warsaw Pact centre around naval forces, with the West worried about the build-up and redeployment of the Soviet Navy and the Soviet Union unhappy about the world-wide presence of the United States Navy. Finally, ceilings on naval forces could head off costly and perhaps unsettling arms races, since the Soviet Navy is continuing to build new vessels, and the United States Navy is scheduled to add attack submarines and to increase the number of major surface combat ships in operation.[4]

One way to impose a ceiling on naval forces would be to limit the numbers of ships by class, as was done at the Washington Naval Conference of 1922. This, however, would be very difficult, because the naval forces of the major powers are less homogeneous today than they were then, and differ markedly from one another. The imposition of limitations by class would require a definition of each class, as well as considerable bargaining over what each limit should be. An alternative which avoided this difficulty would be to set limits on tonnage, as was done for cruisers at the London Naval Conference of 1929, thereby enabling each signatory to build what ships it chose. Such ceilings would favour countries with large numbers of small but deadly patrol craft and few requirements for deep-ocean operations.

Another problem is that ceilings on the forces of each country would ignore both the existence of alliances and the effects of geography, which almost automatically give the Warsaw Pact predomin-

[4] *Rumsfeld Report, 1976*, p. 264.

ance in the Baltic and the Black Seas. If, however, ceilings took into account alliance relationships, either by adjusting national limits to reflect them or by setting totals for each side, NATO would either have to be granted much higher ceilings than the Warsaw Pact, thereby perpetuating its advantage, or it would have to make drastic reductions in naval forces. (See Table 4, p. 251.) Ceilings by region might be equally difficult: the Soviet Union would have only the Pacific to deploy ships withdrawn from Europe, whereas NATO could presumably transfer West German or Italian warships to the North Atlantic and could certainly add to those of the United States in home waters.

This suggests that any comprehensive arrangements for ceilings on naval vessels would be complex in nature and almost certainly asymmetrical in their impact, even if they simply froze navies at present levels. It also suggests that formal agreements to constrain naval vessels would be difficult to negotiate and slow in coming. For these reasons, it is recommended that one look instead to tacit understandings rather than formal agreements, to measures which would affect primarily the United States and the Soviet Union rather than to more widespread controls, and to concentration on a few types of ships rather than to comprehensive limitations. Since it is easier to halt further build-ups than to scrap existing warships, this approach might be tried first.[5]

Constraints on military budgets

Another measure which might be considered for limiting armed forces is the imposition of constraints on military budgets. Such constraints would be popular, since the cost of defence is increasing almost everywhere, even if not at the same rate as gross national product.[6] It is also at first sight a simple measure, since cutting the resources available to the military will obviously reduce military capabilities. For both these reasons, and because money saved on defence could be reallocated either for domestic purposes or for development aid to the Third World, there has been widespread support for this kind of measure.

In fact, constraints on military budgets are one of the most complex and difficult kinds of controls to apply. Firstly, not all expenditures for military purposes are found in the budgets of the defence ministries. In the United States, for example, some 20 per cent of the

[5] One reason for this is, of course, that it does not so directly threaten service interests. Another is that it enables modernization, through the construction of new ships and the retirement of old ones, and hence may be more acceptable—if less valid.

[6] *The Military Balance 76–77*, pp. 78–9.

annual budget of the Energy Research and Development Administration (ERDA) goes towards work on the production or upgrading of nuclear weapons, while it is believed that in the Soviet Union as much as 70–80 per cent of the All Union Science budget may be concerned with defence. Secondly, these budgets themselves include costs incurred on behalf of other agencies, with the American Navy providing both ships and men for the United States Hydrographic Service. Finally, it is very simple not only to hide items within the defence budget (as is commonly done for the intelligence services of most countries) but also to provide hidden subsidies to the military establishment, by, for example, the attachment of personnel without cost to the defence ministry, by the procurement of goods and services by other agencies, through measures for the remission of taxes, and in many other ways. All this means that verification of constraints on military budgets requires a considerable knowledge of the budgetary procedures of other countries, access to their records, the right to raise questions concerning the correlation between these records and what actually went on, and at least a limited right of inspection of both military and supporting facilities. And, even then, such verification can only be of an approximate nature.

Even if these problems were overcome, constraints on military budgets would still affect countries in different ways. Money used for military purposes does not have the same purchasing power as that spent in the open market: sometimes, as in countries with controlled economies, it will buy more, and frequently, as in countries with 'free' economies, it will buy less. The purchasing power of the defence dollar (or rouble) will also vary with what it buys; in some countries soldiers are paid very little, whereas in other countries, which rely on volunteers, they are paid considerably more, both actually and in relative terms. (For instance, it is estimated that manpower costs account for over 50 per cent of the American defence budget, against 30–35 per cent for the Soviet, even though the Soviet Union has almost 50 per cent more men under arms.) This suggests that one should consider constraints on military budgets which would hurt rather than cripple, would be general rather than detailed, and could conceivably withstand some of the stresses already noted.

One such measure might be a freeze on military budgets as a percentage of gross national product (GNP). This would affect directly only those countries planning new defence programmes of such an order as to require major increases in expenditure, as may be true of the Soviet Union and is likely to be true of the United States.[7] Such a

[7] Department of Defense expenditures for FY 1976 went up by about $9 billion or 10 per cent, more than the real increase in GNP for the same

freeze might also pinch when the cost of defence is rising faster than GNP, either because of inflation or because of 'gold-plating' weapons and equipment (i.e., incorporating refinements in design which are of marginal utility). Since the percentages of GNP allocated to defence by the NATO countries and those of the Warsaw Pact have in most instances either remained constant or declined, this type of freeze would not be unduly restrictive and for this reason might be acceptable. There are, however, problems in determining GNP over and above those incidental to verifying any constraints on military budgets. For example, the Soviet Union uses instead a concept called net material product (NMP), which does not allow for depreciation of capital equipment or for services. Even in those countries declaring their GNP, its true value is obscured by taxes imposed at various stages of production and by subsidies. Thus, both economists and accountants might have their work cut out to verify a measure of this sort.

An alternative approach would be to freeze budgets in terms of constant dollars (or roubles or marks), as this would more seriously constrain defence programmes. Such a freeze would largely mean that new programmes would have to be adopted at the expense of old ones, or as the outgrowth of more efficient administration of military establishments. It would also mean that an inflation of defence costs greater than that of the economy as a whole would have an adverse effect on defence programmes—more markedly so in 'free' economies than in controlled ones, where prices can be manipulated and where inflation tends to be hidden rather than reflected in the cost-of-living indices. Moreover, since very different programmes are undertaken within each defence establishment, the rate of cost increases is not the same as for the country as a whole, which raises the question of how to adjust for this—if, indeed, it is possible to do so. Even if these technical problems could be resolved, and effective controls instituted, they would probably have more of an impact on some countries than on others, and thus might not be acceptable.[8]

A more extreme measure would be to freeze budgets at their present levels, regardless of future increases in GNP or in costs. This would probably affect NATO much more than the Warsaw Pact, although

[8] For example, French defence expenditures increased by more than 70 per cent between 1970 and 1975, but the real value of these expenditures went up by only 13 per cent (*The Military Balance 76–77*, p. 82).

period. Outlays are scheduled to increase by about $10 billion a year over the next five years; however it is impossible to say whether defence spending as a percentage of GNP will also rise. (*Rumsfeld Report 1976*, pp. 252–3.)

even there the costs of equipment have been rapidly rising.[9] It would, moreover, have a serious effect on programmes requiring increased expenditures for personnel, like the American switch to an all-volunteer army. And while the Soviet defence budget has ostensibly shown a slight falling off over the last few years, one might expect that a budget freeze would also 'pinch' the Soviet Union, already engaged in an extensive programme of modernization. Partly because of the asymmetrical effects, partly because countries which control prices can evade it, such a freeze may not meet with universal approval.

Another possibility would be to freeze only one budget item, such as procurement costs or all capital expenditures. This would allow expenditure for pay and allowances to increase and would equalize major cost differences between the countries of Eastern and Western Europe–although at some risk that expenditures earmarked for personnel could be diverted to other purposes. It would hit hardest those countries with new weapons under development or with large forces in need of modernization, consequently having a marked impact on programmes of vital concern and serving as a useful complement to other means of limiting modernization, such as controls over research and development. It would, of course, be less effective than an overall freeze, especially as regards manpower. Moreover, additional problems might be expected in determining procurement budgets or the costs of capital expenditure. In fact, current American practice is to estimate the Soviet budget from the number of weapons produced and the types of facilities constructed, and, if this remains the only way of verifying a freeze on procurement budgets, it might be simpler to attempt to limit production in a direct manner.

If various types of 'freeze' on defence budgets are difficult to apply, reductions in defence budgets are an even worse problem. Defence expenditures are so uneven, both in absolute and in relative terms, that cuts which one country could absorb with little difficulty would impinge heavily on the military capabilities of another. Again, the greater strains resulting from tighter curbs on defence budgets may increase the pressures to offset these by manipulating prices and adjusting taxes, or by outright 'cheating' on the agreement. A further difficulty is to choose a basis for reductions which would not have an unequal impact on the two Alliances–thereby violating the principle of 'undiminished security'.[10]

---

[9] The price of tanks rose 250 per cent between 1959 and 1969, of aircraft 320 per cent, and of motor torpedo boats almost 500 per cent, according to Siegfried Schönherr, in *Wirtschaftswissenschaft* (East Berlin), 8 August 1969, pp. 1161–74, cited in Erickson, *Soviet Military Power, op. cit.*, in Chap. 2, note 5, p. 103.

[10] Although each side started out by stating its objectives differently,

In general, therefore, it is impossible to be optimistic about the practicality of constraints on military budgets, which are bound to be complicated, inequitable, intrusive, and difficult to apply in any satisfactory manner. This does not mean that budgetary constraints may not be imposed on a partial and voluntary basis, only that formal agreements to this effect are unlikely. Nor does it mean that countries may not make token reductions – perhaps in the form of mutual announcements of budget cuts, perhaps in the form of payments to the UN which would amount to a fixed percentage of expenditures for defence[11] – it means only that budgetary constraints offer little promise as a major instrument for the control of armaments.

Controls on research and development

An alternative way of limiting the capabilities of armed forces would be to place constraints on research and development (R&D) which would slow down the process whereby new weapons are introduced into national armouries. Since R&D leads not only to the design of new weapons systems but also to alterations which make old ones more efficient, and to greater speed of production, constraints on research will obviously adversely affect military capabilities. They will also affect other advantages gained for R&D, such as the ability to guard against advances which an adversary might achieve, the possibility of designing round the legal and political inhibitions on certain types of weapons (for example, by developing nauseous gases instead of toxic ones), and the capacity to influence allies and neutrals by the sale of advanced weapons and the transfer of military technology. Expenditure on R&D also serves to maintain a technological base which can support defence programmes and can strengthen and placate various interest-groups benefiting from these. Thus, constraints on R&D can result in a variety of consequences, some desirable, some undesirable.[12]

[11] The advantage of this proposal is that it would penalize those countries which keep up or increase their expenditure for defence, whereas the proposals to pay to the United Nations a percentage of monies cut from defence budgets would penalize those which reduce these expenditures.

[12] For many of the ideas in this and subsequent paragraphs I am

the Soviet Union and her associates seeking 'equal security' and the United States and her allies 'the present degree of security at reduced costs', both have apparently adopted the phrase 'undiminished security' as a guiding principle – even though they may interpret it differently. *See*, in this connection, the article in *Pravda*, 17 December 1973, reported by the *New York Times*, 18 December 1973, p. 3, and the statement by Ambassador Stanley R. Resor, *op. cit.* in Chap. 6, note 22, p. 4.

One reason for imposing constraints upon R&D is that these could alleviate concerns about the possible development of weapons which could upset the military balance, with MIRV and MARV (Manoeuvrable Re-entry Vehicles) as prime examples.[13] Another is that they might head off 'research races' between adversaries which could lead to suspicion as to each other's motives and intentions, creating further obstacles to the improvement of East–West relations–to say nothing of the prospect for agreements on the limitation of armaments. A further reason is that they could to some extent lessen the discrepancies between the resources and skills which the super-powers devote to military R&D and those available to the countries of Europe, consequently improving the relative position of European countries. And, as side-benefits, constraints may reduce costs and enable civilian authorities to gain a tighter control of programmes for weapons development.

There are, unfortunately, several problems involved in any attempt to constrain R & D. Firstly, research in itself is hard to control, since it is impossible to tell what knowledge may be relevant in an uncertain future and to prevent people from having ideas which may affect that future. (How could one conceivably have prevented Einstein developing his equation $E=MC^2$ for the conversion of matter into energy?) Again, if one attempts to impose constraints on a broad front, these will affect a wide range of activities, and lead to consequences which may not be intended, whereas to impose constraints on a narrow field requires accurate knowledge of the 'state of the art' in that field–including the state of the enemy's art. Another difficulty is that asymmetries in both knowledge and methods of research make it hard to design and install measures which would be mutually effective, and therefore even potentially acceptable.

The imposition of constraints on development would be just as difficult. Many weapons are being developed for civilian as well as military uses, like nauseating gases, or are the subject of research in both civilian and military laboratories, as is the case with the use of lasers for air and missile defences. Furthermore, some of the work on weapons systems carried out in military laboratories might have civilian applications, for example in the use of radar for tracking aircraft. And even if one could differentiate between military and civilian applications it would be impossible, without opening every

---

[13] For a fuller discussion of weapons which could be destabilizing, and why, see Chapter 4, pp. 70–6.

---

indebted to Dr Harry G. Gelber of Monash University, Clayton, Victoria, Australia.

laboratory to an adversary, to assure him that work on weapons development was not being carried on.

This suggests that new weapons should be caught in the stages between development and testing, or between testing and procurement. Those in the first stage are harder to catch but easier to stop, those in the second easier to catch but more difficult to stop, because one reason for tests is to enable decisions on procurement to be made.

One method of halting development before the testing stage would be to discuss with an adversary those innovations in weaponry which could be destabilizing—as could those leading to a first-strike capability. However, such a method would necessitate revealing to an adversary one's knowledge of potential weapons and concern at their implications, and implies enough trust in the adversary to do so. Alternatively, one could pass to that adversary reassuring information about development programmes, and perhaps permit him to monitor certain weapons tests on a reciprocal basis. This, again, might make him a free gift of one's own knowledge and techniques, and it assumes a degree of reciprocity which might be unreal, at least so far as major weapons systems are concerned.

Another possible approach would be to open defence laboratories, on an expanding and reciprocal basis, to visits from and exchanges of scientists and technicians, to the transmission of reports, and so on, as has been suggested by Dr Herbert F. York.[14] If successful, this would have two consequences: it would bring back into the mainstream of scientific endeavour those now engaged in military research; and it would insure both sides against military-technical 'surprises'. Such success would, however, depend on a high degree of trust, on more or less symmetrical application of the principle, and on a change of heart such that no country would build secret laboratories in unsuspected areas.

All this suggests that, whatever the desirability of measures intended to inhibit weapons development, they may be neither feasible nor acceptable. It also suggests that one must rely primarily on stopping these weapons at the test stage. There are essentially two ways of achieving this. One way is to impose limits on the number of tests or to ban certain types of tests; this would ensure that particular weapons cannot be developed to the point where they could be 'destabilizing'— this being the rationale for constraints on the testing of MIRV outlined in Chapter 4.[15] This can only be effective if it is known which

[14] 'Controlling the Qualitative Arms Race', in *Bulletin of the Atomic Scientists*, vol. XXIX, no. 3, (March 1973), p. 8.

[15] Chapter 4, pp. 72–3.

weapons systems are to be headed off. The other way is to permit tests of new weapons, perhaps under conditions and circumstances which would make monitoring by other nations easier, with the aim of pre-:luding production and/or deployment rather than development. This approach has also been taken up at the Strategic Arms Limitations Talks, where both the United States and the Soviet Union undertook to discuss and negotiate limitations on ABM systems based on different physical principles from those now in operation.[16] This, however, allows competition in the development of weaponry until such weapons have been tested, until both sides agree that they may be destabilizing, and until the side with the weapon decides that it is unlikely to secure a significant military or political advantage by going ahead with procurement. While this coincidence of interests may extend to laser missile defences, it remains doubtful whether it will extend to many other weapons.

An alternative approach would eschew openness and selectivity in favour of broad-based constraints, such as cutting funds for R&D. But, as has already been suggested, budgetary constraints are hard to monitor. Moreover, there is no essential correlation between cuts in funds and the development of particular weapons; a country may simply eliminate lower priority projects or concentrate on those where the research is nearer completion and the prospects for success appear more certain. On the other hand, it may make for fewer tests before procurement, with consequent effects on knowledge about the reliability of the weapon but with no hindrance to the design, which could, if required, be modified in the light of operational experience.

Probably the best that could be done (apart from limiting the numbers of weapons produced or prohibiting their deployment to particular areas) would be to adopt a combination of measures which would inhibit the production of new weapons. These might include freer exchanges of information and more extensive discussions of fears arising from technological innovations (it is possible to discuss the potentially undesirable implications of 'mini-nukes' without knowing, or saying, anything about their design). They might encompass limitations on weapons systems based on certain physical principles, as with laser anti-missile systems; even though this stimulated research into ABM based on other principles, the resultant weapons might be less efficient and hence less destabilizing. They could also include a possibly very effective constraint: the provision of advance information concerning tests of agreed types of weapons, coupled with authorization to observe and record such tests. Finally, they could, of course,

[16] Agreed Interpretations Concerning the ABM Treaty, the *New York Times* and *Survival*, *op. cit.* in Chap. 4, note 2.

include bargaining over the construction of such weapons. To a certain extent the United States and the Soviet Union are moving in this direction, but they still have a long way to go, even in the area of strategic weapons systems, and no other country has taken the first step.

Obviously, such measures would have but little effect upon the R&D programmes of the two super-powers: their funds would remain untouched, most of their progress would continue untrammelled, and only a few weapons would meet the criteria of importance and visibility which would warrant (and make possible) the monitoring of test firings. The impact upon military R&D in the countries of Europe would be even smaller, since none of these countries, with the possible exception of France, are building new weapons which might be called 'threatening'. In fact even more stringent controls over European R&D would have but little effect, since these countries depend heavily on both super-powers for advanced weapons and new technology.

This means that the United States and the Soviet Union have it in their power to inhibit weapons development by other countries with fewer resources and smaller research programmes. They could do this first of all by withholding information about technological innovations in weaponry–especially nuclear warheads, 'smart bombs', and active sonar, where R&D might be both costly and difficult. They could inhibit improvements in the military capabilities of other countries to an even greater extent by limiting the sales or grants to them of advanced equipment. Britain's nuclear force, for example, might be less effective if the United States refused to sell her *Poseidon* SLBM, and the air defences of Czechoslovakia and East Germany might be less efficient if the Soviet Union denied them SA-5 surface-to-air missiles. If, however, such restrictions are to be constructive rather than destructive, they would require a definition of areas where shifts in military capabilities presented a threat to European peace and security. More importantly, they would require a common awareness of this threat, sufficient to overcome all the influences working for the sale or transfer of military equipment. And they would require a system of monitoring which would comprehend not only weapons sales but also transfers of information–something much easier to conceal.

It is, therefore, difficult to imagine that the super-powers would apply such limitations on any scale. For one thing, their refusal to sell advanced weapons to their allies could have serious military–and political–consequences. Furthermore, such sales are sources of revenue for both the United States and the Soviet Union, help to keep their own production lines going, and are, in Eastern Europe at least, a major contribution towards the standardization of equipment. Moreover, there is a tendency among the advanced countries to co-operate in research, development and procurement projects, something which restrictions on the transfer of technology could curtail. Lastly, countries providing weapons and information gain some influence over countries acquiring them, and a certain control over the ways in which they may be used – advantages they might well be reluctant to forgo.

Evaluation

It would, therefore, seem that most of the measures intended to constrain armed forces and their capabilities bear more thorns than fruit, in the sense that their potential advantages are more than offset by the undoubted difficulties of implementing them, and by their asymmetrical effects upon the states which might be involved. Moreover, the interests of these states differ; the United States and the Soviet Union are seeking maximum flexibility in their defence establishments and are primarily concerned in bargaining with one another, while the lesser powers are uncomfortable about super-power 'decisions' and would like to impose constraints on the super-powers to match or offset any that they may accept in the course of mutual force reductions.

This means that there may be some pressure towards the establishment of force ceilings, with all their imperfections. The Warsaw Pact is certainly interested in setting overall ceilings which would help to equalize the numbers of men in the armed forces, where NATO still has a numerical edge despite the major reductions that were made to American strength following the end of the Vietnam war.[17] At the same time, certain of the Western Allies recognize that force ceilings afford one way of imposing constraints on the Soviet Union, and also that the ability of NATO to bargain over such force ceilings might diminish if and when changes in force structures like those proposed for West Germany come into effect.[18]

NATO is, however, likely to resist efforts to establish overall force ceilings which would erode its advantages in numbers, for three reasons. The first is that some of the men in these NATO totals are

[17] *The Military Balance 1976–1977*, p. 101.

[18] These would expand the Army from 33 to 36 brigades but would simultaneously reduce manning levels in the companies and battalions comprising twelve of these brigades. The net result would be to cut active duty personnel by 30,000 men (about 6 per cent), this phase-down being accompanied by a corresponding increase in the number of trained reservists available for immediate recall. See *The German White Paper 1973/1974, op. cit.* in Chapter 6, note 7, pp. 70 and 78.

largely irrelevant to conflict in Europe (for example, the Portuguese Army is not only geographically isolated but most of it is armed, organized and trained for anti-guerrilla operations rather than for combat in Europe). The second is the belief that the present imbalances are needed to rectify geographical differences between the alliances, differences which require some NATO member countries to keep troops in distant areas and all of them to maintain much larger navies than the contiguous and largely land-locked countries of the Warsaw Pact need. The third reason is, of course, that it is impossible to verify such force ceilings, even if one is talking only about counting men in uniform.

Conversely, there is no good reason for the members of the Warsaw Pact to accept force ceilings which would perpetuate such disparities, especially since they are being asked to cut back their troops in Europe disproportionately under mutual force reductions.[19] As the Soviet Union has noted, geography also imposes hardships on her, and she also must keep large numbers of troops in distant areas, notably along the frontier with China.[20] Thus the best one can hope for in the near future is force ceilings which would apply to specific regions, such as Central Europe, or perhaps to larger areas where the forces of the two alliances are in reasonable balance, as might be the case if the example of President de Gaulle was followed and one looked at the territory stretching 'from the Atlantic to the Urals'.[21]

Whether or not regional force ceilings are established, the super-powers (and especially the United States) would find it difficult to argue that their forces should remain intact while those of other countries are reduced. Moreover, there are economic reasons why each super-power might like to cut its own forces, and there are psychological, as well as military, incentives to seek reductions in the troop strength of the other. It is, therefore, conceivable that the United States and the Soviet Union might be willing to make phased cuts in their own military establishments, perhaps in the following manner:

[19] See Chapter 6, pp. 152–3.
[20] Y. Kostko, *op. cit.* in Chap. 6, note 18.
[21] NATO forces in Europe–excluding the Portuguese troops–total approximately 2·8 million men, compared to about 1·6 million for the Warsaw Pact of which about 560,000 are Soviet. Although the Soviet Union probably has more than half of the remaining 2·9 million men in her armed forces deployed west of the Urals, the difference in total strengths within the territory described is not so great as to rule out a possible decrease in Soviet force levels or some form of accommodation, such as the transfer to Central Siberia of a dozen Soviet divisions.

1. The demobilization of any units or men withdrawn from Europe pursuant to agreements on mutual force reductions.
2. Small annual cuts for a prescribed period of years.

The net result of the first measure under any of the proposals for MFR advanced so far would be to diminish somewhat the Soviet advantage in numbers of men under arms, of the order 3:2 now, over the United States. The net result of the second would be to establish *de facto* ceilings on an asymmetrical basis, the degree of asymmetry depending both on the magnitude of the cuts, and on whether they were made on a proportional or an equal basis. Although NATO might prefer the former, it should, given the overall balance in its favour and the desirability of placing some constraints on Soviet military manpower, settle for the latter.

As mentioned above, overall force ceilings, or those covering very large areas and forces, will be more important psychologically than militarily, since there are many ways of offsetting the effects of constraints on the number of men under active service and also serious difficulties in monitoring the effectiveness (and effects) of these constraints. To some extent, the military impact of any force ceilings could be enhanced by agreement on ancillary measures, such as the provision of information concerning the induction and release of conscripts, or the imposition of limits on the call-up of reservists. By and large, however, the problems of establishing and verifying limitations on numbers of men under arms are so enormous that such value as they may have is very limited.

Ceilings on classes of weapons are a more promising approach, partly because these are easier to implement technically, and partly because of the precedent of SALT. With weapons ceilings, however, one comes up against the problem that the interests of the two alliances are very different. Above all, the Warsaw Pact would presumably like ceilings on, or cuts in, NATO tactical nuclear delivery vehicles, especially strike aircraft. In addition, the Soviet Union has indicated some desire to safeguard her missile submarines, whose vulnerability could be decreased if NATO anti-submarine warfare (ASW) forces were constrained.[22] Moreover, the Soviet Union may have a special interest in restricting the number of American aircraft-carriers, which give the United States an advantage in any naval conflict and enable her to support military operations in distant areas.

Obviously, NATO would prefer to keep these weapons intact, since the land-based and carrier-borne aircraft outside Europe can quickly be redeployed to that area, should the need arise, and the ASW forces are considered essential to keep the sea lanes open. If weapons ceilings

[22] See Chapter 4, p. 82.

are to be imposed, NATO would presumably like them to cover tanks, guns and attack submarines, and not fighter-bombers, escort vessels and other categories of weapons in which it has both an advantage and a military reason for maintaining such advantage.

At first sight, this would seem to render unlikely the imposition of a ceiling on weapons, even if the problem of ascertaining the number of tanks and guns in the possession of an adversary could be solved. There may, however, be some overlapping interests which could lead to the establishment of a ceiling on selected classes of weapons which are more easily verifiable. Among these might be:

1. A ceiling on the number of aircraft-carriers the Soviet Union might construct, in return for which the United States would keep her attack carriers at the level of 13 and would limit the number of vertical/short takeoff and landing 'V/STOL support ships'[23] she would build. Although this would leave the United States with an advantage (and NATO as a whole with an even greater one) it would go some way towards equalizing the present imbalance.[24] And although the ASW missions of the two carrier forces are very different (with the United States concerned about protecting sea lines of communication and the Soviet Union with making strategic strikes by American and other missile submarines more difficult) there are ways of modifying those missions which might make agreement to curb carriers possible—one being restrictions on the deployment of SLBM and another, discussed below, being ceilings on attack submarines.

2. Rather tight ceilings on attack submarines, this time on a NATO–Warsaw Pact basis. As of this moment, the two alliances have almost equal numbers of attack submarines, with the advantage on the side of the Warsaw Pact only when submarines carrying SLCM are also counted.[25] If these fleets could be kept at present levels and

---

[23] The 'V/STOL support ship' is envisaged as a comparatively small, multi-purpose carrier employing V/STOL fighter/attack aircraft, ASW helicopters and perhaps assault helicopters for Marines or V/STOL strike aircraft. It would replace the smaller and less offensively oriented Sea Control Ship, eight of which had been programmed previously.

[24] The United States has 13 attack carriers, one of which is to be maintained only on a stand-by basis; she has no ASW carriers as such, but plans to construct an undetermined number of 'V/STOL support ships'. The Soviet Union has 2 ASW helicopter cruisers (the *Moskva* and the *Leningrad*) and one ASW carrier (the *Kiev*). She has under construction 2 additional ASW carriers. (*Rumsfeld Report, 1975–1976*, pp. 100 and 127.)

[25] As of mid-1975, NATO had 72 nuclear-powered attack submarines

old submarines scrapped as new ones were built, the Soviet Union could benefit in terms of the survivability of her missile submarines and the Western Alliance would benefit in terms of reduced vulnerability of surface ships and convoys. Given this, it is conceivable that ceilings on the numbers of attack submarines could have a 'ripple' effect, with NATO reducing or freezing its ASW forces rather than expanding them further,[26] and with the Warsaw Pact reducing the number of SLCM and the submarines carrying them.[27] Indeed, this area is so promising for so many reasons that it might well be the subject of special negotiation leading to reductions in present forces and/or to limitations on qualitative improvements, as by slowing the rate of replacement of old submarines by new or the shift from diesel-electric to nuclear-powered ships.

All this is, of course, highly problematical. Moreover, even if it came to pass, it would at best freeze certain types of ships, and might do no more than limit increases in these categories. However, given the asymmetrical interests of the two alliances and their differing perceptions of threat, a limited freeze on the number of warships is about as much as can be expected—or even desired—at the first stage of an attempt to impose ceilings on classes of weapons.

Greater pressure for constraints on budgets than for ceilings on weapons might be expected. Some of this pressure will come from

---

[26] Anti-submarine warfare was one of the areas singled out under the European Defense Improvement Program (EDIP), on which the West Europeans are spending approximately $1·5 billion annually. It is also an area wherein the United States has recently expanded her efforts, at an increase in costs from $2·6 billion to $3·6 billion per year. (The *New York Times*, 17 January 1974, p. 12.)

[27] One difficulty here is that the United States has under development a new SLCM which can be launched through a torpedo tube, thereby obviating the need to build special submarines to carry cruise missiles. (*Rumsfeld Report, 1976*, p. 69.) Since this development would significantly increase the strategic and tactical capabilities of American (and, in due course, other) submarine fleets, the Soviet Union may be reluctant to cut back on her cruise missiles while the West is deploying newer and better ones. And although the United States might agree to limit deployment, it is hard to see how any constraints could be verified. Once again, technology has outstripped arms control!

---

and 141 diesel-engined ones, and the Warsaw Pact 34 nuclear-powered and 173 diesel-engined attack submarines, exclusive of the 66 submarines armed with SLCM, which can also carry torpedoes or mines. Not all of these on either side are ocean-going, and, of course, not all of them would be available for operations in European waters.

countries which can control their own price structures, and hence manipulate their defence costs, in fact, the Soviet Union has proposed to the United Nations a 10 per cent reduction in all defence expenditures. More pressure will come from Third World countries, which see such constraints as both curbing the growth of super-power military capabilities and making resources available for foreign aid and investment to their advantage. Most of the pressure will come from the ordinary public in all countries, which may see budgetary constraints as acting as a curb to the military both in its domestic context and in its role as an arm of foreign policy, thus enabling a greater allocation of resources to be made for non-defence programmes – an attitude particularly strong in Western countries.

A probable reaction might be a series of pledges by various NATO or Warsaw Pact countries to freeze their budgets as percentages of GNP or in terms of constant dollars. Strenuous efforts might be made to hold down increases in costs, perhaps through tacit bargaining; to take one instance, the United States might announce that, all else being equal, she would have had to increase next year's defence budget by 10 billion dollars but that, thanks to self-imposed limitations on the Soviet defence budget, she will only require an additional 5 billion dollars. There might also be token reductions in defence budgets (although the trend in many countries is away from this)[28] or diversions of resources from them in the form of payments to the United Nations, as suggested earlier. However, in view of the unworkability of budgetary constraints and of their markedly unequal effects on different countries, one cannot expect these to go very far.

The same could be said of controls on research and development, not because these are in themselves undesirable but because they are largely impractical. Moreover, the individual interests of countries tend to move them in markedly different directions. Most of the Western Allies would like to modernize their armed forces but to inhibit the Warsaw Pact countries from doing likewise – probably the reverse is also true. Nor are European members of NATO likely to accept restrictions either on their own research or on the transfer of technology, resulting in their falling further behind in a military capacity or in handicapping the establishment of a European Nuclear Force. The United States may wish to maintain disparities in certain fields, like nuclear weapons technology, but not in, say, air-defence radar, and here may be equally unwilling to accept broad controls.

[28] One reason for the upward trend in some Western defence budgets is inflation, which makes increases largely meaningless. Thus, United States defence expenditure from 1970 to 1975 went up by 14·3 per cent in current dollars, but down by 17·5 per cent in constant dollars (*The Military Balance 76–77*, p. 82).

Given both the technical and the political obstacles to the imposition of realistic constraints on R&D, one might have to settle for something less. This 'something less' should at the very least consist of arrangements to define those categories or types of weapons which could have a destabilizing effect, either because they could alter the military balance significantly or because of their psychological impact. This process could be undertaken by a Committee on European Security, if one were established, by the Twenty-Five Nation Disarmament Committee or by *ad hoc* groups including the five nuclear powers–though not, at any rate for the present, all in the same group! The participant countries should also make provision for the monitoring of weapons tests which fall into the designated categories, perhaps by the super-powers themselves, with the results being made available to each country, or by relatively small teams with the super-powers contributing personnel and equipment. They should also try to develop an understanding that, should weapons falling into the dangerous categories be tested, negotiations in an appropriate forum would be opened immediately on measures to preclude their production or deployment.

Although other restrictions might be imposed, they do not seem very probable–nor really very rewarding. Whether we like it or not, we must look to internal economic, political and bureaucratic pressures, and to interactions between East and West, to set limits on the sizes and the capabilities of the armed forces of the two alliances. In this case, at least, arms control will follow *détente*, not precede it.

RESTRICTIONS ON THE DEPLOYMENT OF FORCES

Limiting the size and the capabilities of armed forces is admittedly the most permanent way of reducing their utility, but not the only one. It can also be achieved by precluding the establishment of new bases, by imposing restrictions on deployment and by requiring advance notice of major troop movements, of the conduct of manoeuvres, and so forth. As I suggested earlier, such measures can inhibit the application of force, an achievement which may be all the more significant in view of the difficulty of constraining military capabilities. More importantly, they might increase confidence in the intent of an adversary, and hence enhance a country's sense of security–as most recently shown by the restrictions on the deployment of Egyptian and Israeli troops and weapons in the area east of the Suez Canal. In this section, therefore, I will look at the attractions and the disadvantages of these kinds of measures, with particular reference to their possible application in Europe and/or to the forces of the two super-powers in other parts of the world.

Precluding the establishment of new bases

Bases in other countries can obviously serve a variety of purposes. They can provide facilities for overhauling ships and other major items of equipment, obviating the necessity of taking them home for rehabilitation. They can provide for the storage of arms and equipment which might be urgently required in areas far from the source of supply. They can house troops which might be needed to defend an ally, or can service aircraft shadowing the movement of naval vessels. They can serve as communications centres, as places from which to monitor test firings of missiles, or as sites for carrying out these and similar tests. In a variety of ways, then, bases overseas both extend and multiply military capabilities.

They may also extend and multiply political influence. This follows in part from the common interests and the shared perceptions of threat which led initially to the establishment of such bases. It reflects the fact that the mere presence of foreign troops enables the state providing them to limit the options open to the host country. It stems also from the money spent and the opportunities for employment offered at these bases, and from the economic and military aid which almost invariably accompanies their establishment. And, while this influence is by no means one-sided, it may be important enough to justify the retention of bases long after their military usefulness has declined.

In the post-war period it was the Western Allies—and in particular the United States—who built and manned such bases, and the Soviet Union who protested at this activity. She tended to see these bases as being directed against herself (as in some sense they were, particularly during the early 1950s) and to inveigh against the 'ring of steel' which the 'imperialists' were attempting to forge around her. Partly for military reasons, therefore, and partly for political and psychological ones, she has called over the years for the withdrawal of all foreign troops and for the abolition or curtailment of bases on foreign soil. The Soviet Union, moreover, put pressure on different countries to revoke the base rights granted to the Western Allies or to restrict their use, as did Mr Khrushchev when he threatened to bomb the Pakistani airfield from which U-2 reconnaissance planes took off for their flights over the Soviet Union.

In the past, the members of the Western Alliance have rebuffed or turned a deaf ear to these threats and have encouraged their supporters in the Third World to resist Soviet pressures. The situation has, however, changed. With the granting of independence to most colonial areas, and with the accession to power there of nationalist governments, Western base rights have been cancelled or curtailed, as in the case of Algeria, Libya, and Kenya. The facilities which the Western Allies are now building are on a relatively small scale and for specialized purposes. Furthermore, the United States, which has easily the most, and the most widely scattered, of these bases, has been voluntarily relinquishing or reducing some of them in accordance with the 'Nixon Doctrine' for the Pacific. At present it is the Soviet Union which is probably interested in finding air and naval bases, to replace those lost in Egypt, to substitute for the open anchorages occupied by her Mediterranean squadron, and the better to enable her to maintain a sizeable naval presence in the Persian Gulf and the Indian Ocean. Should she significantly extend her system of bases, this might induce intensified counter-action by the West and could lead to political confrontations (if not military ones) east of Suez, where the Soviet Union is already diplomatically and economically active.

It is obviously too much to expect that the Soviet Union will give up her efforts to penetrate this or other areas, but the undesirable consequences of emphasizing the military aspects of Soviet foreign policy and the difficulty of maintaining an effective military presence in the face of Western opposition may incline her to proceed cautiously. Equally, it is perhaps too much to expect the members of the Western Alliance to abandon their bases, a measure which, if taken literally, could mean the end for American troop deployments in Europe. However, the problems confronting the West, in the Mediterranean and elsewhere, are so severe that some members of the Alliance might be willing to strike a bargain with the Soviet Union over bases. In this way both sides could proceed, tacitly if not formally, to alter the nature of any competition for influence and to minimize the possibilities of confrontations which would extend back into Europe itself.

Although any such bargains can only be in the realm of hypothesis, it would seem that it might be in the interests of both sides:

1. to recognize the existence of areas considered vital to each, where they would not establish new bases, as distinct from naval forces on more or less permanent station.
2. to refrain from deploying to these areas selected weapons which could be considered particularly threatening by the other side: a move which could preclude the reappearance of Soviet missile submarines off Cuba, the basing of American F-111E strike aircraft in Greece or Turkey, and the stockpiling of nuclear warheads in any additional countries.
3. to give notice of changes in deployment patterns at existing bases, where these would involve major shifts in the numbers of men and arms there.

4. to discuss in advance the establishment of any new bases, explaining their nature, their purpose and the duration of the period for which they would be active.

This could conceivably lead ultimately to a ban on all new bases (at least where these are to house combat elements, as distinct from units concerned with communications and supply) and to a phase-down of selected Western bases in areas close to the Soviet Union.

If such a bargain were struck it could markedly alleviate Western concerns at the establishment of Soviet bases in such key places as Mers-el-Kebir and Aden, and could reduce worries about possible Soviet naval operations in the Persian Gulf. It could head off tests of determination such as occurred in 1971, with the 'on-off' construction of shore facilities in Cuba for Soviet submarines. On the other hand, it could enable the Soviet Union to preclude any build-up of American strike-aircraft in the Eastern Mediterranean, or any establishment of a base for American missile submarines in the Indian Ocean, so lessening her perception of threat.

Admittedly, both sides would have problems with such a bargain—one being the difficulty of reaching agreement on those areas designated as vital. More specifically, the Soviet Union might have to sacrifice not only some of her ability to exercise political influence, but also something of her capability for counter-intervention or for operations against American missile submarines. Moreover, she would, virtually of necessity, have to accept asymmetries in base structures, since she is a late-comer in establishing overseas bases. As for the United States, on whom the brunt of the constraints would fall, she might have to resort to more expensive and time-consuming measures for the maintenance of naval forces in distant waters, and would certainly lose some of her capacity for reassuring anxious allies or influencing doubtful neutrals. And those allies who are already anxious might become more so, even if the restrictions on the redeployment of American forces were not so tight as to prevent demonstrations of support in the event of a new crisis in the area.

It may be hoped, however, that the measures I have outlined could serve to avoid confrontation and to induce restraint in the exercise of force, thus obviating the likelihood of the agreement restricting the establishment and use of bases—and other agreements as well—being denounced. Furthermore, one may hope that such measures might establish a pattern of co-operation having implications far beyond the geographical and technical areas initially covered. For example, restrictions on a permanent military presence in 'vital' areas could be extended to elements not covered in the initial agreement, such as naval forces. Inhibitions on the deployment of 'threatening' weapons to new areas considered vital could be applied to old areas like Central Europe. Additionally, notification of changes in deployment patterns at existing bases outside Europe could also extend to those countries in Europe where troops are currently stationed.

Setting up restricted areas

As I suggested above, there are undoubtedly geographical areas which may be vital for the security of NATO and the Warsaw Pact, either because denial of access would cripple members economically–as in the case of a Soviet blockade of the Persian Gulf–or because an enemy presence in the area would constitute a clear and present danger–as would stationing American air and naval forces in northern Norway. The establishment of even narrow zones from which particular forces would be barred, or within which particular types of weapons could not be deployed, could provide reassurance as to enemy capabilities–and hence, in this suspicious world, as to enemy intentions. Broader restrictions, either on a unilateral or an agreed basis, could have even more important effects on capabilities and more favourable ones on perception of intentions.

One measure which could have these effects would be the imposition of restrictions on the deployment of offensive ground-force units along the borders between two countries. As an illustration, the deployment of tank divisions well to the rear means that they are both less menacing to an opponent and the better positioned for a defensive role, which might involve their moving to threatened parts of the front once fighting began. To a lesser extent this is also true of self-propelled artillery, units transporting mobile bridges and all those other elements essential for the support and maintenance of offensive operations; in fact, their concentration in forward areas is generally considered as an indication that an attack is imminent, and consequently as a cause for concern. Similarly, landing craft which are only four to eight hours away from prospective target areas are more of a threat than those at a greater distance, and amphibious troops kept close to these landing craft (and hence ready for action) may appear more threatening than those which are dispersed. Again, short-range nuclear-capable delivery vehicles deployed at some distance from frontiers are less able to shatter enemy strong-points and pave the way for assaults by mobile forces, and may therefore seem less of a danger.

To some extent, restrictions on the forward deployment of aircraft can have a similar effect. If strike aircraft are based far to the rear, this means that they cannot reach certain targets without redeploying, a factor which reduces both military utility and psychological visibility. Furthermore, even if they attack without redeploying, an adversary will have longer warning of their employment than he would if they were stationed well forward, and can conceivably prevent their penetrating deeply into his air space, with or without nuclear weapons. On both these counts, rearward basing has a more reassuring aspect. As an illustration, the Soviet light bombers which are stationed in the western Soviet Union are less of a threat to NATO than are their counterparts in Central and Southern Europe. Similarly, the aircraft aboard an American aircraft carrier deployed in the western Mediterranean are less of a threat to the Soviet Union than those on one in the Aegean Sea. (Admittedly, the carrier in the western Mediterranean is less reassuring to the allies in the eastern Mediterranean and less able to enter into action quickly, should this be required; however, it may be possible to give reassurances, without losing all the advantages of carrier-borne aircraft, by reducing the complement of planes when the ship sails into certain restricted waters.)

However, given the mobility of aircraft (and, to a lesser extent, of ships which carry them), restrictions on forward deployment may have to be complemented by limitations on military aircraft stationed in a particular theatre. The observance of ceilings on numbers of aircraft in a region, and the avoidance of unexplained fluctuations in numbers (such as precede an attack or go with an attempt to overawe an opponent) may both be helpful in reassuring that opponent. And even those who take little comfort from these efforts to be reassuring may find this disadvantage offset by the ability to communicate intent and to signal resolve in time of crisis by the redeployment of aircraft.

Restrictions on the deployment of naval forces could present more considerable difficulties. For one thing, these forces are to some extent tied to bases, which means that they cannot be denied access to, or passage through, the seas adjacent to those bases. Another reason is that they must in some instances be kept in waters distant from their homelands if they are to protect these from attack, as is the case with the Soviet Northern Fleet, which has a mission of precluding strikes by American, British and French missile submarines. A third difficulty arises from the fact that the political utility and visibility of warships is so high that even minor changes in deployments tend to be viewed as important.

This is all the more reason for avoiding any movements which could have disruptive effects, such as the entry of Soviet submarines into Norwegian fjords. It points towards the establishment of both 'sanctuaries' (where only certain types of warship would be permitted) and restricted areas, from which particular types of ships would be barred, except for the right of innocent passage after advance notice has been given. And it suggests that these restricted areas be set up in such a manner as to minimize possible confrontations between opposing navies: for example, by establishing parallel but distant east–west channels through the Mediterranean for the use of the Soviet and American squadrons there.

Restrictions on deployments should apply particularly to any troops, planes or other weapons removed from Europe. Certainly the Soviet Union would not be happy if American fighter-bombers taken from West Europe were transferred to Japan, any more than Turkey would be if two Soviet divisions withdrawn from West Germany ended up in the Trans-Caucasus. In the case of the Soviet Union one might go further and say that the stationing of these divisions deep inside the country would have favourable psychological consequences, even though, given the size of the forces already garrisoned in the western Soviet Union, this might not significantly affect Soviet military capabilities. In short, restrictions on the redeployment of units involved in force reductions might be even more significant than restraints on elements not so involved.

Of similar consequence would be measures for restricting military and naval exercises. Prohibiting manoeuvres in border areas could diminish fears that these manoeuvres could cloak a surprise attack; even if such restrictions inconvenienced military commanders (as the loss of tank ranges in West Germany near the zonal boundary might do), such inconvenience might be overshadowed by their reassuring effect. Setting ceilings on the sizes of manoeuvre forces in forward areas could also help, as those involving 40,000 men may not seem nearly as threatening as those involving 200,000. So could limiting the time span within which manoeuvres are carried out, in order that such manoeuvres could not be used to justify a semi-permanent troop build-up, or to buttress political pressures against another state, as in the summer before the Soviet occupation of Czechoslovakia. And so, of course, could restrictions on the types of forces engaged in manoeuvres–those bringing offensive weapons and elements near the frontiers of another country being obviously more of a threat, as would be the case in the off-loading of Soviet naval infantry near the Norwegian coast, or the movement of American aircraft carriers into the Sea of Okhotsk.

All this is not to say that restrictions on the deployment of forces and constraints on the introduction of weapons have no drawbacks. The partial demilitarization of border areas, or limitations on the size and number of weapons therein, may weaken defences against probes or incursions. Restrictions on the forward deployment of aircraft and naval vessels could reduce the ability to cope with a surprise attack, as well as the ability to launch one. Inhibitions on the redeployment of units may preclude moves which could be reassuring to an ally in a crisis not caused or marked by a military build-up on the part of the adversary (in other words a crisis similar to those which have frequently occurred at Berlin). Furthermore, all these types of constraint may operate unevenly because of military and geographic asymmetries between the two alliances. More importantly, they may have different political and psychological consequences, since each alliance has perceptions of the other which will influence its reactions. It may, however, be possible to test such restrictions in a limited area, extending them if they prove fruitful, halting them if not.

Monitoring deployment restrictions

Along with the imposition of restrictions on deployment should go measures to monitor them. In view of the depth of fears and suspicions in Europe, no country is likely to rely on the word of another that it is faithfully observing all limitations on the deployment of forces. Moreover, given the fact that many of these limitations may be self-imposed, or may be the result of tacit bargaining rather than formal agreement, their implementation may be imprecise and their application misunderstood. It would therefore seem useful to arrange for a flow of information and communication which could minimize uncertainties and allay fears.

Perhaps the easiest way of doing this would be by providing reassuring information. If, for example, country X questioned whether country Y had really withdrawn all tanks from a prescribed border zone, Y could transmit to X aerial photographs of the zone, the validity and timing of which could readily be verified. If the photographs showed no tanks, X would know either that they had not been there at all or that they had been removed before the photographs were taken—which would be a gain of sorts. Alternatively, Y could announce the location of the units suspected of being in the border area, inviting observers from X (or Z) to verify that they were in fact elsewhere. In these and other ways, one state could put to rest the doubts of another without establishing extensive and extra-national inspection systems.

Such reassurance could be more meaningful, and restrictions on deployment more effective, if manoeuvres were announced well in advance (so that they could not be associated with particular crises) and if notice were given of major changes in troop levels in a given area. The movement of two or three Soviet divisions from the Oder to the lower Elbe might not be important to the Russians but would be to the Danes, just as the dispatch of two additional wings of American fighter-bombers to Western Europe would be important to the members of the Warsaw Pact. Where these movements are routine, nothing will be lost by informing the world of what will happen; where they are deliberately designed to indicate determination, something may well be gained. And, while notices of troop movements can be used to influence crisis outcomes (as was the American announcement of the dispatch of reinforcements to the Seventh Fleet in 1958 during the Quemoy crisis), the fact that they can be used to unnerve an adversary argues all the more strongly for not doing so inadvertently.

Additionally, confidence in the effectiveness of restrictions would be increased if the manoeuvres themselves were monitored by observers, or the larger areas covered by deployment restrictions were open to inspection by liaison missions (as, indeed, was agreed at the CSCE). While these measures could help in gathering intelligence–which all military commanders want for themselves but wish to deny to their adversaries–they could also serve to verify troop and weapons levels and to insure compliance with either agreed or self-imposed constraints on deployments. They could provide information independent of that gathered by national intelligence agencies, which would possibly be more meaningful politically. In time, as these observation teams increased in status (and perhaps took on a multi-national character), they could increase the political obstacles to employment of force by giving clear evidence of the responsibility for violations of deployment restrictions.

Finally–and the sequence is deliberate–provision could be made for verification by national means, such as aerial observation. To a certain extent this could be accomplished by agreement not to interfere with aircraft with side-looking radar flying along (but not over) borders, and three (or twelve) miles from coastal frontiers. It could also be done by allowing either periodic overflights of given areas (such as border zones) or a small number of 'on call' flights through these zones, along main lines of communication or over certain prescribed areas which might serve as jump-off points for attacks or sites for the build-up of supplies and equipment. The aim here would be to complement other national means of verification (such as the establishment of observation posts and the use of reconnaissance satellites) in ways which would provide the maximum of reassurance against gross violations of restrictions on deployments without at the same time acquiring the sort of detailed information about weapons systems and military installations which has, quite understandably, been regarded as unacceptable.

Aside from this last possibility, it is hard to see drawbacks to the measures proposed, which are both modest and non-intrusive. This judgment is, however, based on another: that both the countries of Europe and the super-powers are willing to give up certain uses of force in the interest of enhancing security. This may be so in principle, but in practice it may not hold, since definitions of security may differ and beliefs in the utility of force persist.[29] Thus, the major question concerning both the monitoring of deployment restrictions and the restrictions themselves is how acceptable they might be.

Acceptability of restrictions

In the past the Soviet Union and her allies have made strenuous efforts to create nuclear-free zones, to preclude the movement of Western naval vessels through contiguous waters, such as the Black Sea, to bring about the dismantling of bases and to arrange for the withdrawal of all foreign troops to their respective homelands. It is unlikely that this latter proposal will be pushed as hard in the future as it was in the past, since this is happening anyway (at least outside Europe) and since the Soviet Union may not be as ready to reciprocate as she was ten or fifteen years ago. She may, in fact, be less anxious now to see a complete withdrawal of American forces from Europe, partly because they may exert a stabilizing influence and partly because their presence may be reassuring to the other members of NATO-contributing in both ways to the security of the Soviet Union and her allies in Eastern Europe. The Warsaw Pact may still, however, be interested in preventing the establishment of new Western bases and reducing the number of old ones, for which reasons it may espouse arrangements like those suggested earlier, which could speed up the process of withdrawal and would at least limit the uses to which remaining bases could be put.

Presumably the members of the Warsaw Pact would still wish to impose restrictions on the NATO forces remaining in Europe or abutting on their frontiers elsewhere, and on the weapons with which these are armed. If they cannot get agreement on the establishment of broad nuclear-free zones (or weapons-free zones) they might accept narrow ones. They may be willing to engage in tacit bargaining about the deployment of troops and weapons within their own territories and those of NATO countries. Furthermore, the Soviet Union has already agreed at the CSCE that she give advance notice of manoeuvres (if not of troop movements) and to 'invite other

[29] They seem to have persisted in the American–Soviet crisis of 24–25 October 1973, which arose out of an apparent threat by the Soviet Union to intervene unilaterally in the Egyptian–Israeli conflict if the United States did not preclude Israel from exploiting further the military successes gained after the initial (and abortive) armistice of 22 October. This threat, raised by a concentration of Soviet airborne forces in the southern part of the Soviet Union, led the United States to place all her forces, including the Strategic Air Command and the *Polaris/Poseidon* fleet, on a state of alert. See the articles by Bernard Gwertzman and Hedrick Smith in the *New York Times*, 31 October 1973, p. 17.

participating states . . . to send observers to military manoeuvres'.[30] It is perhaps not too far from this to agreements to install observation posts (another long-standing Soviet proposal) and to the acceptance of other means of verifying restrictions on deployment—at least so long as these are small-scale, unobtrusive and not sponsored by the United Nations or some international disarmament organization.

In the past the West has been cool to demilitarized zones, nuclear-free zones, 'seas of peace', and other deployment restrictions—all of which it saw as efforts to reduce Western military power, to inhibit freedom of movement, and to expose some of the Allies to new threats and pressures. It will probably continue to oppose large-scale arrangements such as a Scandinavian Nuclear-Free Zone, but it may be willing to readjust its own ground and air force deployments within the European region in return for similar adjustments by the Warsaw Pact—at any rate so long as these do not rule out a more integrated defence of Western Europe. It may also be willing to experiment with narrow weapons-free zones—if not along the boundary between East and West Germany, then along other frontiers, such as those between West Germany and Czechoslovakia or Norway and the Soviet Union. Restrains on the deployment of naval forces may be less acceptable, partly because of traditional attitudes towards the freedom of the seas, partly because of concern over establishing a precedent, as in the British–Icelandic dispute over the unilateral extension of fishing rights. It is, however, possible that the West would agree to an interpretation of the rules of the sea along the lines of the American–Soviet agreement of 1972, which would minimize the chance of inadvertent confrontations between NATO and Warsaw Pact naval forces.

It is also possible that the allies would be willing to give advance warning of troop movements on a reciprocal basis; however, a favourable response apparently hinges on the resolution of other issues, such as the area to be included. They, like the members of the Warsaw Pact, have agreed to give notice of manoeuvres involving 25,000 men or more held within 250 kilometres of frontiers in Europe, and to invite observers to attend them, and they would probably be willing to hold these manoeuvres away from border areas, an idea advanced in previous Western proposals. Nor would the Allies find it difficult to adopt reasonable measures to monitor any weapons-free zones that might be established, including installing observers, establishing over-flying rights, and so on—all of which they have endorsed in times past.

---

[30] US Department of State, *Conference on Security and Co-operation in Europe: Final Act*, English Language Version, pp. 18–20.

The Western attitude towards bases may be somewhat different. Whatever the desirability of precluding any additional Soviet bases in the Near and Middle East, or any new ones on the North African littoral, there is no sign that the West is willing to limit its own establishments in order to achieve this. It is conceivable that it would be willing to withhold counter-deployments, on the ground that these are not needed militarily or that they would be unduly disturbing politically. At the moment, however, there are no indications that the West would do this much on a unified basis, much less that it would forgo its own freedom to redeploy forces, which is viewed both as valuable in the management of crises and as essential to the operation of a European Defence Force, should one ever be formed.

It may be that the United States, the Soviet Union and their more reluctant allies will be forced into more responsive attitudes by pressures from other countries. There is some interest on the part of the smaller European states in reductions of forces, withdrawals of weapons and the dismantling of bases. Some Europeans, notably in the non-aligned countries, may wish to extend current inhibitions on the use of manoeuvres for political purposes by setting up demilitarized zones, introducing neutral monitors into them, etc., since these are the best—and perhaps the only—ways in which they can enhance their own security when confronted by more powerful nations. How hard they will push one cannot say, but they will certainly try to move in this direction.

How far these various pressures will move the major powers, and to what extent the latter will reconcile their divergent interests, are difficult to forecast; the outcomes are both speculative and uncertain. An optimistic estimate would be that within the next two or three years one might expect acceptance of limitations on the use of present bases such as those outlined earlier, and possibly some unilateral restraint on the establishment of new bases and/or on the kinds of forces stationed there. One could also expect to see within this period some relocation of forces and weapons on both sides which would make them appear less threatening, and perhaps the establishment in Europe of narrow denuclearized or partially demilitarized zones. It is possible that the participants in the CSCE will, as a further step, inform each other in advance about major troop movements, such as the transfer of a division, the displacement of an air wing or the dispatch of a major combat surface ship.[31] Observers are to be

---

[31] At the moment, advance notification of major troop movements is left to the discretion of each participant in the CSCE; however, these are to give 'further consideration ... to the question of prior notification of major military movements'. *Ibid.*, p. 20.

admitted to manoeuvres and, if any demilitarized zones are established, may be allowed in those also. Finally, it is conceivable that other means of verification will be permitted, both for their contribution to reassurance and because they may help to preclude the use of force by or against the nations of Europe—an objective common to all those nations and the super-powers as well.[32]

INHIBITIONS ON THE USE OF FORCE

Prominent among inhibitions on the employment of armed forces are those deriving from the existence of other and countervailing forces. There are, however, a whole range of inhibitions which derive neither from the existence of armed forces nor from curbs on their size, armament and use. Some are legal inhibitions, in the form of treaties, agreements, and understandings, whose breach may not only incur opprobrium but may also cause less faith to be placed in other or future legal arrangements. Others derive from the existence of international organizations such as the United Nations, regional associations like the Organization of American States, and alliances such as NATO and the Warsaw Pact. All of these in varying ways do inhibit the use of force, can mediate in disputes, and may serve to damp conflicts between their members. A third group of inhibitions are political, arising out of concern lest the use of force alienate friends, arouse adversaries and exacerbate differences among nations. Moreover, there is awareness that military measures may create—or recreate —a climate of fear and an atmosphere of uncertainty, both of which can be poisonous. Finally, there are economic inhibitions, some of which derive from the actual costs of preparing for and initiating war and some from the potential costs, which could include the disruption of trade patterns, the imposition of sanctions, an end to flows of technical information, and so on.

In one sense, these should not be covered in a book on arms control, since they exist independently of measures for the control of armaments. In another sense, however, they are a component of arms control as well as a complement to it, since they too serve to 'restrict the deployment of troops and/or weapons' and are the results of understandings with another state or states.[33] Moreover, they contribute to security, by enhancing confidence that force will not be employed. In this section, therefore, we will look at these inhibitions.

[32] The exact words of President Nixon and Mr Brezhnev, on behalf of their respective countries, were that 'ensuring a lasting peace in Europe is a paramount goal of their policies'. (Joint [Nixon–Brezhnev] Communiqué of 25 June 1973. *The Times*, 26 June 1973, p. 6.)

[33] This is part of the definition of arms control used throughout the book. See Chap. 3, note 1.

Legal inhibitions

Many legal inhibitions to the use of force are already operative. International law itself prescribes the circumstances and conditions under which force can be a legal instrument of policy, and the degree to which it can be utilized, whether or not it is legal. The Charter of the United Nations requires all members to eschew the use of force save for legitimate purposes of self-defence or pursuant to decisions by the Security Council. A third inhibition, which merely illustrates a host of bilateral and multilateral legal instruments, is the reaffirmation of the principles of non-intervention and non-use of force passed without opposition by the UN General Assembly in 1970.[34] And a fourth—and particularly relevant—example is the Final Act of the CSCE, in which the participants acknowledge the inviolability of frontiers and the territorial integrity of the countries of Europe, pledge that they will abjure the threat or the use of force, and agree to 'refrain from any intervention, direct or indirect, individual or collective . . . in the internal affairs of the states'.[35]

One advantage which could accrue from the adoption of these principles is that of repetition. The more frequently parties subscribe to such statements, the more they reinforce a set of expectations about behaviour which influence staff officers and decision-makers. The more numerous the legal instruments committing one to the observance of those principles, the more varied the signatories and the greater their number, the greater the likelihood that these declarations may be binding. As in the case of marriage vows, repetition can serve as a strong reminder of rights and obligations.

The second advantage is that of interpretation. The Soviet Union has in the past considered legal inhibitions on the use of force as not precluding measures to safeguard Socialist regimes against 'counter-revolutionary activities', a view enshrined in the so-called 'Brezhnev Doctrine' formulated in the aftermath of Czechoslovakia. Many of the countries attending the CSCE strongly endorsed language which would close this loophole. According to one account, the Rumanians proposed that these pledges apply 'irrespective of membership in military and political groupings', a clear reference to their associates

---

[34] General Assembly Resolutions 2625 (XXV) and 2627 (XXV) of 24 October 1970, cited in Working Group on European Co-operation and Security, 'Some Institutional Suggestions for a System of Security and Co-operation in Europe', *Bulletin of Peace Proposals*, Vol. III (1972), pp. 76–7.

[35] *Conference on Security and Co-operation in Europe: Final Act*, op. cit. in note 30, p. 8.

in the Warsaw Pact.[36] Although the language of the Final Act was not quite so explicit, it did indicate that the ban on intervention applied to states 'regardless of their mutual relations',[37] thereby making clear that the pledge should be unusually applicable.

However, this is not all, for even the most carefully drawn legal instrument may have escape clauses, and even the most explicit interpretation may be no more than just words. A major aim of many participants in the CSCE was to flesh out these declarations of principle with concrete measures for their application. Though they did not wholly succeed in achieving this, those points dealing with the renunciation of the use of force, with advance notification of manoeuvres and with other so-called 'confidence-building' measures are among the most specific in the Final Act. Whether they will be honoured is still to be seen, but there is hope that they will be; as the Hungarian Foreign Minister, Frigyes Puha, said, 'I expect an atmosphere to be created in Europe which will increase confidence'.[38] These and other agreements reached at the CSCE should place new limitations on the use of force in Europe, limitations which could be amplified and strengthened during the reassessment scheduled for 1977. These are not, however, the only agreements tending in that direction. For example, the Nixon–Brezhnev Pact on the Prevention of Nuclear War not only reaffirms the obligations of the signatories under the United Nations Charter to refrain from the threat or the use of force but goes some way towards saying how they propose to do this. Article I commits them to 'act in such a manner as to prevent the development of situations capable of causing the dangerous exacerbation of their relations, [and] as to avoid military confrontations';[39] Article II pledges them to refrain from the threat or use of force 'against the other party, against the allies of the other party and against other countries, in circumstances which may endanger international peace and security'; and Article IV requires them to consult immediately if any situation arises which carries a risk of nuclear war, in order to avert that risk. And, although few would characterize the behaviour of either party during October 1973 as illustrative of how

---

[36] *The Times*, 2 July 1973, p. 4. *See also* Robin A. Remington, 'European Security in the Era of Negotiation', *Current History*, Vol. 64, No. 381 (May 1973), p. 233.

[37] *Conference on Security and Co-operation in Europe: Final Act, op. cit.* in note 30, p. 8.

[38] *Der Spiegel*, 19 May 1975, pp. 88–9, translated and reprinted in Foreign Broadcast Information Service, East Europe (Hungary), 21 May 1975, p. F1.

[39] *Op. cit.* in Chapter 1, note 11.

these clauses should be implemented, at least consultations did take place – and force was not used.

Security cannot, of course, rest solely – or even largely – on agreements for the renunciation of force. For one thing, they may be interpreted by non-signatory states as having been made at their expense – as, in large measure, the countries of Western Europe interpreted the Nixon–Brezhnev Pact.[40] For another, these agreements may, in time of crisis, be considered 'scraps of paper', as German Chancellor Theodor von Bethmann-Hollweg termed the multinational guarantees of Belgian neutrality in 1914. Even scraps of paper may, however, clog up the machinery of war. This is particularly true if legal inhibitions to the use of force are reinforced by institutional arrangements for their interpretation and application, a subject to which we will turn next.

Institutional inhibitions

As noted previously, there already exist many international institutions concerned with inhibiting the use of force. For various reasons – to do partly with their membership, partly with their nature and partly with the mechanisms they are able to employ – these institutions are not as effective in insuring European security as one might wish.[41] One way of enhancing that security would be to establish an institutional framework for Europe, perhaps in the form of a permanent Committee on European Security (CES).

At best, any European Security Committee could play only a consultative role, but even this could be productive. Such a Committee could discuss military doctrines and their implications for security, an item whose importance has been noted previously.[42] It could also consider perceptions of threat and measures to alleviate them, leaving to the Vienna Conference on Mutual Force Reductions, or to other forums, the implementation of desirable measures. It could flash diplomatic 'warning lights' in time of crisis – lights which could be turned on by non-aligned powers as well as by members of NATO and

[40] For a general survey of the concerns aroused by the Nixon–Brezhnev Pact see *The Times*, 23 June 1973, p. 4, and 25 June 1973, pp. 5 and 13, and the article by Herr Hermann Bohle in the *Münchner Merkur*, 3 July 1973, translated and reprinted in *The German Tribune*, No. 588, 19 July 1973, p. 2. For a favourable view of the Pact, see the address by Egon Bahr, Minister of State in the West German Chancellery, 'German *Ostpolitik* and Super-Power Relations', at the Protestant Academy, Tutzing, 11 July 1973, translated and reprinted in *Survival*, Vol. XV, No. 6 (November/December 1973), pp. 299–300.

[41] See Chapter 1, pp. 14–15.

[42] See Chapter 4, p. 94.

the Warsaw Pact. In all these ways it could inhibit not only the use of armed forces but also their development and deployment, which frequently have almost as much effect on perceptions of security.

This goal could be furthered if the Committee on European Security became one of the bodies which received reports on the implementation of the confidence-building measures adopted by the CSCE, and with which complaints about non-compliance could be registered.[43] While the United Nations is, and presumably will remain, the ultimate tribunal for considering 'threats to the peace', the CES could certainly take the initial responsibility for investigating activities in the European region, mediating disputes and possibly taking other actions to damp conflicts. The aim would not be to set up a local Court of International Justice, nor a regional Disarmament Organization, but to provide a basis for exchanges among, and inquiries by, the states most directly concerned with progress towards implementing agreements on the non-use of force and the reduction of armaments in Europe. This would not only focus attention on progress in Europe, or the lack of it, but would afford an opportunity for participation by states which, like Yugoslavia, are not directly involved in the MFR negotiations or which, like Switzerland, are not even members of the United Nations.

One could, of course, go further in establishing institutional inhibitions to the use of force in Europe. Some envisage a European Treaty Organization, with an attached Security Committee for Europe, which could deal with problems of security and arms control.[44] Others foresee the ultimate evolution of the CSCE into a 'true European security system, i.e., a Federation whose central authority would exercise control over all national armed forces, as well as over a Federation Army which could police and secure a neutral Europe'.[45]

The question, however, is not whether one could or should go this far, but whether institutional inhibitions to the use of force can be further strengthened. The answer is that they can, since the mere existence of a European institution to monitor progress on arms control and discuss problems affecting security could have an additional effect on its maintenance. Although such inhibitions may

[43] At the moment there is no forum to which such complaints could be addressed, since the first follow-up session of any kind is not scheduled until June 1977.

[44] 'Some Institutional Suggestions for a System of Security and Co-operation in Europe', *op. cit.* in note 34, pp. 84, 87–8.

[45] Johannes W. Klefisch, 'The Art of Securing Peace Today–Reflections on a European Security Conference', *Frankfurter Hefte*; No. 12 (1971), translated and reprinted in *The German Tribune Quarterly Review*, No. 17 (23 March 1972), p. 5.

not in themselves be enough to preclude the use of force, they can go to make a whole which may be greater than the sum of its several parts.

Political inhibitions

The political climate is another part of the same whole, since it can make possible the erection of legal barriers and the construction of institutional obstacles. It can create or strengthen vested interests in the maintenance of peace by affecting relations among states, outcomes to disputes and expectations of the future, and it can enlarge the political cost (and hence the political difficulty) of altering these relationships.

Europe today exemplifies the process whereby changes in the political climate create vested interests in the preservation of peace. The settlement of territorial issues between West Germany and Poland, and German acknowledgment of the inviolability of post-war frontiers in Europe, relieved fears about 'revanchism' and created new attitudes in Eastern Europe–so much so that West Germany's ratification of the treaties with the Soviet Union and Poland was called a 'turning point' in world affairs.[46] The acknowledgment by West Germany of the existence of an East German state within the German nation, and her declaration that she will work towards a reconstitution of Germany in new ways and over a longer period of time, also improved the political climate in Eastern Europe. And the fact that the CSCE not only ratified these guarantees of the inviolability of frontiers but, in effect, enlarged them to include warranties for the existence of regimes with varying political and social systems can only be reassuring to the Soviet Union and to the countries of Eastern Europe.

These are not the only countries which should be reassured by developments at the CSCE. Although there may be questions about the application of the principle of non-intervention to cultural life and political affairs, there can be little doubt as to what it means militarily: hands off. Attempts by the Soviet Union or any of the countries of Eastern Europe to employ force, directly or indirectly, would re-arouse in the West those fears and suspicions which the countries of the Warsaw Pact are attempting to alleviate. They could shatter all efforts to create a 'new Europe' in which confrontation is ended, blocs disappear, and an organization which is the 'common handiwork of all the countries of Europe...' would be created.[47] Since

---

[46] I. Aseyev, 'Europe 1972: Time of Hopes', *International Affairs* (Moscow), No. 10, 1972 (October 1972), p. 18.

[47] *Ibid.*, pp. 18 and 19.

the positions taken by Soviet spokesmen reflect both an awareness and an acceptance of these factors, it is possible that the future may be more peaceful than many Westerners anticipate.

Similarly, the use or threat of force by the West could end hopes for the freer interchanges, better communications and greater openness which some believe are pre-conditions for real *détente*. It would set back West German attempts to improve conditions in East Germany and to rebuild the ties between the two states. And it would mark a return to the Cold War which no one wants.

These political inhibitions to the use of force arise not only in Europe but outside it. The United States and the Soviet Union are attempting in a variety of ways to improve relations with each other, limit competition and create 'a permanent structure of peace'.[48] These attempts appear to stem from recognition of the futility and the sterility of past policies and the dangers of continuing them. Perhaps more importantly, they represent a commitment on the part of top leaders to a policy whose reversal would represent a marked political defeat; hence both national politics and personal interests seem to combine to favour constraints on the use of force.

Economic inhibitions

The costs incurred by altering the political climate may be not only political but also economic. The last few years have witnessed a marked expansion in East–West trade and the development of plans for further expansion, as noted in the Nixon–Brezhnev communiqué; in fact, the United States and the Soviet Union plan to increase not only sales of commodities but also exchanges of information, cooperation in medical, atomic and oceanographic research, Western financing of Eastern construction projects, and so on.[49] If this process continues, it could provide the Soviet Union and the countries of Eastern Europe with funds for capital development, with new technologies and with advanced machinery, all of which could enable them to increase productivity and improve efficiency. It could provide the United States and other advanced countries with markets (for cereals, as well as machine tools), natural resources which are in short supply (such as oil and gas) and opportunities for investment which– perhaps paradoxically–might be more secure than in many other parts of the world.

[48] Joint [Nixon–Brezhnev] Communiqué of 25 June 1973, Part III, *op. cit.* in note 32.
[49] *Ibid.*, Article IV. *See also* Y. Zakharov, 'An Important Condition for *Détente* in Europe', *International Affairs* (Moscow) No. 10, 1972 (October 1972), p. 29, for an outline of Soviet–West German exchanges.

This is not to argue that economic interdependence will necessarily lead to political interdependence: history suggests otherwise–as in the case of Europe before the outbreak of World War I. One should, however, note that increased exchanges like those mentioned above create economic associations which it can be costly, in terms of both money and productivity, to disrupt. They also create or strengthen interest groups which will argue against policies likely to lead to such disruptions. In these and other ways they make countries more vulnerable to the application of economic leverage, which will increase with the growth of East–West trade.

These economic inhibitions to the use of force could, therefore, be increased simply by a continuation of the process now under way. They could be strengthened by deliberate efforts to secure key positions in one or two crucial areas, thereby increasing the economic leverage which could be applied. And they could be further increased by co-ordinated responses to a major breach of the peace, perhaps organized by the Committee for European Security, if one is established.

There are, of course, both limitations on this process and dangers involved in it. One limitation derives from the fact that for the foreseeable future East–West interchanges will be both low in volume and marginal in their effect on particular segments of the economy, another from the possibility that some countries may be unwilling to exercise even the comparatively small economic leverage they have. The greatest danger is that if this leverage increases it may be used to attain political objectives (as the Arab States used the leverage afforded by controlling a large part of the world's oil), and not simply to punish breaches of the peace. A subsidiary danger is that efforts to arrange concerted action against an 'aggressor' may simply split the institution making the efforts, as the imposition of economic sanctions against Italy split the old League of Nations.

This suggests that one should not rely too much on economic sanctions as a deterrent to the use of force. At the same time, one should not underrate the inhibitions created by policies which aim at increased economic co-operation. As one West German participant put it, after discussions with Mr Brezhnev during the latter's visit to Bonn in 1973, 'this grand panorama of trade, better relations, and cultural exchange is, as far as we can determine, a reflection of a basic, even irrevocable, decision that this man [Brezhnev] is willing to bet on co-operation for decades to come with the West. This means he has to have a security and military policy to match.'[50]

[50] The *International Herald Tribune*, 23 May 1973, p. 1.

THE IMPLICATIONS FOR SECURITY

This look at global restrictions on forces and weapons was prompted in part by awareness that measures which affected only the countries of Europe, and not the super-powers, could lead to greater military imbalances than now exist, especially between the Soviet Union and the countries to the west of her. It was also prompted by recognition that some arms-control measures, like restrictions on the deployment of naval forces, have to apply on a global basis if they are to be meaningful. And it derived from the knowledge that actions outside Europe could threaten European security either directly (by the interdiction of sea lines of communication, for example) or indirectly (by starting conflicts which might ultimately extend to the continent of Europe). The question which still has to be answered is: What effect will those global restrictions which seem both workable and acceptable have on these problems?

The first answer is that measures affecting the size of armed forces which are both workable and acceptable are unlikely to close the gap between the military capabilities of the super-powers and those of their allies. Indeed, this gap may in some instances increase, because reductions likely to be made in the armed forces of the super-powers will not approach the cuts in the indigenous forces of some European countries now under consideration at the Vienna Conference on Mutual Force Reductions. Even if the United States and the Soviet Union demobilized any units withdrawn from Europe, this would only marginally diminish the number of men the two countries have under arms. And even if tacit ceilings on their armed forces were set, these are not likely to be so low as to require drastic reductions by either country.

Furthermore, ceilings on classes of weapons cannot readily be applied to tanks, planes and guns. Hence, it is not possible to eliminate by this means current imbalances in these categories, which derive from differences in the organization and equipment of the forces of the two alliances. Ceilings on naval forces are easier to verify but so difficult to devise and so uneven in their impact that they have been considered feasible in only a few instances. The limitations on the number of aircraft carriers and constraints on attack submarines could curb future threats to European security; however, it must be admitted that they would not markedly affect the current ability of either side to wage war at sea. And, while this may accord with the principle of 'undiminished security', it is scarcely a step towards the goal of achieving it with smaller forces and at lesser cost.

As for budgetary restrictions, those likely to be acceptable will not have much impact, while those with great impact are not likely to be

acceptable. This is equally true of controls on research and development, which can only affect most weapons programmes marginally, if
at all. Furthermore, some kinds of controls, such as those on the sale
of advanced weapons, would adversely alter European military
capabilities and hence may not be deemed desirable. The measures
which were judged potentially acceptable focus on determining which
weapons could be destabilizing militarily or unsettling psychologically,
on the monitoring of tests of such weapons and on the conduct of
negotiations to preclude their deployment. While these measures
could alleviate concern about the introduction of new weapons, they
would do little to redress existing disparities in research capacities or
to slow programmes for modernization (which may now be being
implemented more rapidly by the East than by the West, and by the
two super-powers than by their allies).

However, even partial measures such as these can have some
impact on perceptions of security. The acceptance of lower force levels
by the super-powers, whatever their effect militarily, would affirm
the peaceful intentions of these two states. The adoption of ceilings on
even a few classes of weapons would be reassuring, and reductions in
armaments would be even more so; similarly, constraints on budgets
and agreements to discuss limitations on 'destabilizing' weapons would
reduce anxieties, particularly if they applied mainly to the United
States and to the Soviet Union.

If, however, arms-control measures are to have maximum psychological impact, they must be given great publicity. Unilateral constraints of the past, such as the reductions in Soviet ground forces in
the mid-1950s, or the ceiling on American strategic launch vehicles in
the late 1960s, have not penetrated the consciousness of many officials
and analysts; those who are fearful tend to select information which
supports their fears, not information which challenges them. This
argues for measures which would create their own sound effects, as
would the scrapping of the 1,000-odd T-55 tanks in East Germany
replaced recently by more modern T-62, and the destruction of those
Honest John rockets and *Sergeant* SRBM in West Germany scheduled
to be replaced by *Lance* missiles. The danger of over-stating the
military consequences of such actions is slight by comparison with the
danger of letting each side continue believing that the other is hell-
bent on improving its defence posture, which seems to be the case at
present.

The proposed restrictions on deployments may well have more
effect militarily than will limitations on the size and capabilities of
armed forces. Even partial curbs on the establishment of new bases
and the deployment of 'threatening' weapons to vital areas could
alter Warsaw Pact capabilities to conduct military operations in

distant waters and NATO capabilities to launch nuclear strikes against targets in Eastern Europe and the Soviet Union. The redeployment of forces and weapons to rear areas would diminish the ability of both sides to launch surprise attacks, and increase their capacity to defend against them; the capacity to defend would be further enhanced if restrictions on deployment were formalized by the establishment of narrow zones in which all nuclear warheads and all offensive weapons were banned.[51] Although the effect of such measures would be greatest if they were applied in Europe, their implementation elsewhere could also be valuable. If extended to the Middle East, the Indian Ocean and other areas where the super-powers now maintain forces, they could inhibit these forces from increasing to a level where they could interdict European sea lines of communication or preclude European access to Middle East oil. They could also minimize the chances of a confrontation or conflict between the super-powers which could involve their allies in Europe. In both these ways, therefore, they could enhance European security and improve relations between East and West.

Restrictions on deployment would have even more effect on perceptions of security because of what they would communicate concerning the intentions of the two alliances. These beneficial effects could be further increased by giving advance notice of large-scale manoeuvres and (better still) major troop movements, by allowing greater freedom and scope for action to present liaison missions, by admitting observers to manoeuvres and (possibly on a permanent basis) to border areas, and so on. Their effects would be still more beneficial if the restrictions on deployment were supplemented by the provision, on request, of reassuring information, by the authorization of overflights in border zones and by the other measures for verification recommended earlier, all of which have been accepted in principle by both sides at one time or another—some of them, like the pledge not to interfere with national means of verification which is contained in the SALT agreement, very recently.

Although these judgments may be disappointing to those seeking drastic alterations in the global balance of power, the combined effect of overall limitations on NATO and Warsaw Pact forces and of restrictions on their deployment will not be negligible. Moreover, these will not be the only measures affecting the military capabilities of the two alliances, for these may be altered not only by unilateral decisions but also by bilateral or multilateral arms-control agreements—some of which, like SALT II, could diminish the relative advantages the two super-powers currently enjoy over other nuclear powers. Even more

[51] See Chap. 5, p. 122.

importantly, agreements, which could strengthen legal, institutional and political inhibitions on the use of force, have been reached at the Conference on Security and Co-operation in Europe and others may be adopted as part of any arrangements for Mutual Force Reductions in Europe.

Inhibitions on the use of force will obviously not affect military capabilities directly: this is not their intent. They are designed to strengthen existing obstacles to the use of those capabilities for either military or political purposes by increasing the costs attendant on their employment. This also involves enlarging the rewards of not using them: better relations among states, expanded trade, increased co-operation and the development of alternative means of preserving vital interests–if not of achieving all national objectives.

This emphasizes a point made previously: that improved relations among states may both facilitate arms control and enhance national security. They can do the former by making it easier for states to reduce defence budgets, cancel or defer weapons programmes and practise restraint in the deployment of their armed forces, whether by agreement or as part of tacit bargaining. However, given the impossibility of eliminating weapons which could literally destroy nations, there are limits to what arms control can accomplish, either in reducing military capabilities or in relieving anxieties about the possibility of their use. In these circumstances, patterns of behaviour may have more influence on perceptions of threat than measures to reduce (or to produce) armaments.[52] If this lesson is learned, we can afford to worry less about the difficulty of devising and implementing measures for the control of armaments, on either an overall or a limited basis.

[52] A clear illustration of this (and of the fact that capabilities are not the only things taken into account in devising defence programmes) is given by Dr Kissinger's remark that the United States could afford to limit ballistic missile defences under the SALT agreements because the American *rapprochement* with the People's Republic of China drastically reduced the likelihood of a Chinese nuclear strike against American cities (Congressional Briefing by Dr Henry A. Kissinger, *Congressional Record– Senate*, 19 June 1972, p. S9604).

Chapter 8

SECURITY THROUGH ARMS CONTROL

My intention in this chapter is to summarize what the foregoing analyses tell us about present relations between arms control and European security, and what they suggest for the future. Since the perspectives and interests of West Europeans differ so markedly from those of their fellows in Eastern Europe I will look first at the implications for the security of Western Europe, next at the implications for the security of Eastern Europe, and finally at those for the security of Europe as a whole–which is undoubtedly greater than the sum of all its parts.

WEST EUROPEAN SECURITY AND ARMS CONTROL

As we saw in Chapter 2, West European concerns about security derive from four major sources.[1] One of these is the existence of imbalances in the military capabilities of NATO and the Warsaw Pact, which would enable the latter to launch a massive conventional assault against Western Europe, confronting NATO with the choice of accepting defeat or escalating to nuclear war, neither of which are very palatable alternatives. Whether this appreciation of the threat is valid may be questionable, whether it is salient is perhaps more questionable, since it is hard to find a Western political leader, general, or official who believes that such an assault is very likely. Nevertheless, NATO continues to define the military threat as primarily that of such an assault, and statements by officials of NATO and other agencies concerned with national security affairs are replete with references to the dangers arising from Warsaw Pact advantages in conventional forces and weapons.

Another source of concern is that further improvements in, and the continued extension of, Warsaw Pact (and especially Soviet) armed forces would enable the bloc countries to cut sea lines of communication, deny access to oil, intervene in Third World countries, and otherwise to operate in ways detrimental to Western security interests.

[1] See Chapter 2, pp. 40–4.

Even if such operations did not immediately involve the countries of Western Europe, they might well do so ultimately, either because these countries would have to take countervailing action or because their American ally would have to respond to such challenges. Moreover, if this Warsaw Pact intervention were directed against a nonaligned state in Europe–or even, as in 1968, against an errant member of the Socialist Commonwealth–the likelihood of West European involvement would be still greater.

A related concern is that the growth and extension of Soviet power could make it possible for the Soviet Union to influence Western policy simply by threatening military action. In fact there are those who believe that this power may become so great as to enable the Soviet Union to exercise pressures which could, to requote the 1970 German White Paper, 'narrow the freedom of political decision' of the Western allies.[2] And although the Soviet Union herself has pointed out that 'it is naïve to put the West European countries in the same category [as Finland]',[3] many West Europeans are worried that they may be compelled to practise that degree of responsiveness to Soviet wishes which goes under the name of 'Finlandization'.

Concerns about these changes in the military environment are reinforced by the possibility of other–equally unwelcome–changes in the political environment. Many Europeans are fearful that the United States may, whether because of unwillingness to risk nuclear war, declining interest in Western Europe, desire to promote accommodation with the Soviet Union, or domestic pressures, gradually 'decouple' herself from Western Europe, thereby leaving the countries of that area less able to rebuff Warsaw Pact threats and resist Soviet pressures. This is accompanied by worry lest the process of accommodation between East and West (and particularly between the United States and the Soviet Union) should go so far as to inhibit moves towards the stronger and more integrated European community which some view as desirable in its own right; others deem essential if Western Europe is to compensate for a decline in American support; and many see as of crucial importance to the ability to protect one's own vital interests in an uncertain world.

One would logically expect these fears and concerns to lead to West European concentration on the negative aspects of current and prospective measures for armaments control–as in fact they have. There is widespread concern lest SALT II preclude the sale to Western Europe of advanced weapons, inhibit the transfer of technology, or otherwise

---

[2] *German White Paper 1970, op. cit.* in Chapter 2, note 27, p. 21.
[3] Seymour Topping, 'Answers by Soviet to West's Questions', the *New York Times*, 13 December 1973, p. 14.

set limits to the development of military–and especially nuclear–capabilities. There is apprehension lest any reduction in tactical nuclear delivery vehicles (and especially in the American Forward Based Systems), the redeployment or restructuring of tactical nuclear forces, or understandings concerning their employment, might serve to weaken the deterrent, diminish the utility of the instruments at the disposal of the allies and lower their voices in council. There are also fears lest mutual force reductions not only fail to redress military imbalances–which caused questions about the absence of the word 'balanced' from the Nixon–Brezhnev communiqué dealing with these negotiations[4]–but also have other undesirable side-effects. One, the most prominent, is that forthcoming negotiations could sanction a cutback of the American presence below the level at which the allies would like to see it maintained. Another is that the negotiations may set up additional constraints on the deployment of weapons systems or the size of armed forces which would affect some of the allies unequally, decrease flexibility in adjusting to future military needs, and perhaps give the Soviet Union some leverage over Western defence policies and programmes.

In some respects these concerns are valid, in some respects they may not be. As indicated previously, those measures for the limitation of strategic armaments which seem both feasible and likely would probably not directly affect the countries of Western Europe.[5] Possible exceptions are further restrictions on the deployment of anti-ballistic missiles and constraints on anti-submarine warfare forces; both would marginally improve British and French SLBM capabilities, and the latter might marginally constrain future NATO ASW capabilities. Indirectly, the countries of Western Europe would benefit from the extension of controls over certain other classes of weapons, such as medium bombers and IRBM, but here their arms policy preferences stand in the way–as they may with respect to the imposition of controls over advanced weapons.

As for tactical nuclear forces, the kinds of measures suggested for consideration in any future negotiations[6] would neither restrict British

---

[4] Nixon–Brezhnev Communiqué, *op. cit.* in Chap. 7, note 32, p. 6.

[5] These include cutting down on strategic offensive weapons; inhibiting MIRV – either through constraints on test flights or agreements not to install MIRV on certain types of missiles; imposing curbs on radically different weapons; setting ceilings on hunter-killer submarines and restrictions on their use in tracking other submarines; and discussing further measures to avoid inadvertent nuclear war. For details, *see* Chapter 4, pp. 94–7.

[6] These include 20 per cent cuts in tactical nuclear delivery vehicles; the establishment of narrow zones from which nuclear weapons and/or

and French nuclear forces nor 'decouple' strategic deterrence from the possession of tactical nuclear delivery vehicles. Nor would these measures affect adversely the ability of NATO to wage tactical nuclear war, if such a drastic step were ultimately necessary. They could, however, conceivably reassure the Warsaw Pact about NATO's willingness to start such a war as a matter of policy, and vice versa.

The problem here is that TNW are viewed by many in NATO as the main offset to Warsaw Pact superiority in conventional forces, as well as an important component of the deterrent; hence few West Europeans would like to see them reduced or redeployed. Furthermore, if they are to be used as 'bargaining chips' in any negotiations, there is the question of whether they should be traded for cutbacks in Soviet regional nuclear forces, reductions in conventional capabilities, or both. Given the difficulty of answering this, the potentially divisive effects of negotiations, and the concern that any agreements might impinge on their freedom of action, it is understandable that many West Europeans would like to ignore the issue of controls on TNF.

This, however, the Warsaw Pact will not allow; in fact, their delegates to the Vienna Conference are insisting that cutbacks in aircraft and missiles should be made a part of MFV. At some stage, therefore, the Western allies will have to consider whether to accept restrictions on tactical nuclear forces, either as a *quid pro quo* for Soviet concessions on other matters or as a contribution to *détente*.

Should they choose to move in this direction, there are a number of arms-control measures which commend themselves, as indicated above. While these measures may demand some restructuring of NATO nuclear forces and some shift in NATO thinking (both about the likelihood of attack and the ways of precluding it), they are not out of place in the kind of world towards which we are apparently moving.

The same could be said of the kinds of measures recommended for the first stage of mutual force reductions.[7] These would in fact strike

---

[7] These include cuts of 10–20 per cent in military manpower and certain types of weapons (aircraft, tanks, armoured personnel carriers and self-propelled artillery) in Central Europe, and similar cuts of 10 per cent for NATO forces in Southern Europe and 15 per cent for the smaller Warsaw Pact forces in that area. They also include the establishment in all regions of Europe of measures to guard against surprise attack: narrow zones

---

TNDV might be barred; restrictions on the deployment of these and other 'offensive' weapons; discussions on the effects of introducing new weapons; and consideration of the possible consequences of restricting the employment of TNW in case of war. For further details see Chapter 5, pp. 131–4.

at some concerns about imbalances between NATO and the Warsaw Pact, since equal percentage reductions applied to asymmetrical forces will require larger cutbacks in Warsaw Pact aircraft and tanks than in those of NATO. They could alleviate some of the worries about the ability of the Warsaw Pact to launch a large-scale conventional assault, by increasing *defensive* capabilities at the expense of offensive ones—even if only in the short run, and not after mobilization. They could assuage fears about the ability of the Soviet Union and her allies to exert political pressures backed by the threat of force, both by lowering the Soviet military presence in Eastern Europe and by giving some assurances of Soviet intent.

Admittedly, these measures for mutual force reductions would result in a diminution of the American military presence in Europe, but this may occur anyway. Also, the proposals would impose on some states, but not on others, *de facto* ceilings on forces and weapons and restrictions on deployment. This is true, however, largely because other Western states are unwilling to accept similar restrictions, rather than because any particular countries are accorded 'second-class status'. If and when one proceeds with deeper cuts in forces, further restrictions on the deployment of weapons and additional inhibitions to the build-up of troops close to frontiers, one may also extend these kinds of constraints to new geographic areas; indeed, this is probably essential if one wishes to impose controls on the forces inside the Soviet Union.

This still leaves untouched fears that mutual force reductions may decrease military flexibility and give the Soviet Union leverage on Western defence policies and programmes largely because these fears are valid. The whole aim of arms control is to enable one state to influence the decisions of another, to the betterment of both. The points to be noted here are that Western Europe would also gain some leverage over the countries of Eastern Europe and, to a lesser extent, over the Soviet Union. Furthermore, any leverage the latter acquired under any of the proposals advanced here would not be such as to enable her to prevent West European defence co-operation or the creation of a European Nuclear Force. Finally, any constraints arising out of agreements for the reduction of forces in Europe could be set aside, should 'extraordinary events related to the subject matter

---

from which offensive weapons would be barred, redeployment to rear areas of forces peculiarly suited for mobile offensive operations (tank divisions and amphibious units, to give just two illustrations) and the establishment of observation posts and other means of verifying that these restrictions are in fact observed. For further details *see* Chapter 6, pp. 154, 159, 163, 167–8.

of this Interim Agreement jeopardize supreme interests . . .'–a phrase used in other arms-control agreements.[8]

Mutual force reductions would also leave untouched two other matters of concern to the West: the expansion of Soviet 'globally mobile forces' and their introduction into new areas, and the continued strengthening of the Soviet military establishment. As suggested previously, relatively few arms-control measures aimed at precluding these developments are workable, and even fewer are acceptable to either side.[9] Nevertheless, it might be possible to set ceilings on some types of Soviet warships, and to arrive at some understanding on the size, nature and permanence of future Soviet deployments outside Europe which could alleviate Western fears about the interdiction of their sea lines of communication, intervention in the Third World, and so on. It might also be possible, through tacit bargaining, to persuade the Soviet Union to demobilize some of her men, scrap some of her weapons, and even to exercise some restraint in the development of new ones. Such measures could have a significant psychological effect, and perhaps a limited military one, but they will not preclude further increases in Soviet power, much less redress the imbalances between Soviet capabilities and those of the countries of Western Europe.

This suggests that West European fears about threats to their vital interests, and pressures which could affect their political independence, cannot be eased by measures for the limitation and reduction of armaments: none that pass the double test of feasibility and acceptability are likely to achieve this. To some extent, however, these fears should be assuaged by other kinds of measures, such as the removal of offensive weapons from border areas, a ban on the conduct of manoeuvres near frontiers, advance notification of troop movements and similar steps to make it more difficult for any country to threaten the use of force. They could be reduced even more by strengthening political inhibitions on the use of force, creating institutions which can monitor observance of these inhibitions, erecting additional legal obstacles and enhancing awareness of the potential economic costs of breaking the peace. Their significance lies not so much in their effect in precluding the use of force–though this is not inconsiderable–as in

[8] See Chap. 4, note 1.

[9] The measures deemed feasible and potentially acceptable included cutbacks in Soviet and American troop strength; ceilings on aircraft-carriers and attack submarines; establishment of a group to discuss the development of potentially destablizing weapons, and possibly to monitor any tests of these weapons; limitations on the establishment of new bases; and constraints on the movement of 'threatening' weapons to old ones located in designated areas. See Chapter 7, pp. 194–8, 200–5.

what they may signify concerning the intent to use force, which is all-important.

If all the arms-control measures suggested so far were adopted—a supposition almost certainly Utopian—they could partly alleviate West European concerns about a massive Warsaw Pact assault by reducing the forces immediately available for such an operation, constraining their offensive capabilities and increasing NATO's defensive potential, certainly relatively and perhaps absolutely. They could ease fears of Soviet intervention inside or outside Europe by slowing the build-up of the Soviet Navy, restricting the deployment of ground, air, and naval units, and strengthening inhibitions on the use of force. They could lessen worries about the potential political impact of growing Soviet power by the inhibitions mentioned above, by the proposed cuts in Soviet troop strength and weapons both in Europe and within the Soviet Union, and, above all, by the curbs on Soviet strategic offensive forces. And, taken together with the changes in the political climate associated with them, they may generally mitigate Western nervousness about future Soviet behaviour.

What they will not do, however, is restore confidence in the firmness of the American commitment to the defence of Western Europe and in the permanence of the American military presence there. In large measure this is because the erosion of confidence resulted from factors which have nothing to do with arms control—ranging from the advent of strategic parity to the way in which the United States treated her allies on particular occasions. To some extent, however, it may be because the measures proposed *would* reduce the American presence in Europe (along with the Soviet one) and because negotiations on the measures will undoubtedly expose differences of opinion between the United States and her allies.

This does not, however, mean that arms control should be abjured because it cannot achieve the heart's desire, nor that it should be condemned because it has side-effects which to some seem undesirable. The issue in both instances is whether Western Europe is—and feels—safer with arms control or without it.

EAST EUROPEAN SECURITY AND ARMS CONTROL

The situation in Eastern Europe is somewhat different, in that perceptions of threat are as much political as military. Although the East Europeans (and the Soviet Union) earlier seemed fearful that Western nuclear weapons would be employed by the German 'revanchists' and other 'agents of imperialism', these fears appear to have largely vanished. War today is not seen as a result of a deliberate decision, but rather as a consequence of situations getting out of hand, such as political instabilities in Eastern Europe, which could prompt Western intervention, or super-power conflicts elsewhere which could burn back into Europe. The concentration on measures to reduce or remove TNW from large areas of Europe therefore reflects a desire to prevent Eastern Europe becoming a nuclear battlefield and to head off a European Nuclear Force, a development which could in turn force the East Europeans into greater reliance on the Soviet Union. (It may also, of course, reflect the view that one should not give up something–in this case an advantage in mobile conventional forces–for nothing, as the West has proposed at the Vienna Conference.)

Of greater concern to the East Europeans are political threats to their security. One of these, as already indicated, is that the creation of a more unified Europe might inhibit the kinds of interactions with the West which they would like (or which the Soviet Union would permit), especially if this unity went as far as embracing the establishment of a European Defence Force, with or without nuclear weapons. A second is that some kinds of interactions which the West might like, such as untrammelled exchanges of information, complete cultural freedom, and so on, could undermine stability in Eastern Europe. A third is that the Soviet Union, which has complemented moves towards *détente* with stricter internal controls, may feel impelled at some stage to tighten her grasp on Eastern Europe, if necessary by force of arms.

In this sense, the SALT negotiations are largely irrelevant to the countries of Eastern Europe, since they deal with problems which are not of great concern to them and over whose solutions they can exercise very little influence. The MFR negotiations at Vienna and the Conference on Security and Co-operation in Europe, recessed at Helsinki but scheduled to reopen in Belgrade are, however, of much concern. To some degree this is because cutbacks in conventional forces would reduce burdens (especially in the three countries of the 'Northern Tier'), and would lessen the Soviet presence in Eastern Europe, thereby giving the states of that region somewhat greater freedom of action. The main reason, however, is that these two conferences are grappling with the issues of greatest interest to them: cuts in TNDV, curbs on the use of force, and measures for co-operation and exchanges between East and West.

The measures proposed here for first-stage reductions in tactical nuclear forces (which may not be much different from those put forward at Vienna by the Pact) would only partly achieve the East European objectives of limiting nuclear strike against targets on their territories and precluding the establishment of an European Nuclear Force. Although cuts of 10–20 per cent, especially in nuclear-capable strike aircraft, would be desirable, they leave a long way to go before one reaches levels pleasing to the countries of Eastern Europe. Nor would measures to establish small nuclear-free zones along borders and to redeploy some tactical nuclear delivery vehicles to rear areas prevent a West German contribution to NATO tactical nuclear forces or FRG participation in the establishment of an European Nuclear Force; if they did, the Western allies would not accept them. However, the East Europeans may (rightly) view these as only the first steps in a process which could lead to low levels of nuclear armaments, to tight controls over nuclear weapons, and to significant extensions of the areas from which nuclear weapons and delivery vehicles might be barred.

This may also be true of measures to bar manoeuvres in areas near frontiers, to inhibit troop build-ups, and to interpose barriers to the use of force, to all of which the East Europeans attach great importance. If effectively implemented, these measures would diminish the possibility of intervention by NATO in Eastern Europe, would reduce the likelihood of confrontations and clashes of arms which could escalate into a nuclear war, and would inhibit any Western efforts to 'bargain from strength' for readjustments in East European frontiers or changes in East European institutions. They would also, of course, make it harder for the USSR to intervene, or to exert pressure against its associates, which may be why the Russians attempted at the CSCE to limit the application of the principles which should govern relations between states to those having different political, economic and social systems. In the end, however, they did accept a wording which gave the East Europeans (and Yugoslavia) slightly better legal protection against moves by the Soviet Union.

This outcome may illustrate the importance which the USSR attaches to *détente* but it also underlines the difficulty the East Europeans have in taking the initiative on measures for the control of armaments. As long as the Russians are cold to some proposals (as for advance notification of troop movements) it is hard for their allies to be warm to them. As long as they insist on interpreting pledges of non-intervention in such a way as to preserve their freedom to repeat what they did to Czechoslovakia, it takes a bold Bulgar or a rash Rumanian to say them nay. And while there are rash Rumanians, it is best for both themselves and others that they be not too rash.

The arms-control measures outlined in this book should alleviate East European concerns about the likelihood and the consequences of tactical nuclear war, and ease their fears of Western intervention or a clash between the super-powers. They should give them somewhat greater freedom of action *vis-à-vis* the Soviet Union, and somewhat stronger assurances against the use of force by that country. That these results are far from what they might like must be acknowledged; that they are considerably ahead of what they now have must also be admitted. And although the price the regimes are asked to pay may seem high, in terms of potential political instability, that payment will also buy other things they are seeking, such as freer access to Western technology and expanded trade. All in all, the deal would seem worth while, especially if one considers its potential as well as its actual benefits.

ARMS CONTROL, SECURITY, AND THE FUTURE OF EUROPE

This assessment – necessarily incomplete – of the desires for, and doubts about, initial and not very extensive measures for the control of armaments illustrates the difficulty of enhancing security through arms control when security is defined in so many different ways by so many different countries. This judgment holds even though all the countries involved seem to want an easing of tensions, improved relations among the states of Europe and, of course, peace. It holds despite the fact that these same countries 'recognize the interest of all of them in efforts aimed at lessening military confrontation and promoting disarmament, which are designed to complement political *détente* in Europe and to strengthen their security'.[10]

Thus, even under present circumstances one may get nowhere with the approach currently followed and may have to turn to unilateral measures which could maintain 'undiminished security', reduce fears and, one would hope, induce some response from the other side.

Although it is easier to say this than to do it, there are measures which could meet these objectives – if the states concerned choose to take them. To give one illustration, the redeployment from East Germany of one Soviet Army (4–5 divisions), or its reduction to Category 2 status,[11] should not significantly affect Warsaw Pact defensive capabilities, yet it would communicate peaceful *intent* far more certainly than Mr Brezhnev's verbal assurances that 'the Soviet Union has never threatened and is not threatening anyone . . .'[12] Similarly, an American decision to withdraw voluntarily the 36

[10] *Conference on Security and Co-operation in Europe: Final Act, op. cit.* in Chapter 7, note 30, p. 21.

[11] Soviet Category 2 divisions are at something over half-strength, as contrasted with Category 1 divisions, which range between three-quarters and full strength. *The Military Balance, 1976–1977*, p. 9, footnote.

[12] L. I. Brezhnev's Interview with French television, 5 October 1976, Tass Report in English, teletype, p. 12.

Pershing SRBM with which it is bargaining at the negotiations on Mutual Force Reductions could not fail to signal NATO intentions—as, even more, would a comparable cut in the *Pershings* operated by the *Bundeswehr*. Thus there are ways of proceeding with arms control if political leaders wish to do so.

It may be, of course, that they do not wish to do so, not only because this would deprive them of 'bargaining chips' but because the time in which to cash those chips is over. Even if one discounts campaign rhetoric, it is clear that there has been a change of mood in the United States and to some extent in Western Europe, a change marked by pessimism about *détente*, increased concern over 'shifts' in the military balance and a tendency to draw back from new East–West ventures. Though this change has not, so far, affected the peoples and the policies of Eastern Europe, it may yet do so, and the Soviet Union may already have begun to alter its deeds—if not its words.

Whether this is in fact the case, one cannot rule out a world wherein the Cold War is waged again; indeed, this was one of the three possible outcomes foreseen by Soviet political scientists when they attempted to peer into the future.[13] If in fact this is the kind of future which comes about, it is safe to predict that arms control will at best be a by-product of national decisions about defence programmes and budgets, rather than a way of influencing these. More important, the end to which arms control is a means—that of enhanced security—is very likely to 'go down the drain' simultaneously.

Regrettably, this is not the worst future which one can imagine: there could be a war in Europe, or a series of super-power confrontations in the Third World which could hasten the prospect of such a war—with profound implications for European security. Even futures which one side would find desirable might be disastrous for the other; thus, the collective security system for Europe envisaged by the Soviet Union, marked by the dissolution of blocs, the withdrawal of all foreign troops, reductions in indigenous armed forces, and the renunciation of force, could only insure that Soviet primacy on the Continent would turn into predominance.[14] Thus, whatever the

[13] See N. N. Inozemtsev, '*Les relations internationales en Europe dans les années 1970*' in *Europe 1980: The Future of Intra-European Relations*, Reports presented at the Conference of Directors and Representatives of European Institutes of International Relations, Varna, 3–5 October 1972 (Leiden: A. W. Sijthoff, 1972).

[14] For a discussion of the Soviet model and its implications see Paul Seabury, 'On *Detente*', *Survey*, Vol. 19, No. 2 (Spring 1973), esp. pp. 69–74, and Robert Legvold, 'The Problem of European Security', *Problems of Communism*, Vol. 23 (January/February 1974), particularly pp. 17–21.

sincerity of Soviet pledges, whatever the validity of contracts to renounce the use and threat of force, and whatever the extent to which she might be willing to disarm, security for the Soviet Union might not mean security for others—by any definition of that word.

This is equally true of some of the futures envisioned by (and promoted by) leaders in the West. Neither a full-scale Atlantic Community nor a Federation of Europe, with a central political authority, integrated military power and an independent European Nuclear Force,[15] is likely to be interested in arms control; in fact, given the fallible nature of man, the primary motivation for the establishment of either of those institutions is likely to be a belief that they will enhance [West] European security. Nor is it likely that the East Europeans would, under such circumstances, choose arms control as an instrument of policy; it is more likely that they would feel threatened (particularly by an ENF in which West Germany played a part) and almost inevitable that they would draw (or be drawn) closer to the Soviet Union. Nor would that country welcome the emergence on the Continent of a powerful political and economic competitor, with military potential at least equal to her own. Thus, West European security might be bought at the expense of others—if indeed it can be bought at all by the means described.

A personal perspective

At the risk of seeming to prescribe for others measures on which they should decide, I would suggest that these options should not be taken up at the moment. One reason for this is the difficulty of putting them into effect, even if the European Economic Community achieves by the end of the decade that degree of political unity which it is seeking —an outcome which is by no means certain. Another is that they could be counter-productive both in terms of their effect on relations with the Soviet Union and the countries of Eastern Europe and in terms of the focus which they would provide for West European interests and endeavours. A third is that the exercise of these options may not be necessary, particularly if East–West relations continue to improve, and restrictions on the deployment and the use of force continue to multiply.

The road I suggest goes neither towards Atlantic unity nor to a militarily powerful European Political Community with its own independent nuclear force. Instead West Europeans might simultaneously follow three paths: towards economic integration, which promises to increase their well-being and their influence; towards the building of a

[15] Alastair Buchan (ed.), *Europe's Futures, Europe's Choices: Models of Western Europe in the 1970s* (London, New York: Chatto and Windus for the IISS, Columbia University Press, 1969), esp. pp. 124–6.

more cohesive political community; and towards arrangements for co-ordinating of national security policies and programmes which would give that (embryonic) community both strong defence forces and greater influence within NATO. Such outcomes would not be entirely to the liking of the Soviet Union and her associates, but they have accepted the first, they can scarcely object to the second (particularly if accompanied by increased interchanges between West and East) and, since they apparently envisage a continuation of NATO and the Warsaw Pact over the foreseeable future, there may be circumstances which would dispose them to tolerate the third. One of these circumstances would, of course, be that the military measures taken did not include a significant build-up of West European national nuclear forces, nor arrangements for their co-ordination which would give West Germany a markedly stronger voice in decisions on their employment. Another would be that the measures did not preclude steps towards the reduction and limitation of armaments.

Although no one can forecast the policies of an organization yet unborn, it is possible that even a partially developed European Community could bolster the confidence of its members to such a degree that they would be willing to take steps over which they now hesitate.[16] It is certain that progress towards a peaceful and co-operative Europe will require that the allies be more aware of, and more responsive to, the fears and concerns of other Europeans than is sometimes the case today. As already suggested, this would require efforts to avoid the development of weapons, the establishment of defence postures, and the approval of military programmes which are likely to exacerbate Warsaw Pact fears and stimulate responses which, in turn, would seem threatening to the members of NATO. It would also require efforts to provide satisfactory assurances about West European intentions—for example, by careful selection of the scale and type of West European interactions with the peoples of Eastern Europe. This does not mean that one has to accept the current regimes as presently constituted, nor cease trying to induce them to improve the lot of their peoples, but rather that one should avoid adopting extreme and potentially counter-productive positions, such as that propounded by the Secretary-General of NATO that 'NATO, because it is defensive in military terms, can well afford to be on the political offensive'.[17]

[16] Although I arrived at this judgment separately I find that it closely parallels the one reached by Francois Duchêne. See his 'Europe's Role in World Peace', in Richard Mayne (ed.), *Europe Tomorrow: Sixteen Europeans Look Ahead* (London: Collins, 1972), pp. 41–3.

[17] Joseph M. A. H. Luns, 'NATO View of Security Conferences', talk to the North Atlantic Assembly, Bonn, 22 November 1972, reprinted in *The Atlantic Community Quarterly*, Vol. II, No. 1 (Spring 1973), p. 63.

All this is, of course, equally true of the Soviet Union and her allies in Eastern Europe. They need to be more aware of the interpretations placed on measures to restrict individual freedoms which, however necessary from the perspectives of their governments, seem to some in the West incompatible with *détente*.[18] They need also to understand the meanings attached to other measures which, however valid as solutions to Warsaw Pact defence problems, are seen as a threat by the West–notable examples being the heavy reliance placed on armour in Eastern Europe and the redeployment of strong Soviet naval forces to advanced areas. They (like those in the West) need to realize that massive and continuing expenditures on modernizing and upgrading their armed forces can arouse concerns and stimulate reactions which may be contrary to Warsaw Pact interests; as the former Chairman of the US Joint Chiefs of Staff, Admiral Moorer, testified, 'It is against these capabilities of our principal adversaries that our [American] military force requirements have been developed.'[19] Thus at the end of this study, as at the beginning, it may be said that arms control can contribute to security–not least by helping to damp the cycle in which each side continuously upgrades its defences in response to measures taken by the other.

[18] See, in this connection, the statement of Harold Wilson, then British, Prime Minister, at Helsinki that '*détente* means little if it is not reflected in the daily lives of our peoples'. (*The Times*, 31 July 1975, p. 1.) This feeling is apparently shared by the leader of the Conservative Party, Margaret Thatcher, who attacked the Soviet Union for her 'ruthless opposition to all domestic forms and expressions of dissent', adding that '*détente* must be a reality which the Soviet Union supports in actions as well as words'. (*The Times*, 28 July 1975, p. 1.)

[19] *Statement by Admiral Thomas H. Moorer, USN, Chairman, Joint Chiefs of Staff, on United States Military Posture for FY 1974 before the Defense Appropriations Subcommittee, Committee on Appropriations, US House of Representatives, 93rd Congress, on 3 April 1973, mimeograph, p. 59.*

SELECT ENGLISH LANGUAGE BIBLIOGRAPHY

Arms Control (General)

Biddle, W. F. *Weapons Technology and Arms Control.* London: Pall Mall, 1973.

Blechman, Barry M. *The Control of Naval Armaments: Prospects and Possibilities.* Washington, D.C.: The Brookings Institution, 1975.

Carter, Barry. 'What Next in Arms Control?' *Orbis* 17, No. 1, (Spring, 1973), pp. 176–196.

Dougherty, James E. 'The Soviet Union and Arms Control.' *Orbis* 17, No. 3 (Fall, 1973), pp. 737–777.

Edwards, David V. *Arms Control in International Politics.* New York: Holt, Rinehart and Winston, 1969.

Gelber, Harry G. 'Technical Innovations and Arms Control.' *World Politics* 26, no. 4 (July 1974), pp. 509–541.

Greenwood, T. *Reconnaissance, Surveillance and Arms Control.* Adelphi Paper no. 88. London: International Institute for Strategic Studies, June 1972.

Holst, Johan Jorgen. 'Arms Control and the European Political Process.' *Cooperation and Conflict, Nordic Journal of International Politics* 10, no. 2 (1973).

Myrdal, Alva. 'It's the Qualitative Arms Race that Frightens Us Most.' *War/Peace Report* 13 (June 1975), pp. 3–7.

Ognibene, Peter J. 'Hard Choices in the Defense Budget.' *Commonwealth* 102 (6 June 1975), pp. 169–172.

Pastusiak, Login. 'East–West Relations and Arms Control: Achievement and Prospects.' *East European Quarterly* 9, no. 1 (Spring, 1975), pp. 1–13.

Pfaltzgraff, Robert L., Jr. *Contrasting Approaches to Strategic Arms Control.* London: Lexington Books, 1974.

Rathjens, G. W., *et al. Nuclear Arms Control Agreements: Process and Impact.* Washington, D.C.: Carnegie Endowment for International Peace, 1974.

Reford, Robert W. 'Problems of Nuclear Proliferation.' The Canadian Insitute of International Affairs (Toronto), *Behind the Headlines* 34, no. 1 (1975), pp. 1–22.

Russett, Bruce M. and Cooper, Caroline C. *Arms Control in Europe: Proposals and Political Constraints.* Monograph Series in World Affairs 4, no. 2. Denver: Social Science Foundation and Graduate School of International Studies at the University of Denver, 1966–1967.

Schelling, Thomas and Halperin, Morton. *Strategy and Arms Control.* New York: The Twentieth Century Fund, 1966.

Schilling, Warner R., *et al. American Arms and a Changing Europe: Dilemmas of Deterrence and Disarmament.* New York: Columbia University Press, 1974.

Szulc, Tad. 'Have We Been Had? Soviet Violations of the SALT Deals.' *New Republic,* 7 June 1975, reprinted in the *Congressional Digest,* 94th Congress, 1st Session, Vol. 121, no. 103 (26 June 1975), S 11718.

Mutual Force Reductions in Europe

The Atlantic Community Quarterly 2, no. 1 (Spring, 1973), pp. 7–54. 'Conference on Security and Cooperation in Europe and Negotiations on Mutual and Balanced Force Reductions.' Contributions by Joseph W. Harned, Laszlo Hadik (Rapporteur), Wolfgang Klaiber, James Sadler and Stanislaw Wasonski.

Bertram, Christoph. *Mutual Force Reductions in Europe: The Political Aspects.* Adelphi Paper no. 84, London: International Institute for Strategic Studies, January 1972.

Caldwell, Lawrence T. *Soviet Security Interests in Europe and MBFR.* Los Angeles: University of Southern California Arms Control and Foreign Policy Seminar, January 1974.

Coffey, J. I. 'Arms Control and the Military Balance in Europe.' *Orbis* 17, no. 1 (Spring, 1973), pp. 132–154.

Erickson, John. 'MBFR: Force Levels and Security Requirements.' *Strategic Review* 1, no. 2 (Summer, 1973), pp. 28–43.

Holloway, David. *The Soviet Approach to MBFR.* The Waverley Papers, Series 1, Occasional Paper 5, Edinburgh: The University of Edinburgh, March 1973.

Khlestov, D. 'Mutual Force Reductions in Europe.' *Survival* 16, no. 6 (November/December 1974), pp. 293–298.

Kostko, Y. 'Mutual Force Reductions in Europe.' *Survival* 14, no. 5 (September/October 1972), pp. 236–238.

Multan, W. and Towpik, A. 'Western Arms Control Policies in Europe. Seen From the East.' *Survival* 16, no. 3 (May/June 1974), pp. 127–132.

Pierre, Andrew J. 'Limiting Soviet and American Conventional Forces.' *Survival* 15, no. 2 (March/April 1973), pp. 59–64.

Ranger, Robin. 'MBFR: Political or Technical Arms Control?' *The World Today* (October 1974), pp. 411–418.

Smart, Ian. *MBFR Assailed: A Critical View on the Proposed Negotiations on Mutual and Balanced Force Reductions in Europe.* Ithaca: Cornell University Peace Studies Program, 1972.

Sukovic, Olga. *Force Reductions in Europe.* Stockholm: Stockholm International Peace Research Institute, 1974.

Wolfe, Thomas W. *Soviet Attitudes Towards MBFR and the USSR's Military Presence in Europe.* Santa Monica: Rand Corporation, April 1972.

Yochelson, John. 'MBFR: The Search for an American Approach.' *Orbis* 17, no. 1 (Spring/Summer, 1973), pp. 155–175.

Strategic Arms Control and Europe

Booth, Kenneth. 'The Strategic Arms Limitation Talks: A Stocktaking.' *World Survey* no. 73 (January 1975), pp. 1–17.

Burt, Richard. 'Soviet Sea-based Forces and SALT.' *Survival* 17, no. 1 (January/February 1975), pp. 9–13.

Clemens, Walter C., Jr. *The Superpowers and Arms Control.* Lexington: Lexington Books, 1973.

Coffey, J. I. *Strategic Power and National Security.* Pittsburgh: University of Pittsburgh Press, 1971.

Coffey, J. I. and Laulicht, Jerome H. *The Implications for Arms Control of Perceptions of Strategic Weapons Systems.* United States Arms Control and Disarmament Agency Paper ACDA E-163. Pittsburgh: Graduate School of Public and International Affairs and Research Office of Sociology at the University of Pittsburgh, 1971.

Daurs, K. Jacquelyn; Lehman, Christophor; and Wessell, Nils H. *SALT II and the Search for Strategic Equivalence.* Philadelphia: Foreign Policy Research Institute, 1975.

Doty, Paul. 'Strategic Arms Limitations After SALT I.' *Daedalus* (Summer, 1975), pp. 63–74.

Garthoff, Raymond L. 'SALT and the Soviet Military.' *Problems of Communism* 24, no. 1 (January/February 1975), pp. 21–37.

Gray, Colin S. 'SALT and the American Mood.' *Strategic Review* 3, no. 3 (Summer, 1975), pp. 41–51.

Hamlett, Bruce D. 'SALT: The Illusion and the Reality.' *Strategic Review* 3, no. 3 (Summer, 1975), pp. 67–78.

Kaplan, Morton. *SALT: Problems and Prospects.* Morristown: General Learning Press, 1973.

Kemp, Geoffrey. *Nuclear Forces for Medium Powers, Part 1: Targets and Weapons Systems.* Adelphi Paper no. 106. London: International Institute for Strategic Studies, Autumn, 1974.

Kemp, Geoffrey. *Nuclear Forces for Medium Powers, Parts 2 and 3: Strategic Requirements and Options.* Adelphi Paper no. 107. London: International Institute for Strategic Studies, Autumn, 1974.

Kemp, Geoffrey; Pfaltzgraff, R. L., Jr.; and Ra'anan, Uri. *The Superpowers in a Multinuclear World.* Lexington: Lexington Books, 1974.

Kintner, William R. and Pfaltzgraff, R. L., Jr. (editors). *SALT: Implications for Arms Control in the 1970's.* Pittsburgh: University of Pittsburgh Press, 1973.

Kruzel, Joseph. 'SALT II: The Search for a Follow-on Agreement.' *Orbis* 17, no. 2 (Summer, 1973), pp. 334–363.

Leitenberg, Milton. 'The Race to Oblivion: The Superpowers Talk

Peace While Preparing for War.' *The Bulletin of the Atomic Scientists* 30, no. 7 (September 1974), pp. 8–20.

Metcalf, Arthur G. *SALT II: Some Principles*. Washington, D.C.: United States Strategic Institute, 1973.

Nacht, Michael L. 'The Delicate Balance of Error.' *Foreign Policy* no. 19 (Summer, 1975), pp. 163–177.

Nacht, Michael L. 'The Vladivostok Accord and American Technological Options.' *Survival* 17, no. 3 (May/June 1975), pp. 106–113.

Newhouse, John. *Cold Dawn: The Story of SALT*. New York: Holt, Rinehart and Winston, 1973.

Nitze, Paul H. 'The Vladivostok Accord and SALT II.' *Review of Politics* 37 (April 1975), pp. 147–160.

Pierre, Andrew J. 'The SALT Agreement and Europe.' *The World Today* (July 1972).

Survival 17, no. 1 (January/February 1975), pp. 14–24. 'SALT and MBFR: The Next Phase'. Report of a Trilateral Conference.

Walsh, John. 'Strategic Arms Limitation II: "Leveling Up" to Symmetry.' *Science* 187 (21 February 1975), pp. 627–634.

Westervelt, David. 'The Essence of Armed Futility.' *Orbis* 18, no. 3 (Fall, 1974), pp. 689–705.

Willrich, Mason (editor). *SALT: The Moscow Agreement and Beyond*. New York: Free Press, 1975.

Yale Law Journal 84 (April 1975), pp. 1078–1100. 'The SALT Process and Its Use in Regulating Mobile ICBM's.'

European Security (General)

Asevev, I. 'Europe 1972: Time of Hopes.' *International Affairs* (Moscow) no. 10 (October 1972), pp. 16–20.

Birnbaum, Karl E. 'Ways toward European Security.' *Survival* 10, no. 6 (July 1968), pp. 193–199.

Birnbaum, Karl E. *Peace in Europe: East–West Relations 1966–1968 and the Prospect for a European Settlement*. London: Oxford University Press, 1967.

Bromke, Adam. *Current European Perspectives. Current Comment Series* no. 5. The Norman Patterson School of International Affairs, University of Kentucky, 1975.

Brown, Neville. *European Security 1972–1980*. London: Royal United Services Institute for Defence Studies, 1972.

Buchan, Alastair (editor). *Europe's Futures, Europe's Choices: Models of Western Europe in the 1970s*. London: Chatto & Windus for the Institute for Strategic Studies; New York: Columbia University Press, 1969.

Freymond, Jacques, *et al. Europe 1980: The Future of Intra-European Relations*. Presentation at the Conference of Directors and Representatives of European Institutes of International Relations at Geneva. Leiden: A. W. Sijhoff, 1972.

Hunter, Robert E. *Security in Europe*. Second edition. Bloomington: Indiana University Press, 1972.

Mayne, Richard (editor). *Europe Tomorrow: Sixteen Europeans Look Ahead*. London: William Collins, 1972.

Väyrynen, Raimo. *Two Approaches to European Security: Arms Control and Cooperation*. Tampere: Tampere Peace Research Institute, 1974.

European Security: The Outlook from the East

Bender, Peter. *East Europe in Search of Security*. London: Chatto & Windus, 1972.

Brown, J. F. 'Detente and Soviet Policy in Eastern Europe.' *Survey* 25, no. 2–3 (Spring/Autumn, 1974), pp. 40–58.

Bykov, Vladimir L. 'The USSR and Security in Europe: A Soviet View.' *The Annals of the American Academy of Political and Social Science* 414 (July 1974), pp. 96–104.

Campbell, John C. 'European Security Prospects and Possibilities for East Europe.' *East Europe* 19, no. 2 (November 1970), pp. 2–8.

Holloway, David. 'The Warsaw Pact in the Era of Negotiations.' *Survival* 14, no. 6 (November/December 1972), pp. 275–279.

Johnson, Ross. *The Warsaw Pact 'European Security' Campaign*. Santa Monica: Rand Corporation, November 1970.

King, Robert R. and Dean, Robert W. (editors). *East European Perspectives on European Security and Cooperation*. Washington, D.C.: Praeger, 1974.

Klaiber, Wolfgang. 'Security Priorities in Eastern Europe.' *Problems of Communism* 19, no. 3 (May/June 1970), pp. 32–44.

Lambeth, Benjamin S. *Soviet Views on European Security 1965–1970*. Cambridge: MIT Center for International Studies, 1972.

Legvold, Robert. 'The Problem of European Security.' *Problems of Communism* 23, no. 1 (January/February 1974), pp. 13–33.

Lendvai, Paul. 'How to Combine Detente with Soviet Hegemony.' *Survey* 17 (Autumn, 1970), pp. 74–92.

Lippmann, Heinz. *Honecker and the New Politics of Europe*. London: Angus and Robertson, 1973.

Pavlov, V. and Gorelov, G. 'The Soviet State's Struggle for European Security.' *International Affairs* (Moscow) no. 2 (February 1967), pp. 17–19.

Pipes, Richard. 'Operational Principles of Soviet Foreign Policy.' *Survey* 19, no. 2 (Spring, 1973), pp. 41–61.

Sinanian, Sylva; Deak, Istvan; and Ludz, Peter C. (editors). *Eastern Europe in the 1970's*. London: Praeger, 1972.

Ulam, Adam B. 'The Destiny of Eastern Europe.' *Problems of Communism* 23, no. 1 (January/February 1974), pp. 1–12.

Whetten, Lawrence L. 'Recent Changes in East European Approaches to European Security.' *The World Today* 25, no. 7 (July 1970), pp. 277–289.

Wolfe, Thomas W. *Soviet Power and Europe: 1945–1970.* Baltimore: Johns Hopkins Press, 1970.

European Security: The Outlook from the West

Burrows, Bernard and Irwin, Christopher. *The Security of Western Europe– Towards a Common Defense Policy.* London: Charles Knight, 1972.

Debré, Michel, 'The Defense of Europe and Security in Europe.' *The Altantic Community Quarterly* 2, no. 1 (Spring, 1973), pp. 93–118.

Foster, Richard B.; Beaufre, André; and Joshua, Wynfred (editors). *Strategy for the West: American–Allied Relations in Transition.* New York: Crane, Russak, 1974.

Fox, William T. R. and Schilling, Warner R. *European Security and the Atlantic System.* London: Columbia University Press, 1973.

Geiger, Theodore. *The Fortunes of the West: The Future of the Atlantic Nations.* London: Indiana University Press, 1973.

Gladwyn, Lord. 'The Defense of Western Europe.' *Foreign Affairs* 51, no. 3 (April 1973), pp. 588–597.

Goodman, Elliot R. *The Fate of the Atlantic Community.* Springfield: Praeger, 1975.

Groom, A. J. R. *British Thinking About Nuclear Weapons.* London: F. Pinter, 1974.

Hadley, Guy. *Transatlantic Partnership and Problems: An Inquiry into Relations Between Western Europe and the United States.* Tunbridge Wells: Free Trade Association Trust, 1974.

Holst, Johan Jorgen. 'Five Roads to Nordic Security.' *Cooperation and Conflict, Nordic Journal of International Politics,* Special Issue on Nordic Security (3/4, 1972), pp. 133–138.

Luns, Joseph. 'The Future of the Atlantic Alliance in the Light of Present European Developments.' *The Atlantic Community Quarterly* 10, no. 2 (Summer, 1972), pp. 194–202.

Luns, Joseph M. A. H. 'NATO View of Security Conferences.' *The Atlantic Community Quarterly* 2, no. 1 (Spring, 1973), pp. 55–64.

Kaiser, Karl. *Europe and the United States: The Future of the Relationship.* Washington, D.C.: Columbia Books, 1973.

Kaplan, Morton A. *The Rationale for NATO.* Washington, D.C.: American Enterprise Institute for Public Policy Research, 1973.

Kohl, Wilfrid L. and Trubman, William. 'American Policy Toward Europe: The Next Phase.' *Orbis* 17, no. 1 (Spring, 1973), pp. 31–50.

Petersen, Nikolaj. 'Danish Security Policy in the Seventies: Continuity or Change?' *Cooperation and Conflict, Nordic Journal of International Politics,* Special Issue on Nordic Security (3/4, 1972), pp. 139–170.

Pfaltzgraff, Robert L., Jr. 'The United States and Europe: Partners in a Multipolar World.' *Orbis* 17, no. 1 (Spring, 1973), pp. 7–30.

Pierre, Andrew J. 'Can Europe's Security Be "Decoupled" from America?' *Foreign Affairs* 51, no. 4 (July 1975), pp. 761–777.

Serfaty, Sium. 'America and Europe in the 1970's: Integration or Disintegration?' *Orbis* 17, no. 1 (Spring, 1973), pp. 95–109.

Tucker, Gardiner L. 'Standardization and the Joint Defense.' *NATO Review* 23, January 1975, pp. 10–14.

European Security: The Outlook From the Sidelines

Andren, Nils. 'Sweden's Security Policy.' *Cooperation and Conflict, Nordic Journal of International Politics*, Special Issue on Nordic Security (3/4, 1972), pp. 133–138.

Archer, Clive. 'Scandinavian Security: Its Background and Development.' *Royal Air Force Quarterly* 15 (Spring, 1975), pp. 35–41.

Pajunen, Aimo. 'Finland's Security Policy in the 1970's: Background and Perspectives.' *Cooperation and Conflict, Nordic Journal of International Politics*, Special Issue on Nordic Security (3/4, 1972), pp. 171–192.

Johnson, A. Ross. 'Yugoslav Total National Defence.' *Survival* 15, no. 2 (March/April 1973), pp. 54–59.

Remington, Robin Alison. 'Yugoslavia and European Security.' *Orbis* 17, no. 1 (Spring, 1973), pp. 197–226.

Military Balance in Europe

A. General

Cliffe, Trevor. *Military Technology and the European Balance.* Adelphi Paper no. 89. London: International Institute for Strategic Studies, August 1972.

Dupuy, Trevor N. *Almanac of World Military Power* (Third edition). Arlington: R. R. Bowker Company, 1974.

Luttwak, Edward. *The U.S.–U.S.S.R. Nuclear Weapons Balance.* The Washington Papers 2, no. 13. Center for Strategic and International Studies. Beverly Hills: Sage Publications, 1974.

International Institute for Strategic Studies. *The Military Balance 1975–1976.* London: International Institute for Strategic Studies, 1975.

Netherlands Institute for Peace Questions. *Nuclear Weapons for Western Europe?* The Hague: Netherlands Institute for Peace Questions, 1974.

B. Western Strategy and Forces

Alberts, D. J. 'Counterforce In An Era of Essential Equivalence.' *Air University Review* 26, (March/April 1975), pp. 27–37.

Brayton, Abbott A. 'The Transformation of U.S. Mobilization Policies: Implications for NATO.' *Journal of the Royal United Services Institute for Defence Studies*, no. 120 (March 1975), pp. 48–55.

Canby, Steven L. *Damping Nuclear Counterforce Incentives: Correcting NATO's Inferiority in Conventional Military Strength.* Santa Monica: California Arms Control and Foreign Policy Seminar, August 1974.

Dairs, Paul C. 'A European Nuclear Force: Utility and Prospects.' *Orbis* 17, no. 7 (Spring, 1975), pp. 110–131.

Hunt, Kenneth. *The Aliance and Europe: Part II: Defence With Fewer Men.* Adelphi Paper no. 98. London: The International Institute for Strategic Studies, Summer, 1973.

Joshua, Wynfred and Hahn, Walter P. *Nuclear Politics: America, France, and Britain.* The Washington Papers 1, no. 9. Beverly Hills: Sage Publications, 1973.

Lawrence, Richard and Record, Jeffrey. *U.S. Force Structure in NATO: An Alternative.* Washington, D.C.: The Brookings Institution, 1974.

Nailor, Peter, *et al. The Roles of Maritime Forces in the Security of Western Europe.* Southampton: Department of Extra-Mural Studies, University of Southampton, 1972.

Newhouse, John; Croan, Melvin; Fried, Edward R.; and Stanley, Timothy W. *U.S. Troops in Europe: Issues, Costs, and Choices.* Washington, D.C.: The Brookings Institution, 1971.

Pick, Otto. 'Defense and Strategic Questions: Altantic Defense and the Integration of Europe.' *The Atlantic Community Quarterly* 10, no. 2 (Summer, 1972), pp. 174–184.

US Congress. Senate Committee on Foreign Relations. *U.S. Forces in Europe. Hearing Before the Subcommittee on Arms Control. International Law and Organization.* Ninety-Third Congress. First Session, 1973.

White, William D. *U.S. Tactical Air Power Missions, Forces and Costs.* Washington, D.C.: The Brookings Institution, 1974.

Williams, Alan Lee. 'Is a European Nuclear Force Desirable?' *Atlantic Community Quarterly* 10, no. 2 (Summer, 1972), pp. 184–187.

C. *Warsaw Pact Doctrine and Forces*

Blechman, Barry. *The Changing Soviet Navy.* Washington, D.C.: The Brookings Institution, 1973.

Erickson, John. *The Soviet Military: Soviet Policy and Soviet Principles.* Washington, D.C.: United States Strategic Institute, 1973.

Fairhall, David. *Russian Sea Power: An Account of its Present Strength and Strategy.* Boston: Gambit Incorporated, 1971.

Gouré, Leon; Kohler, Foy D.; and Harvey, Mose L. *The Role of Nuclear Forces in Current Soviet Strategy.* Coral Gables: Center for Advanced International Studies, University of Miami, 1974.

Holloway, David. 'Technology and Political Decision in Soviet Armament Policy.' *Journal of Peace Research* 11, no. 4 (1974), pp. 257–279.

Host, Johan Jorgen. 'The Soviet Build-up in the North-East Atlantic.' *NATO Review,* October 1971. Reprinted in *Survival* (January/February 1972), pp. 37–48.

Jacobsen, D. G. *Soviet Strategy–Soviet Foreign Policy*. Glasgow: Robert Maclehose, 1972.

Jacobsen, D. G. 'The Emergence of a Soviet Doctrine of Flexible Response?' *The Atlantic Community Quarterly* 12, no. 2 (Summer, 1974), pp. 233–238.

MccGwire, Michael. 'Soviet Naval Capabilities and Intentions.' *The Soviet Union in Europe and the Near East: Her Capabilities and Intentions.* London: Royal United Services Institute for Defence Studies, 1970.

MccGwire, Michael (editor). *Soviet Naval Developments: Capability and Context.* London: Pall Mall, 1973.

MccGwire, Michael K.; Booth, Kenneth; and McDonnell, John (editors). *Soviet Naval Policy: Objectives and Constraints.* New York: Praeger, 1975.

Mackintosh, Malcolm. 'The Warsaw Pact Today.' *Survival* 16, no. 3 (May/June 1974), pp. 122–126.

Polmar, Norman. *Soviet Naval Power: Challenge for the 1970's.* New York: Crane, Russak, 1974.

Sidorenko, A. A. *The Offensive (A Soviet View).* Moscow: 1970, translated and published under the auspices of the United States Air Force. Washington, D.C.: Government Printing Office, 1973.

Williams, E. S. 'Soviet Military Thought and the Principles of War' (Part V). *Royal Air Forces Quarterly* 15 (Spring, 1975), pp. 17–22.

Wolfe, Thomas W. *Soviet Military Capabilities and Intentions in Europe.* Rand Paper P-1588. Santa Monica: Rand Corporation, March 1974.

Wolfe, Thomas W. *Soviet Power and Europe, 1945–1970.* Baltimore: The Johns Hopkins Press, 1971.

Wolfe, Thomas W. *Military Power and Soviet Policy, 1975.* Santa Monica: Rand Corporation, March 1975.

Wolfe, Thomas W. *Role of the Warsaw Pact in Soviet Policy.* Rand Paper P-4975. Santa Monica: Rand Corporation, March 1975.

Tactical Nuclear Weapons in Europe

Brenner, Michael. 'Tactical Nuclear Strategy and European Defense: A Critical Reappraisal.' *International Affairs* 51, no. 1 (January 1975), pp. 23–42.

Cohen, S. T. and Lyons, W. C. 'A Comparison of U.S.–Allied and Soviet Tactical Nuclear Force Capabilities and Policies.' *Orbis* 19, no. 1 (Spring 1975), pp. 72–92.

Enthoven, Alain. 'U.S. Forces in Europe: How Many? Doing What?' *Foreign Affairs* 53, no. 3 (April 1975), pp. 513–533.

Gray, Colin. 'Deterrence and Defence in Europe: Revising NATO's Theatre Nuclear Posture.' *Journal of the Royal United Services Institute for Defence Studies* (December 1974), reprinted in *Strategic Review* 3, no. 2 (Spring, 1975), pp. 58–69.

Heisenberg, Wolfgang. *The Alliance and Europe: Part I: Crisis Stability in*

Europe and Theatre Nuclear Weapons. Adelphi Paper no. 96. London: The International Institute for Strategic Studies, Summer, 1973.

Lawrence, Robert M. 'On Tactical Nuclear War.' *Revue Militaire Generale.* Part I (January 1971), pp. 46–63; Part II (February 1971), pp. 237–265.

Record, Jeffry; with Anderson, Thomas I. *U.S. Nuclear Weapons in Europe: Issues and Alternatives.* Washington, D.C.: The Brookings Institution, 1974.

East–West Relations

A. *Détente*

Cox, Mike. 'Detente: Perspectives and Problems.' *Critique* (Autumn, 1974), pp. 89–97.

Griffiths, Franklyn. 'Cooperation as a Form of Conflict: The Soviet Approach.' *NATO Review* 22, no. 5 (October 1974).

Hassner, Pierre. 'Detente: The Other Side.' *Survey* 19, no. 2 (Spring, 1973), pp. 76–100.

Kohler, Foy D., *et al. Soviet Strategy for the Seventies: From Cold War to Peaceful Coexistence.* Coral Gables: Center for Advanced International Studies, University of Miami, 1973.

Korbel, Josef. *Detente in Europe: Real or Imaginary?* Princeton: Princeton University Press, 1972.

Laquer, Walter. 'Detente: Western and Soviet Interpretations.' *Survey* 19, no. 3 (Summer, 1973), pp. 74–87.

Seabury, Paul. 'On *Detente.*' *Survey* 19, no. 2 (Spring, 1973), pp. 62–75.

Steibel, Gerald L. *Detente: Promises and Pitfalls.* New York: Crane, Russak, 1975.

Survey 20, nos. 2 and 3 (Spring and Summer, 1974), pp. 1–27. 'Détente: An Evaluation.' Contributions by Robert Conquest, Brian Crozier, John Erickson, Joseph Godson, Gregory Grossman, Leopold Labedz, Bernard Lewis, Richard Pipes, Leonard Shapiro, Edward Shils, P. S. Vatikiotis.

US Congress. Senate. Committee on Foreign Relations. *Detente: U.S. Relations with Communist Countries. Hearings Before the Committee on Foreign Relations.* 93rd Congress, 2nd Session, 1974.

B. *CSCE*

Bromke, Adam. *The Eastern Conference on Security and Cooperation and Eastern Europe.* Current Comment Series no. 6. The Norman Patterson School of International Affairs, University of Kentucky, 1975.

Klaiber, Wolfgang; Hadik, Laszlo; Harned, Joseph; Sattler, James; Wasowski, Stanislaw. *Era of Negotiations: European Security and Force Reductions.* Lexington: Lexington Books, D. C. Heath, 1973.

Povalny, Mojmir. 'The Soviet Union and the European Security Conference.' *Orbis* 18, no. 1 (Spring, 1974), pp. 201–230.

Soviet Analyst 4 (5 June 1975), pp. 3–6. 'The CSCE: Progress or Platitudes?'

The World Today (May 1975). 'The CSCE and Eastern Europe.'

US Department of State. *Conference on Security and Co-operation in Europe: Final Act. Helsinki, 1975.* Washington, D.C.: Government Printing Office, 1975.

Yefimov, A. 'European Conference and Detente in Europe.' *International Affairs* (Moscow), no. 5 (May 1975), pp. 25–31.

APPENDIX: TABLES

Table 1: *Strategic Offensive Forces, Mid-1976*

A. *Global*

	United States	Soviet Union
Intercontinental ballistic missiles (*ICBM*)	1,054	1,527
Submarine-launched ballistic missiles (*SLBM*)	656	845
Bombers	453	135
Total launch vehicles	2,163	2,507
Deliverable warheads	10,622	3,300
(of which independently targetable)	(10,302)	(3,300)
Deliverable Megatonnage	3,672	8,520
Megaton equivalents	3,968	4,055

B. *Regional (Europe)*

	Britain and France	Soviet Union
Medium-range ballistic missiles (*MRBM*)	—	400[a]
Intermediate-range ballistic missiles (*IRBM*)	18	60[a]
SLBM	112[b]	—[c]
Bombers	36[d]	509[e]
Total launch vehicles	166	969
Deliverable warheads	330	2,827
(of which independently targetable)	(202)	(2,827)
Deliverable megatonnage	76	2,827
Megaton equivalents	120	2,827

[a] Assumes that 100 of the 500 Soviet *MRBM* and 40 of the 100 *IRBM* are not targeted against Europe.

[b] To be increased by 1976 to 128 *SLBM* and by 1979 to 144 *SLBM*, as France completes two missile-submarines now under construction.

[c] Soviet *SLBM* are counted under global forces, Soviet submarine-launched cruise missiles (*SLCM*) under tactical nuclear forces.

[d] Exclusive of 20 French *Mirage* IVA bombers in reserve, and 56 British Vulcan B2 bombers assigned a tactical role but which could attack strategic targets in the Soviet Union.

[e] Includes 170 Tu-22 *Blinder* strike aircraft assigned to the Long-range Air Force, but excludes 280 Tu-16 *Badger* aircraft in the Naval Air Force, configured for attacks on shipping but which could in theory carry nuclear weapons.

For further details, see table 5, *Strategic Nuclear Forces, 1976–1982*, pp. 252–5.

Table 2: Nuclear-Capable Tactical Delivery Vehicles in Europe, Mid-1976[a]

Region	Artillery[b]	Rockets	VSRBM[c]	SRBM[c]	Strike Aircraft[a]	Total
Northern						
NATO[e]	102				62	164
Warsaw Pact [including forces inside the Western Part of the USSR]	–	[8][f]	[8][g]	[12][h]	[25][l]	[53?]
Central						
NATO[e]	1,361	94	56	180	645[j]	2,336
Warsaw Pact	234	217	167	16[h]	771[k]	1,405
[Including forces inside the Western part of the USSR]	[360]	[266]	[223]	[32]	[1,321]	[2,205]
Southern						
NATO	336	34	6	–	219 land-based 60 carrier-based	655
Warsaw Pact	36	106	49	?	55[l]	246
[Including forces inside the Western part of the USSR]	[126]	[130]	[89]	[87?][h]	[150]	[503]
Western						
NATO	–	–	1	–	338	338
(including France)	–	–	(24)	–	(533)	(557)
Total						
NATO	1,799	128	62	180	1,324	3,493
(including France)	(1,799)	(128)	(86)	(180)	(1,519)	(3,712)
Warsaw Pact	270	323	216	16	826	1,651
[Including forces inside the Western Part of the USSR]	[486]	[407]	[320]	[52]	[1,496]	[2,761]

Sources: (1) *The Military Balance, 1976-1977,* pp. 6-7, 9-10, 12-17, 18-26.
(2) *Interchanges with the International Institute for Strategic Studies.*

Notes:

^a Only those weapons-systems listed as nuclear-capable in *The Military Balance, 1976–1977* and/or Trevor Cliffe, *Military Technology and the European Balance*, Adelphi Paper No. 89 (London: IISS, August, 1972), pp. 41–42, are counted here, even though this excludes weapons such as the 175mm gun and the *Mirage* VF which other analysts consider nuclear-capable.

^b Dual-capable (i.e. capable of delivering conventional or nuclear warheads). The Soviet Union's artillery figures are derived by assuming 36 203mm howitzers for each of the 5 field armies in East Germany and the field armies in Czechoslovakia and Hungary and by assuming 18 203mm sp. how. for the (half-strength) field army in Poland. Although these are shown in the table, it is uncertain whether the Soviet Union has nuclear shells for its 203mm artillery.

^c All figures for aircraft count only those operational in organized units; excluded are squadron reserves (3–7 aircraft per squadron) and war reserves. All figures for missiles count only launchers, and exclude those extra missiles carried in battery trains or maintained in war reserves.

^d Only those aircraft in bomber or fighter-bomber squadrons are counted, here and elsewhere; thus nuclear-capable aircraft in fighter-interceptor or reconnaissance squadrons are omitted.

^e Norway and Denmark do not allow nuclear warheads to be stored in their territories; hence these figures represent potential rather than actual capabilities.

^f Based on one *FROG* battalion of four launchers per division, from Kenneth Hunt, *The Alliance and Europe: Part II: Defence with Fewer Men*, Adelphi Paper No. 98 (London: IISS, Summer, 1973), p. 24.

^g Based on one missile brigade at full strength (16 launchers) for each of the five Soviet Armies in East Germany, and one brigade at half strength for the three Soviet armies in Poland, Czechoslovakia and Hungary. The 104 Soviet *Scud* deployment represents over 1/5 of the total Soviet *Scud* deployment, and may therefore be high.

^h All figures for *Scaleboard* launchers are assumptions.

ⁱ Assumes that 240 of the 300-odd Soviet aircraft deployed on the Kola Peninsula belong to the Naval Air Force and the remaining 65 are distributed by type as are the total planes available for operations against northern and central Europe, i.e., about 40 per cent are nuclear-capable (*The Military Balance, 1976–1977*, pp. 10 and 24).

^j These figures are based on equipment levels of 24–25 aircraft per squadron, rather than the 18 given for fighter-bombers by *The Military Balance, 1976–77*, p. vii; however, the latter levels do not jibe with the total number of aircraft given in *Ibid.*, p. 7, which has been deemed overriding.

^k In calculating Soviet aircraft in Eastern Europe it is assumed that there are no MIG-17 FGA aircraft in the Soviet squadrons in Poland, East Germany and Czechoslovakia (i.e. all Soviet strike aircraft are nuclear-capable). Moreover, it is assumed that the percentage of FGA planes among the 1,300 Soviet aircraft deployed in the NATO Guidelines Area (*The Military Balance, 1976–77*, p. 104) is the same as among the 2,500 aircraft immediately available for operations in that area (*Ibid.*, p. 102).

^l The figures for Soviet aircraft in the Southern Region are derived by subtracting from the 400 Soviet tactical aircraft in Southern Europe (*The Military Balance, 1976–77*, p. 102) the 250 tactical aircraft in the Odessa Military District. (R. Meller, 'Europe's New Generation of Combat Aircraft, Part I, the Increasing Threat', *International Defense Review*, 1975, No. 2, p. 180.)

Table 3: *NATO and Warsaw Pact Ground and Air Forces Immediately Available for Operations in Europe, Mid-1976*

Region		Divisions	Equivalents[a]	Troops	Tanks in Formations[b]	Aircraft[c,f]
Northern:	NATO[d]	0 [2⅓][e]	2 [2⅓][e]	32,000 [30,000][e]	250 [510][e]	250 [65][e]
	Warsaw Pact	20⅔ (22⅔)[g]	26 (28)[g]	603,000 (645,400)[g]	6,430 (6,755)[g]	1,320 (1,320)[g]
Central:	NATO	58 [71][e]	54 [67][e]	727,000 [865,000][e]	15,700 [18,876][e]	3,000 [4,225][e]
	Warsaw Pact	33⅓	41⅓	549,000	4,050	850
Southern:	NATO	28 [34][e]	27 [33][e]	302,000 [345,000][e]	5,815 [7,460][e]	865 [1,115][e]
	Warsaw Pact	1 (9)[g]	1 (8)[g]	21,000 (190,600)[g]	250 (850)[g]	510 (980)[g]
Western:	NATO[h]	56 (66)[g]	70⅔ (79⅓)[e]	1,196,000 (1,403,600)[g]	10,980 (11,905)[g]	2,930 (3,400)[g]
Total:	NATO	86 [107⅓][e]	81 [102⅓][e]	1,029,000 [1,240,000][e]	21,515 [26,846][e]	3,865 [5,405][e]

[a] 'Division Equivalents' reflect the fact that some divisions have only two brigades, rather than the customary three, and that others are manned at considerably less than operational levels. (See, for example, the note concerning Warsaw Pact formations in *The Military Balance, 1976–1977*, p. 12.) It also reflects the fact that some armies have independent brigades, i.e. units which are not organized into divisions.

[b] Including 550 tanks earmarked for American dual-based or NATO-committed divisions but exclusive of NATO and Warsaw Pact tanks held in war reserve.

[c] Exclusive of squadron reserves or war reserves.

[d] Danish and Norwegian forces only; the West German division assigned to the Northern Command is included in the total for the Central Region.

[e] Figures in [] include those units inside the western military districts of the USSR which are combat-ready and which could be employed in operations outside the Soviet Union, such as Category I divisions, squadrons of the Tactical Air Force, etc.

[f] Exclusive of American dual-based squadrons and of naval aircraft on both sides.

[g] Forces in () include those of France.

[h] Forces deployed in Britain, Spain and France.

Warning: No two unclassified sources agree; hence all figures are approximations and must be treated as such.
Sources: See Tables 6, 7 and 8, pp. 256, 258 and 260.

Table 4: *NATO and Warsaw Pact Naval Forces Available for Operations in Europe, Mid-1976*

		Attack Carriers	ASW Carriers or through-deck Cruisers[a]	Other Major Surface Combat Ships	Attack Submarines	Combat Aircraft	Remarks
North Atlantic excluding Portugal	NATO	1	1	81[b] (106)[c]	46 (58)[c]	55 (80)[c]	Includes 30 carrier-based aircraft
	WTO	–	–	51	126	265;?[d]	Includes 25 carrier-based aircraft
Baltic Sea	NATO	–	–	24 (24)	30 (30)	135 (135)	
	WTO	–	–	47	12	141?[d]	
Black Sea and Mediterranean	NATO	2 (4)	–	64 (88)	34[e] (45)	160 (260)[d]	160 (240) carrier-based aircraft
	WTO	–	2	59	19	160?[d]	
Immediately available	NATO	3 (5)	1	169 (218)	110 (133)	350 (475)	
	WTO	–	3	155	157	565?	
Available as reinforcements[f]	NATO	5 (5)	–	71 (71)	48[e] (48)	400 (400)	US carrier-based aircraft only
	WTO	–	–	–	–	–	
Total	NATO	8 (10)	1	240 (289)	158 (181)	750 (875)	
	WTO	–	3	155	157	565?	

Legend: Including France ().
Source: The Military Balance, 1976–1977, pp. 6–7, 9, 12–14, 18–26.

Notes:

[a] Exclusive of US Helicopter Assault ships (LHA) which compare in size to the Soviet ASW carrier *Kiev*. One of these will be deployed in forward areas in 1977, and eventually two. (*Rumsfeld Report, 1976,* p. 127.)

[b] Excluding British surface ships and submarines in reserve or undergoing refit.

[c] Assumes that French naval aircraft, surface ships (save for carriers) and attack submarines are divided evenly between the Atlantic and the Mediterranean, with one ship on permanent detail in the Indian Ocean.

[d] It is assumed that ⅔ of the 645 combat aircraft of the Soviet Naval Air Force (or 40 planes) are deployed in the West and that of these ⅓ (240 planes) are based in the North, ⅛ (80 planes) in the Baltic area and ⅓ (180 planes) near the Black Sea.

[e] It is assumed that the US normally deploys 6 carrier attack submarines in the North Atlantic and 4 in the Mediterranean, and that these will be built up to a total of 55 out of the 75 US attack submarines.

[f] Considers only the Canadian forces based in the Atlantic and the US Second (Atlantic) Fleet, and not the ships held in reserve by the US and the UK. Some (but not all) of these active forces could be deployed to European waters as rapidly as elements of the Soviet Fleet which are considered immediately available.

Table 5: *Strategic Nuclear Forces, 1976–1982*

A. *Global Forces*

	United States			Soviet Union	
Launch Vehicle Type	*1976*	*1982*	Launch Vehicle Type	*1976*	*1982*
ICBM			*ICBM*		
LGM-25C Titan 2	54	54	SS-7 Saddler	140	0[e]
LGM-30F			SS-8 Sasin	19	0[e]
Minuteman II	450	450	SS9-Scamp	252	0
LGM-30G			SS-11 Sego	900	0
Minuteman III	550	550[a]	SS-13 Savage	60	0
			SS-X-16	—	60[c]
			SS-17	20	165[d]
			SS-18	36	300[d]
			SS-19	100	825[d]
TOTAL ICBM	1,054	1,054	TOTAL ICBM	1,527	1,350
SLBM			*SLBM*[h]		
TRIDENT II	—		SS-N-8	64	208
TRIDENT I	—	144[e]	SS-N-8	156	180
TRIDENT I (in	—	160[f]	SS-N-6	544	544[i]
Poseidon)					
Poseidon C 3	496	336	SS-N-5 (Serb)	33	18[j]
Polaris AA 3	160	160[g]	SS-N-4 (Sark)	27	0[j]
TOTAL SLBM	656	800	TOTAL SLBM	845	950
Bombers			*Bombers*		
B-52 (D-F)	146	80[k]	TU-95 (Bear)	100	100
B-52 (6-H)	241	250	MYA-4 (Bison)	35	0[m]
FB-111A	66	60			
B-1	—	156[l]			
TOTAL BOMBERS	453[n]	546	TOTAL BOMBERS	135	100
TOTAL LAUNCH			TOTAL LAUNCH		
VEHICLES	2,163	2,400	VEHICLES	2,507	2,400
TOTAL MIRVS	1,046	1,190	TOTAL MIRVS	120	1,320
Deliverable warheads	10,622[o]	17,478	Deliverable warheads	3,300[p]	9,330
(of which indepen-			(of which indepen-		
dently targetable)	10,302[o]	17,158	dently targetable)	3,300[p]	9,330
Deliverable			Deliverable		
megatonnage	3,672[o]	6,480	megatonnage	8,520[p]	5,925
Megaton equivalents	3,968[o]	7,728	Megaton equivalents	4,055[p]	6,545

B. *Regional Forces*

Launch Vehicle Type	Western Europe		Launch Vehicle Type	Soviet Union	
	1976	*1982*		*1976*	*1982*
IRBM			IRBM[a]		
SSBS-S-2	18	18	SS-5 Skean	60	—
			SS-X-20	—	60
MRBM	—	—	MRBM[a]		
			SS-4 Sandal	400	400
TOTAL MR/IRBM	18	18	TOTAL MR/IRBM	460	460
SLBM			SLBM[s]	—	—
Polaris A-3	64	64			
MSBS M-1	32	32			
M-2	16	16			
M-20	—	32[r]			
TOTAL SLBMS	112	114	TOTAL SLBMS	—	—
Bombers			Bombers[v, w]		
Mirage IVA	36	36[t]	TU-16 Badger	450	300
			TU-22 Blinder	170	100
			TU-25 Backfire	30	210
TOTAL BOMBERS	36	36[u]	TOTAL BOMBERS	650	610
TOTAL LAUNCH VEHICLES	166	198	TOTAL LAUNCH VEHICLES	1,110	1,070
TOTAL MIRV	0	0	TOTAL MIRV	0	0
Deliverable warheads (of which independently targetable)	330 (202)	36 (234)	Deliverable warheads[x] (of which independently targetable)	2,827 2,827	2,880 2,880
Deliverable megatonnage	76	95	Deliverable megatonnage	2,827	2,880
Megaton equivalents	120	144	Megaton equivalents	2,827	2,880

[a] The yield of MMIII could double by 1982 if the US decides to go ahead with procurement of the new MK 12A re-entry vehicle, which will also be more accurate than present RVs. (Kosta Tsipis, *Offensive Missiles*, SIPRI Paper 5, Stockholm: Stockholm International Peace Research Institute, 1974, p. 27.)

[b] It is assumed that as the Soviets increase their SLBMs to the maximum of 950 allowed by SALT I, they will retire SS-7's and SS-8's for each SLBM over 740 (as they have already begun to do). This means the eventual retirement of the 159 SS-7's and SS-8's currently deployed.

[c] It is assumed that the SS-X-16 (with a single warhead) will replace the 60 SS-13 at the rate of 15 per cent per year beginning in 1976. See General George S. Brown, USAF, Chairman, Joint Chiefs of Staff, *United States Military Posture for FY 1976*, Statement before the Senate Armed Services Committee, no date, pp. 13–15.

d These figures are derived by assuming the Soviets will retrofit 15 per cent or a sixth of their force each year starting in 1975 and completing that retrofitting about 1981 (as suggested by James R. Schlesinger in testimony before the Committee on Foreign Relations, United States Senate). It is assumed the approximately 1,000 SS-11 will be retrofitted with SS-17 and SS-19 favouring the latter (which is reported to be the preferred missile) in a ratio similar to that exhibited in current Soviet deployment. Also it is assumed the nearly 300 SS-9 will be converted to SS-18 (Mod 2 with 8 RVs). *US–USSR Strategic Policies: Hearings before the Subcommittee on Arms Control, International Law and Organization, of the Committee on Foreign Relations, United States Senate* 93rd Congress, 2nd session, Washington, USGPO, 4 March 1974, pp. 43–44.

e This assumes that the construction schedule for *Trident* submarines of 1-2-1-2- a year continues and that FY 1979 will see the first *Trident* submarines and *Trident* I missiles operational. *Rumsfeld Report, 1976*, p. 66.

f The United States plans to retrofit the *Trident* I missile into ten of the *Poseidon* submarines. *Schlesinger Report, 1975*, p. 31.

g The two lead *Polaris* classes of 5 ships each, because of their size, cannot be converted to either *Poseidon* or *Trident* missiles. Since, however, the ceiling on SLBM set at SALT I expires in 1977, these missile submarines can be continued within the overall limit of 2,400 launch vehicles set at Vladivostok.

h It is assumed that the Soviets halt production on the Y-class submarines at 34 and stop production of the D-class submarines at 15 in order to shift entirely to production of the new longer D-class submarine. If the Soviets continue at production rates of 6–8 per year (as indicated in the *Schlesinger Report, 1974*, p. 47) they would be easily able to build the two current D-class and 13 new and longer D-class submarines by 1982, giving a total of 62 modern submarines allowed by the SALT I accords. (The H-class nuclear submarines do not count against the 62 limit.)

i Since the SS-N-8 has not been tested with either MRV or MIRV it is assumed it will remain deployed in a single warhead version. (*Rumsfeld Report, 1976*, p. 53.) The SS-N-6 has been tested in a Mod 3 version carrying 3 MRVs similar to the US *Polaris* A-3; however, no MIRV-ed RVs have been tested and it is assumed that none will be introduced –largely because of the probable US–Soviet agreement to count *all* missiles of a given type as MIRV-ed once one has been deployed.

j It is assumed the Soviets would retire two H-class boats and 6 SLBMs to stay within the 2,400 launcher limit set at Vladivostok. It is assumed that the SS-N-5 (Serb) and SS-N-4 (Sark) will be phased out by 1982 to allow for more modern launchers under the 2,400 limit set at Vladivostok.

k The US plans to complete the installation of structural modifications on 80 B-52D aircraft in FY 1976 to extend their safe life service into the 1980s. *Schlesinger Report, 1975*, p. II-36.

l This figure assumes that authorization for the B-1 bomber is given and that production begins in FY 1977, as planned, with only 6 planes. Additionally it assumes that the programme will run according to schedule, producing approximately 30 planes per year from 1978–1985. *Ibid.*, p. 38.

m It is assumed the Soviets will convert all of the MYA-4 (Bison) bombers into tankers in order to retain the 100 TU-95 bombers and stay under the 2,400 limit set at Vladivostok. See Brown, *United States Military Posture for FY 1975*, pp. 31–32.

n This figure does not accord with Mr Rumsfeld's (earlier) count of 497 bombers; however, the data available do not permit accounting for the difference. (*Rumsfeld Report, 1976*, p. 44.)

o Including 1,500 short range attack missiles (SRAM) armed with a 200 KT warhead, but excluding weapons which would be mounted on the 71 B-52 used in training.

p Including 50 ASM not counted by IISS but excluding 60 SS-N-4 and SS-N-5 SLBMS counted by IISS–these not being considered 'strategic' under the terms of the SALT Agreement. (See *The Military Balance, 1976–1977*, pp. 8 and 100–7.)

q The Soviets have retained a constant number of MRBM and IRBM throughout the seventies and it is assumed this will continue till 1982. During 1975 the Soviet Union tested a new IRBM, the SS-X-20, with a range of 2,500 miles and 3 independently targeted warheads. It is assumed that any deployment will replace existing SS-5s; as yet there is no basis for judging whether it will also replace the SS-4 MRBM. This count assumes 100 of the 500 Soviet MRBMs and 40 of the 100 Soviet IRBMs are not targeted against Europe.

r Assumes a fifth submarine, now under construction, will be completed in 1979. A sixth, previously planned, is being reconsidered.

s Soviet SLBMs are counted under global forces, Soviet SLCMs under tactical nuclear forces.

t It is reported that the *Mirage* IVA will remain in service until 1985 and then be replaced gradually by an aircraft now known as the '*Avion de Combat Futur*' (ACF). *Le Monde*, 12 February 1974, cited in the Netherlands Institute for Peace Questions, *Nuclear Weapons for Western Europe*, The Hague, November, 1974, p. 71.

u Exclusive of 16 French *Mirage* IVA bombers which are presently in reserve and 50 British *Vulcan* B-2 bombers which are assigned in a tactical role and are expected to remain so.

v Figures for Soviet medium-range bombers were derived by assuming that the TU-16 *Badger* are retired at a rate of 24 per year and the TU-22 *Blinder* at a rate of 12 per year from 1977–1982. It is also assumed that the TU-25 *Backfire* is deployed at a rate of 30 per year for this same period.

w Exclusive of medium bombers assigned to the Naval Air Force, which are to be used for attacks on shipping.

x It is assumed that those TU-16 *Badger* not equipped to carry ASMs will be retired first.

Table 6: *NATO and Warsaw Pact Forces in Central Europe, Mid-1976*

	United States	Other Stationed Forces	Indigenous	Total NATO	Soviet Union	Other Warsaw Pact	Total Warsaw Pact
Ground Forces							
Divisions	4	3	13¾	(22¾)[a]	27	31	58
Division-equivalents[b]	5⅝	2⅜	18	(28)	27	27	54
Manpower in Divisions[e]	84,200	24,000	203,925	(347,125)	336,000	251,250	587,250
Combat and Direct-Support troops[d]	169,400	52,000 (94,400)	381,600	603,000 (645,400)	437,000	290,000	727,000
Personnel	189,000	58,000 (116,000)	487,000	734,000 (792,000)	455,000	444,000	899,000[e]
Tanks[f]	2,500	650 (975)	3,280	6,430 (6,755)	7,900	7,800	15,700
Air Forces							
Personnel	41,000	–	149,800	190,900 (199,900)	45,000	142,000	187,000
Combat aircraft[g]	260	136	924	1,320 (1,320)	1,300[h]	1,700[i]	3,000
light bombers	–	25	–	25 (25)	100	30	130
fighter/ground attack	150	72	658	880 (880)	550	420	970
fighter/interceptors	70	24	151	245 (245)	500	1,100	1,600
reconnaissance	40	12	118	170 (170)	150	150	300
Naval Forces[j]							
Personnel	–	–	61,500	61,500 (61,500)	–	41,000	41,000
Major Surface Combat Ships	–	–	35	35 (35)	–	5	5
Attack Submarines	–	–	30	30 (30)	–	6	6
Combat Aircraft	–	–	135[k]	135 (135)	–	51[l]	51
Total men under arms	230,000	58,000 (116,000)	698,300	986,400 (1,044,400)	500,000	627,000	1,127,000
Tactical Nuclear							
Delivery Vehicles[m]	879	130	1,332	2,336	1,054	351	1,405
artillery	498	70	793	1,361	234	–	234
rockets	–	8	86	94	108	109	217
VSRBM	36	–	20	56	96	71	167
SRBM	108	–	72	180	16?	–	16
strike aircraft	232	52	361	645	600	171	771

Legend: Including France ( ).

a Exclusive of British, French, and American troops in Berlin (some 6,000 and equivalent in combat power to about two brigades).

b 'Division-equivalents', reflects the fact that some divisions have only two brigades rather than the customary three (as do those in the British Army of the Rhine) and that others are at cadre strength only – a factor which reduces the Polish Army from a nominal strength of 15 divisions to an actual one of 13 'division-equivalents'. It also reflects the fact that some brigades are independently organized, as are the three infantry brigades of the US Seventh Army. The figures for the US include 2 Army cavalry regiments which the IISS counts but the US does not.

c Calculated from the table on p. vii of *The Military Balance, 1976–1977*. Soviet units are assumed to be at full strength and other Warsaw Pact forces assumed to be at three-quarters strength (see p. 12, *Ibid.*). All NATO forces are assumed to be at full strength except the US armoured cavalry regiments, Canadian battle group, and the NATO units in Berlin.

d Computed on the basis of 29,100 men per American division and 21,200 for other NATO divisions, and including 7,000 American and British personnel in Berlin which are not reflected in the division totals. The Soviet combat and direct support troops are computed from the information provided by *The Military Balance, 1976–1977*, p. 99. (Those Soviet figures seem somewhat high in that they allow for only 18,000 troops in all administrative and logistic support positions).

e The strength of the Warsaw Pact ground forces in Central Europe has reportedly been given at 805,000 in information passed to NATO at the Vienna Conference. *New York Times*, 4 February 1977, p.1.

f Including approximately 550 stock-piled for US dual-based or immediate reinforcing formations, as indicated in *The Military Balance, 1976–1977*, p. 101, but not reserve stocks held by either NATO or Warsaw Pact forces.

g The breakdown by types is based on primary mission, as given in the country section of *The Military Balance, 1976–1977*, rounded off to the nearest five. Since many planes are dual-purpose, this breakdown is illustrative only; for example, 60 of the West German fighter-bombers double as interceptors and the 120 G-91 can be used as ground attack planes or for reconnaissance.

h The breakdown by types of Soviet aircraft was derived by assuming that the 1,300 planes in Central Eastern Europe were structured similarly to the overall total of 2,500 given in *The Military Balance, 1976–1977*, p. 102.

i The breakdown by type of other Warsaw Pact aircraft was derived from country data, rounded off to the nearest five.

j One difficulty in dealing with regional force reductions in general, and naval forces in particular, is that the areas covered do not necessarily correspond with those which make sense militarily. The Dutch Navy should be considered as operating in the Atlantic, and the Danish, together with the Soviet Navy, as operating in the Baltic. If these shifts were made the balance would be as follows:

	Major Surface Combat Ships	Attack Submarines	Combat Aircraft
NATO	24	30	135[k]
Central Warsaw Pact	52	19	141[l]

k About 85 are F-104G fighter-bombers of the West German Naval Air Arm; the remainder are maritime reconnaissance aircraft.

l Of these, about 50 are Polish MiG-15 and MiG-17 fighter-bombers, the remainder Polish light bomber/reconnaissance planes and similar planes of the Soviet Naval Air Force.

m For details about tactical nuclear delivery vehicles, see Table 2, p. 248

Source: *The Military Balance, 1976–1977*.

Warning: No two unclassified sources agree; hence all figures are approximations, and must be treated as such.

Table 7: *NATO and Warsaw Pact Forces in Southern Europe,*[a] *Mid-1976*

	United States	Other Stationed Forces	Indigenous	Total	Soviet Union	Other Warsaw Pact	Total
Ground Forces							
Divisions	–	–	33	33⅓	4	24	28
Division-equivalents[b]	–	–	41	41⅓	4	23	27
Manpower in Divisions	–	2,000	308,950[c]	310,950	50,000	140,250[d]	190,250
Combat and Direct-support Troops[e]	3,000	2,000	535,000	549,000	62,000?	240,000	302,000
Personnel	5,000	3,000?	775,000	783,000	65,000?[f]	356,000	421,000
Tanks	–	–	4,050	4,050	1,165[g]	4,650	5,815
Air Forces							
Personnel	7,000?	2,000?	137,000	146,000	8,000?	70,000	78,000
Combat aircraft	–	–	850	850	150[h]	715	865
light bombers			–	–	20	–	20
fighter/ground attack		–	440	440	35	150	185
fighter/interceptor		–	265	265	75	515	590
reconnaissance			145	145	20	50	70
Naval Forces							
Personnel	32,000[i]	(10,000?)	99,500	131,500 (141,500)	15,000	19,500	34,500
Attack Carriers	2	(2)	–	2 (4)	–	–	–
ASW Carriers	–	–	–	–	2	–	2
Major Surface Combat Ships	14[j]	(24)	48	62 (86)	14[l]	2	16
Attack Submarines	4[k]	(11)	30	34 (45)	10[i]	4	14
Combat Aircraft	160	(100)	12	172 (272)	–	–	–
Total men under arms	44,000	5,000 (15,000)	1,011,500	(1,060,500)	83,000	445,500	528,500

Tactical Nuclear Delivery Vehicles[m]						
artillery	60	—	595	655	115	135	250

Tactical Nuclear Delivery Vehicles[m]	60	—	595	655	115	135	250
artillery	—	—	336	336	36	—	36
rockets	—	—	34	34	16	94	110
VRSBM	—	—	6	6	8	41	—
SRBM	—	—	—	—	—	—	49
strike aircraft	60	—	219	279	55	—	55

Legend: Including France ( ).

a 'Southern Europe' includes Italy, Greece, Turkey, and Cyprus; Hungary, Rumania, Bulgaria, the Mediterranean and, for non-Soviet Europe, the Black Sea.

b 'Division-equivalents' reflect the fact that some divisions have only two brigades rather than the customary three and others are manned at cadre strength only – a factor which reduces the Hungarian Army from a nominal strength of 5 divisions to an actual one of 3 'division-equivalents'. It also reflects the fact that some countries, like Turkey, have a large number of independent brigades.

c Although The Military Balance, 1976–1977, p. vii, indicates that Greek, Turkish, and Italian formations have totals similar to those of Germany, this is impossible to reconcile with the numbers of men in combat and direct-support troops (Ibid., pp. 23–26); accordingly the number of men in divisions has arbitrarily been reduced by one-half.

d Computed on the basis that Soviet divisions are at full strength and that other WTO divisions are at ¾ strength if not cadre and at ¼ strength if cadre, as indicated in Ibid., p. 12.

e Computed on the basis of 13,000 men per division-equivalent for NATO, 10,000 men for WTO divisions other than Soviet and 15,500 for Soviet division-equivalents. These figures were in both cases obtained by dividing the revised number of division-equivalents into the combat and direct support troops listed on p. 97 of The Military Balance, 1976–1977.

f This and the previous figures are suspect, since the number of Soviet troops in Hungary is consistently reported as 'around 40,000'.

g Computed on the basis of two armoured divisions with 325 medium tanks each and two mechanized divisions with 255 medium tanks each, from the Tables of Organization on p. vii of The Military Balance, 1976–1977.

h The figures for Soviet aircraft in the Southern Region are derived by subtracting from the 400 Soviet tactical aircraft in Southern Europe (The Military Balance, 1976–77, p. 102) the 250 tactical aircraft in the Odessa Military District. P. R. Meller, 'Europe's New Generation of Combat Aircraft, Part I, The Increased Threat', International Defense Review, 1975, No. 2, p. 180.

i Including about 4,000 on shore duty in Greece.

j Deployment varies. In addition, British, and occasionally French, ships sometimes deploy to the Eastern Mediterranean.

k Deployment varies.

l Drawn in part from the Soviet Black Sea Fleet which, including such detachments, normally numbers 59 major surface combat ships and 19 attack submarines. In addition, about 160 of the 645 combat aircraft of the Naval Air Force are deployed along the coasts of the Black Sea.

m For details concerning tactical nuclear forces, see Table 2, p. 248.

Source: The Military Balance, 1976–1977.

Warning: No two unclassified sources agree; hence all figures are approximations, and must be treated as such.

Table 8: *NATO and Warsaw Pact Forces in Northern Europe, Mid-1976*

	United States	Other Stationed Forces	Indigenous	Total	Soviet Union	Other Warsaw Pact	Total
Ground Forces							
Divisions	—	—	1	1	[2½]	—	[2½]
Division-equivalents[b]	—	—	2	2	[2½]	—	[2½]
Manpower in Divisions[c]	—	—	11,700	11,700	—	—	—
Combat and Direct-support Troops[d]	—	—	32,000	32,000	[30,000]	—	[30,000]
Personnel	—	—	41,800	41,800	?	—	?
Tanks	—	—	250	250	[510]	—	[510]
Air Forces							
Personnel	—	—	17,100	17,100	?	—	?
Combat Aircraft	—	—	250	250	[65][f]	—	[65]
light bombers	—	—	—	—	[8]	—	[8]
fighter/ground attack	—	—	160	160	[25]	—	[25]
fighter/interceptors	—	—	60	60	[25]	—	[25]
reconnaissance	—	—	30	30	[7]	—	[7]
Naval Forces							
Personnel	—	—	14,800	14,800	[60]	—	[60]
Major Surface Combat Ships	—	—	12	12	[110]	—	[110]
Attack Submarines	—	—	21	21	[270]	—	[270]
Combat Aircraft	—	—	—	—	?	—	?
Total men under arms	—	—	73,700	73,700	?	—	?

Tactical Nuclear Delivery Vehicles						
artillery	—	—	164[g]	164[g]	[53]	[53]
rockets	—	—	102	102	—	-
VSRBM	—	—	—	—	[8][h]	[8]
SRBM	—	—	—	—	[8][h]	[8]
strike aircraft	—	—	62	62	[12][h]	[12]
	—	—	—	—	[25][h]	[25]

Legend: Including forces inside the western USSR [ ].

[a] Northern Europe includes only Denmark, Norway and the Kola Peninsula, which adjoins Northern Norway.

[b] 'Division-equivalents' reflects the fact that some divisions are not at full strength and that some armies maintain independent brigades.

[c] Calculated from the table on p. vii of *The Military Balance, 1976–1977*.

[d] Computed on the basis of 14,500 men for Soviet divisions. NATO figures are derived from information in *The Military Balance, 1976–1977*, p. 99 by subtracting NATO troops in the Central region from the total provided. This suggests 16,000 men for Danish and Norwegian Division-Equivalents.

[e] These Soviet forces are deployed in the Kola Peninsula.

[f] The 65 aircraft are obtained by calculating support ratios for the two Army divisions on the Kola Peninsula at two-thirds of that for the Soviet divisions in Central Europe. The break-out by types is the same, in terms of percentages, as that given on p. 102 of *The Military Balance, 1976–1977*.

[g] The Danish and Norwegian TNDVs are without nuclear warheads.

[h] See Table 2, p. 248, notes f, g, h and i.

Source: The Military Balance, 1976–1977
Warning: No two unclassified sources agree; hence all figures are approximations, and must be treated as such.

INDEX

A-7D, 65, 86, 163
ABM *see* Limitation of Anti-Ballistic Missile Systems
Adriatic Sea, 35
Aegean Sea, 36, 162, 203
airborne warning and control systems (AWACS), 75
aircraft-carriers, 65, 166, 194, 195, 203
air forces, 31–3, 225, 226, 250, 251, 252–5, 256–7, 258–9, 260–61; constraints on TNF and, 100, 108–9, 110, 111, 115, 122–3; MFR and, 141, 142, 143, 148–9, 159, 161, 163, 164, 166, 167, 171; overall restrictions on armaments and, 180–82, 202–3; SALT and, 76–7, 87, 90; *see also aircraft types and* conventional forces; forward-based systems; strategic forces; tactical nuclear forces
Albania, 34, 35, 36
Algeria, 200
Alma Ata, 24
amphibious forces, 34, 78, 202; DRG, 53, 167; limitations on, 50, 226n.; Polish, 53, 166, 167
Anglo-French co-operation, 43, 56
anti-aircraft weapons, 147
anti-submarine rocket (ASROC), 99n.
anti-submarine warfare (ASW), 33, 77–8, 82–3, 90–91, 96–7, 164, 194, 195–6, 224; *see also* submarines
anti-tank weapons, 29; MFR and 147, 160
Arab states, 12, 14, 18, 42, 162, 201, 217, 220
arms build-up, forces contributing to, 52, 53, 57, 81
arms control, bureaucratic factors affecting, 57; complexity of, 54; economic factors affecting, 67–8, 80, 81, 139, 172, 173, 183, 210, 216–18, 227; institutional means to, 210, 213–15, 227; legal means to, 210, 211–13; 227; military capabilities and, 47–52; peaceful intention and, 52–3; political

factors affecting, 53, 57, 80–81, 139, 172, 173, 215–16, 227, 228; scope of, 47–58; social factors affecting, 172, 173; unilateral measures for, 52, 53, 231; *see also* Limitation of Anti-Ballistic Missiles; Mutual Force Reductions; Nixon-Brezhnev Agreement; Non-Proliferation of Nuclear Weapons; Scandinavian nuclear-free zone; Security and Co-operation in Europe; Strategic Arms Limitation Talks; tactical nuclear forces; weaponry, limitations on qualitative improvements in
arms sales, 191–2
artillery, 128, 129; dual-capable, 52, 117; MFR and, 147, 159, 160, 163, 169; self-propelled, 108, 132, 147, 159, 169, 202, 225n.; towed, 148; tube, 148; *see also under specific weapons*
Atlantic, 35; North, 34, 55, 82, 83
Atlantic Alliance, see North Atlantic Treaty Organization
Aseyev, I., 215n.
Attack carriers, 33, 195
Austria, 10, 34
Azores, 9n.

B-1 bombers, 67, 68, 80, 82
B-52 bombers, 69, 79, 95
Backfire, 65, 69, 79, 108
Bahr, Egon, 213n.
Bahrein, 42
balance of forces in Europe, 22–46, 143–4
Balkans, 162
Baltic Sea, 33, 36, 50, 55, 118, 166, 183
Barents Sea, 50
bases, 199–202, 207, 209, 227n.
Beaufre, General André, 11
Bechhoefer, Bernhard G., 177n.
Beecher, William, 100n.
Belgium, 30, 136n., 158, 169
Bender, Peter, 13n.
Berlin, 91, 125, 205